Searching for Oedipus

Searching for Oedipus

How I Found Meaning in an Ancient Masterpiece

Kenneth Glazer

HAMILTON BOOKS
Lanham • Boulder • New York • London

An imprint of The Rowman & Littlefield Publishing Group, Inc.
4501 Forbes Boulevard, Suite 200, Lanham, Maryland 20706
Hamilton Books Acquisitions Department (301) 459-3366
www.rowman.com

Unit A, Whitacre Mews, 26-34 Stannary Street, London SE11 4AB

British Library Cataloguing in Publication Information Available

Library of Congress Cataloging-in-Publication Data Available
Library of Congress Control Number: 2018955007

ISBN 978-0-7618-7045-6 (pbk. : alk. paper)
ISBN 978-0-7618-7046-3 (electronic)

∞™ The paper used in this publication meets the minimum requirements of American National Standard for Information Sciences Permanence of Paper for Printed Library Materials, ANSI/NISO Z39.48-1992.

Printed in the United States of America

For Elisa, with undying love.

Contents

The Backstory

It begins with a prophecy. Laius, the king of Thebes, receives an oracular warning that it is his destiny to die at the hands of any child he might have with his queen, Jocasta. The queen eventually gives birth to a son, and when the infant is three days old, his ankles are cruelly pinned together, and he is handed to a servant who is told to leave the child to die on a mountain outside the city—Mount Cithaeron.

The servant, pitying the infant, cannot carry out these orders. Instead, he gives the child to a passing shepherd, who in turn takes the boy to Corinth. When they arrive, the shepherd gives him to the city's king and queen, Polybus and Merope, who are childless. They adopt him and raise him as if he were their natural-born son. He grows up as a prince of Corinth, ignorant of his true heritage.

Many years later, when the boy is a young man, a drunken stranger at a party implies that he is not his father's son. The young man approaches his parents about this alarming suggestion, and they assure him it's untrue. But he remains troubled, and one day he decides to consult the oracle at Delphi. Offering the story's second prophecy, the oracle tells him that he is destined to kill his father and marry his mother. He flees Corinth to avoid fulfilling the prophecy.

On his journey, the prince comes to a narrow, wooded place where three roads meet. Coming toward him from the direction of Thebes is a horse-drawn chariot carrying a somewhat important-looking older man. The charioteer tries to push the prince off the road to make way for the vehicle. An altercation ensues and escalates, and in short order, the prince kills the man seated in the chariot, the driver, and several other attendants.

After this fatal encounter at the crossroad, the prince continues on his journey. As he approaches the city of Thebes, he encounters the Sphinx, a terrifying creature who has blocked all traffic in and out of the city. To exit or enter, one must answer her riddle, on pain of a gruesome death. No one yet has guessed correctly. The prince decides to take his chances, and the Sphinx poses the following riddle to him: What creature walks on four feet in the morning, on two feet in the middle of the day, and on three feet at night? A wrong answer would spell his death. He guesses correctly, however: man himself, for in the morning of his life, as a baby, he crawls on all fours; in the midday of his life, as a grown man, he stands proud and tall on two legs; and in the twilight of his life, when he is an old man, he needs the aid of a stick.

The Sphinx throws herself off a cliff. The prince is hailed as the city's savior and is given the city's crown and its queen, whose husband (the king) was recently killed on his way to Delphi. They marry and have several children together. He leads the city as a wise and benevolent ruler.

Time passes. A plague descends on Thebes, killing many of its citizens and destroying livestock and crops. The ruler—the hero who defeated the Sphinx—sends a messenger to the oracle at Delphi to ask what can be done about the plague. The messenger returns with an unexpected answer: Somewhere within the city reside the man who killed the previous king. To end the plague, that man must be found and driven from the city.

And that's when things really start to get interesting.

Introduction

The Riddle of Oedipus

The year is circa 430 BC, and you are walking with some friends to the great open-air arena on the southeastern slope of the Acropolis to attend the annual spring festival in honor of Dionysus, the god of wine and fertility. The festival consists mostly of performances of new plays, primarily tragedies. The weather is good, and you are looking forward to the theatrical offerings, of which there will be many, occupying several days.

You are happy to be here. In fact, you are happy to be anywhere, for last year a terrible plague swept through Athens, killing many of your fellow citizens, including some of your friends. The plague also killed the city's great leader, Pericles. But despite the plague and some wars, you are living through what will eventually be known as the Golden Age of Greece. You don't know that, just as you don't know that you are living in 430 BC. But you do sense that the city is going through an extraordinary period of creativity and is truly alive with great artists and thinkers of all kinds—sculptors, architects, philosophers, actors, and, of course, dramatists.

You and your friends find a good place to sit within the rows of benches that look down on the stage. Surrounded by thousands of other Athenians, you spend many enjoyable hours watching one play after another by the greatest playwrights of the day. The music and dancing accompanying the choruses feature prominently in each play, and the performances are made even more memorable by their delivery in iambic trimeter.[1]

After watching a number of plays, you learn that the next one to be performed is called *Oedipus*, by the great Sophocles, many of whose plays you've already seen and enjoyed. You think of Sophocles as one of the Big Three of Greek tragedy, alongside Aeschylus and Euripides. They write the best plays and have won the most awards.

Sophocles has already written scores of plays and has many more in him. By the time he dies, he will have written perhaps 120 or 130, mostly tragedies. Of course, you don't know that. Nor do you know that of all these plays, only six besides *Oedipus* will survive intact: *Antigone*, *Oedipus at Colonus*, *Electra*, *Ajax*, *Philoctetes*, and *Women of Trachis*. Altogether, of the more than one thousand tragedies that were performed at Dionysian festivals, only thirty-three will survive intact, all of them authored by one of the Big Three.[2]

Almost all the plays you see at the festival are based on preexisting myths, which means you know the background of each character in them. Still, you are intrigued by how the playwrights handle the mythical material on which they draw. That's true of the play you are about to see, as the story of Oedipus is part of a very old myth known as the Theban Saga, which is based around the fortunes of the Greek city of Thebes (pronounced "Theebz"), a real city-state located in the Boeotian region, about thirty-three miles northwest of Athens.

The saga begins with Cadmus, the legendary founder of Thebes, who, as the legend goes, creates an army from dragon's teeth planted in the ground. Cadmus is succeeded by his grandson Labdacus, who is followed by his son, Laius. Laius and his wife, Jocasta, also have a son, Oedipus, who famously kills his father and marries his mother, all without knowing their true identities because he had been cast away as an infant. The sad story of Oedipus is followed by calamitous events involving his and Jocasta's children. The saga even extends to the children of their children, six generations down from Cadmus.[3]

Normally, the plays performed at this festival are part of a unified trilogy by the same author on a related subject. Aeschylus's trilogy *The Oresteia*, about the fortunes of the mythological king Agamemnon and his family after his return from the Trojan War, is the most well-known example of this three-part model. But the play you are about to see by Sophocles is not part of any trilogy; it is a stand-alone work—an exception to the general rule. This is just one of many exceptional things about the drama, as you will soon see.[4]

In any event, you are familiar with the Theban saga, just as you are familiar with other great myths, such as those involving the heroes Heracles and Achilles and Jason and Odysseus. You know about the Theban saga through the poetry of Homer and Hesiod, whose great epics in the late eighth and early seventh centuries BC laid the foundations of the story, as did some later epic poems like *The Oedipoedia* and *The Thebais*.[5] At least twelve Greek poets wrote epics about Thebes, and Aeschylus also covered the subject in various plays. Many years ago, you saw his trilogy consisting of *Laius*, *Oedipus*, and *Seven against Thebes* (only the last of which will survive, another fact you don't know).

You know the basics of the Oedipus story, starting with the warning to Laius that his child would someday kill him, but you're a little fuzzy on some of the details. For example, you're not terribly sure how Jocasta ended up pregnant. In one version you've heard, Laius is said to have raped Jocasta while he was drunk.[6] But the chorus in Aeschylus's *Seven against Thebes* says that Jocasta was the instigator, using her feminine charms to get Laius into bed.

Of course, you also know about the Sphinx, one of those terrifying creatures from Greek mythology whose parts are taken from different animals—in this case, a lion and an eagle. Appended to this monstrosity is the head of a woman. Adding to the terror of her appearance, she kills anyone who cannot answer her riddle, perhaps by strangling. You've heard different explanations for why the Sphinx came to torment Thebes—for example, that she was sent by Hera, the queen of the gods, because Thebes took in Semele, one of her rivals for the affection of her husband, Zeus. But there are other versions, and you're not sure which one to credit.[7] It's your understanding that "Sphinx" is derived from the word for "strangle," as in "sphincter."[8] It's possible, though, that it comes from the Greek version of an Egyptian word, because, after all, Egypt also has a famous sphinx, which you know from various accounts. However, you don't know what relationship there might be between the two creatures (nor will anyone else, even 2,500 years later).

Speaking of derivations, you also know where the name Oedipus comes from. It's one of those combination names: "Oed" is the root for "swell" (as in "oedema" or "edema," the medical condition in which fluid builds up in a part of the body), and "pus" or "pous" is the root for "foot" (as in "octopus")—hence, the name means "swollen foot." In the myth, Oedipus was supposedly given this name by the people who rescued him because his feet were swollen from being pinned together with something sharp, like a nail. (In the story, this feet-pinning was done so that, after he is dead, the infant's ghost will be hampered from taking any revenge.)[9] Such an injury would have given him lifelong scars on his feet.[10]

You know your Homer well enough to recall the passage from *The Odyssey* in which the mythological hero Odysseus meets Oedipus's mother, Jocasta, in the underworld: "And I saw the mother of Oedipus, beautiful [Jocasta]. What a monstrous thing she did, in all innocence—she married her own son . . . who'd killed his father, then he married her! But the gods soon made it known to all mankind."[11] Accordingly, the horrors of Oedipus's story are not unfamiliar to you.[12]

In fact, ten years ago you saw a different play by Sophocles called *Antigone*, which chronicles the tragic death of Oedipus's daughter Antigone after her two brothers, Eteocles and Polyneices, are killed battling each other for control of Thebes. Though written by Sophocles before he wrote the play you are about to see, it covers a later period in the mythological saga—thus, chronologically speaking, it's a sequel. Two decades from now, if you live long enough, you will be able to see Sophocles's play *Oedipus at Colonus*, which covers Oedipus's final hours on earth. Set after the events in *Oedipus* and before the events in *Antigone*, that play will portray Oedipus as a blind old man, guided by Antigone, whose search for a place to rest has finally come to an end.

As you watch this new play about Oedipus, you realize that Sophocles has cleverly zoomed in on a part of Oedipus's life that nobody has yet covered in any depth—the part in which Oedipus finally figures out the truth about who he is and what he has done. In *The Odyssey*, Homer wrote that "the gods soon made it known to all mankind," but nobody before Sophocles has thought to tell the story of precisely how the truth was made known.[13] When the play begins, Oedipus has already ruled over Thebes for many years in peace and prosperity and has had four children with Jocasta. But now Thebes is enduring a terrible plague—a chilling reminder of the plague you have just lived through in Athens. Oedipus learns from an oracle that the plague has been brought on by the presence within the city of the men responsible for killing the city's previous king. You and everyone else in the audience, of course, know that Oedipus himself is responsible for the murder, but Oedipus doesn't. You watch with fascination as Oedipus conducts his investigation and eventually learns the horrifying truth about his own life—that the man he killed all those years ago at the crossroad was actually his father, Laius, the previous king of Thebes. Further complicating things, the woman whom Oedipus married was his own mother, Jocasta, Laius's widow. The shocking discovery leads Jocasta to commit suicide and Oedipus to blind himself. Within the space of one hour, he goes from beloved ruler to blind beggar.

By the time the play is over, you feel as though you have seen something extraordinary, something well beyond any of the other plays you have seen at these festivals. As you walk home from the arena with your friends, you can't stop thinking about it.

That imagined ancient Athenian theatergoer knew the play simply as *Oedipus*. Today, we usually call it *Oedipus Rex*—"Oedipus the King"—the name it was given centuries later by the Latin-speaking world ("rex" is a Latin word, while the Greek equivalent would have been "basileus").[14] By any name, it is universally regarded as one of the supreme masterpieces of Western art and literature.

About a hundred years after that first performance of *Oedipus Rex*, Aristotle would hold it up as the model on which all other tragedies should be based. The seventeenth-century English poet John Dryden would call it "the most celebrated piece of all antiquity."[15] Friedrich Schiller, the eighteenth-century German poet and author of *William Tell*, would write that it is "its own genus" to which there belongs "no second species."[16] D. H. Lawrence would call it "the finest drama of all times."[17]

Scholars in the twentieth and twenty-first centuries would be no less effusive, claiming that it "has established a sort of standard for all time,"[18] "[has] no equal in world literature,"[19] "[is] an unsurpassable masterpiece of construction,"[20] and plays a role in literature "something like that of the *Mona Lisa*."[21]

In other words, that ancient theatergoer's instinct would have been right. He *had* seen something special—more than he could possibly have imagined.

* * * * * * *

I first encountered *Oedipus Rex* in high school. As for so many students before and after me, the play was required reading. But I was captivated from the first page, and as I kept reading, my excitement continued to mount. When Oedipus begins to divine the truth about his life, I had an almost visceral reaction, as if I were rounding the top of a steep roller coaster before a final descent. I was spellbound. To this day, even after a lifetime of reading great works, I consider *Oedipus Rex* the most powerful piece of literature I've ever read and the figure of Oedipus the greatest character ever presented on stage or the page.

I have spent many years pondering this great work, exploring its meaning and asking myself why it has stuck with me for so long. I've been a lawyer my whole adult life, not an academic, and this exploration has been strictly a sideline passion for me. But the more I've studied *Oedipus Rex*, the more meaningful I have found it. This book is the story of how, over the years, I have come to understand why it has had such an enormous impact on me and why, even after 2,500 years, it has such enduring power.

At the outset I should be clear that I'm talking about the play—a particular work by a particular man—and not the myth. To be sure, the myth has much going for it: patricide, incest, regicide, attempted infanticide, suicide by hanging, self-blinding, a plague, power struggles, prophecies, blind seers, hideous monsters with insidious riddles, and more. If it were a film, the advertising for it would scream, "*This is the movie that has it all!*"

But most of those elements underlie every telling of the myth, not just the Sophoclean version. In fact, there have been many additional tellings since Sophocles. The great Roman statesman and Stoic philosopher Seneca (4 BC–65 AD) wrote a famous version. So, according to the ancient historian Suetonius, did Julius

Caesar (100 BC–44 BC).[22] Oedipus has also been revisited in the modern era, and often. In the seventeenth century, John Dryden and Pierre Corneille wrote plays based on the myth of Oedipus, as did Voltaire in the eighteenth. In fact, there were at least seventeen adaptations created in eighteenth-century France alone, including two parodies and two operas.[23] One eighteenth-century Frenchman, M. de La Tournelle, wrote no fewer than nine plays on the subject of Oedipus.[24]

In the twentieth century, André Gide and Jean Cocteau wrote plays about Oedipus. Gabriel García Márquez wrote a screenplay on the subject, and Igor Stravinsky and Carl Orff wrote operas. It's not too much of an exaggeration to say, as did one scholar, that "in modern literature nearly every major poet has, at some time or another, drawn on an aspect of the legend as a meditation on the human condition."[25] At the time he wrote his play, Gide referred to a veritable "Oedipemic" of works involving Oedipus.[26] No doubt even as I'm writing these words, a new poem or play or opera based on the Oedipus story is in the works. In fact, as I was putting the finishing touches on this manuscript, a play titled *Oedipus El Rey*, which sets the story in the contemporary gangland of South-Central Los Angeles, premiered in New York and LA.

Yet if someone in the twenty-first century—2,500 years after that performance in 430 BC—were to say, "I saw *Oedipus*" or "I read *Oedipus*," that person would almost certainly be referring to the Sophocles version.[27] Despite addressing just one slice of the overall Theban saga, *Oedipus Rex* by Sophocles has eclipsed everything else written on the subject for millennia and is usually the first Greek tragedy that comes to people's minds.[28] It is the version that captivated me and is the subject of this book.

But *why*? What's so exceptional about Sophocles's version? Why is it so powerful?

This is a very old question and one that has been debated endlessly, including by some of the real heavyweights of intellectual history, from Aristotle to Hegel, Schopenhauer, and Nietzsche, and from Freud, Jung, and Heidegger to Claude Lévi-Strauss and Milan Kundera.

There is an air of mystery around *Oedipus Rex*, arising from the longstanding difficulty in answering this question. The puzzle of its power has even been given a name: "the Riddle of Oedipus."[29] It's a meta-riddle, referring not to the riddles within the play but the riddle *about* the play. All of the luminaries named above agree that there is something inexpressibly captivating about it. But what that *something* is has been a tough nut to crack, as is the question of what it all means. As the classicist Michael O'Brien has put it, "The question of the play's meaning has been embroiled in seemingly hopeless controversy."[30]

Over the years its meaning has been interpreted in countless different ways. We've been told that it's a tragedy of fate, because it's about a man whose destiny was determined from the day he was born, and that it's a reminder of the fragility of our fortunes in life. We've been told that it symbolizes the horror of the human condition. Some claim it's really about the gods, others that it's about the meaninglessness of life, and yet others that it's about the way societies use scapegoats to cleanse themselves. Still others, such as Freud and his followers, argue that it's about our deepest psychosexual anxieties. Some have even argued that *Oedipus Rex* *has* no meaning—not even "life is meaningless"—and that it just *is*.

If you were to explore the vast Oedipus literature, as I have done, you would encounter some awfully strange theories; one psychoanalyst, for example, has argued that the story is actually about the fact that Oedipus and his father are homosexuals fighting over the affections of a young man. You would run across mystifying statements such as, "The Oedipus myth is a transformation of the monomythic plot via a systematic disruption of the canonical schema of the triple ordeal that is correlated with the hero's three sins."[31]

It's often said that each generation comes along and imposes its own world view on the great classics, and that's true of *Oedipus Rex* to an extreme degree. Anthropologists have found it full of anthropological significance. Marxists read it from their perspective, feminists from theirs, and deconstructionists from theirs.

Every single aspect of *Oedipus Rex* you can imagine has been debated, down to the width of the road on which Oedipus and his father had their fatal encounter. (To summarize the many debates and controversies over the play, I created a table, which can be found in the appendix.)

All of which raises another question: Why another book on *Oedipus Rex*? Hasn't everything already been said on the subject (and then some)? And why a book by someone who isn't a scholar of ancient Greece or even an academic?

The answer lies partly in the very fact that I am *not* a scholar or academic. I come at *Oedipus Rex* from no particular academic or theoretical perspective; as far as I know, this is the first extended treatment of *Oedipus Rex* by a non-specialist. (Actually, I am a specialist in the law, but fear not: I am not analyzing the play from a legal perspective.) The twentieth-century French statesman Georges Clémenceau reportedly said, "War is too serious a business to be left to the generals." I think that something analogous can be said about *Oedipus Rex*—namely, it's too great a work to be left to the specialists alone.

By this I don't mean that the story of Oedipus needs to be rescued from scholarly obscurity. To the contrary—even if you don't remember much, if anything, about the play from your high school days, you know that Oedipus is the man in mythology who killed his father and married his mother. And there are so many cultural touchpoints involving *Oedipus Rex*: the idea of the "tragedy of fate"; the Sphinx's riddle, which is perhaps the most famous riddle of all time; the image of Oedipus contemplating that riddle, most famously depicted by Jean-August-Dominique Ingres, whose painting *Oedipus Explaining the Enigma of the Sphinx* hangs in the great salon of the Louvre; the image of Oedipus with his eyes gouged out, and the one of him as a blind beggar being led by his daughter/sister Antigone—among the most iconic depictions of suffering in Western culture; and Oedipus as a man with a "tragic flaw."

And then, of course, there's Freud. Thanks to him, Oedipus has been indelibly linked with psychosexual dysfunction. Just the mention of his name brings to mind a strange relationship with one's mother and a hostile attitude to one's father or other male authority figures.

If anything, *Oedipus Rex* may well need to be rescued from overexposure, so encrusted is it with misconceptions and scholarly exegeses. One almost has to peel away the layers before one can see it for what it is—one of the most moving and human works of literature ever created. This book is about one person's attempt to peel away those layers, come to terms with this ancient and timeless masterpiece, and solve his own personal Riddle of Oedipus.

I've lived with and thought about Oedipus for a long time. His story has become personal with me. By "personal," I don't mean there's anything special or idiosyncratic about me. This is not a confessional; I didn't learn late in life that I was adopted or that I had unknowingly slain a family member. You're not going to hear anything scandalous about my relationship with my mother. My fascination with *Oedipus Rex* is based on nothing peculiar to me, no out-of-the-ordinary experience setting me apart from others. I learned about *Oedipus Rex* through the normal vicissitudes of a normal life, the kinds of changes and experiences we all go through.

At the same time, my pursuit of Oedipus has involved a kind of self-analysis. I have felt deeply moved by the play and have asked myself *why*—why is it so meaningful to me? This book tells the story of how I have come to answer that question.

It took me a long time to make sense of *Oedipus Rex*; actually, a whole lifetime. Like most things in life, it was a process. The Oedipus literature helped some, but ultimately, I learned the most about *Oedipus Rex* from other works of imaginative fiction—novels, short stories, plays, movies. Some were stories that would seem to have not the least bit in common with an ancient Greek drama about a dysfunctional royal family dealing with monsters, plagues, and unpleasant oracles. Enlightenment came from unexpected places: a movie starring Bruce Willis about a dead psychologist, a Bible epic starring Charlton Heston as Moses, a science-fiction classic about an astronaut who wrongly thinks he has travelled to another planet, a French drama about a man concealing the source of a spring from his young neighbor, an Arthur Miller play about a father and son and a terrible crime from the past, and even an episode from the Harry Potter series.[32]

As I explain throughout the book, *Oedipus Rex* has spoken to me in different ways during different periods of my life, touching multiple chords. Accordingly, my interactions with it are presented as an unfolding story, which is appropriate given that *Oedipus Rex* is fundamentally a story about an unfolding.

At first, I was interested in the mystery angle. The play begins as a detective story. It becomes a very peculiar kind of whodunit, however, because the detective, it turns out, is also the very suspect he is searching for. I call this the theme of the Circular Detective. It's reflected in innumerable other stories throughout the ages, and it occupied my thinking about *Oedipus Rex* for many years. This aspect of the story had the biggest impact on me early on, as I explored the theme's psychological and philosophical implications.

About a third of the way through, the play shifts into a different kind of story, one about a man asking that most existential of questions: Who am I? During certain stages of my life, *that* was the question that drew me in most. I was intrigued by what has been called the "return of the repressed"—the way Oedipus came to learn the truth of his own existence, and the specific discoveries he made: who he was, what he had done, what he hadn't done, what had been done to him, and where he was. His discoveries lead us to explore ideas such as the role of fate in our lives, the self-fulfilling prophecy, the inherent tendency of the truth to make itself known, the circularity of our lives, and the nature of tragedy in real life.

Then, at other periods in my life, especially in middle age, I turned more of my attention to what *Oedipus Rex* says about leadership, character, and heroism, in the most meaningful sense, because, for my money, Oedipus is the greatest hero in all of literature.

To be moved and thrilled by *Oedipus Rex*, you don't have to have accidentally killed your father, committed unintentional incest, or blinded yourself. Its appeal is universal, not dependent on peculiar life experiences. You don't have to be a scholar to understand it and find it mesmerizing, just as you don't have to know ancient Hebrew or Greek to be moved by the Bible.

That's because, ultimately, *Oedipus Rex* is about some of the most important things in life. It's about men and women confronting the truth about their lives and themselves, and how they respond to that truth. It's about playing the hand that life has dealt you.

I will start my story with the aspect of *Oedipus Rex* that first grabbed me so many years ago—the story of a strange detective who didn't know he was searching for himself.

Chapter One

The Circular Detective

In a sense, my fascination with Oedipus began long before I read or even heard of *Oedipus Rex*.

When I was twelve or so, I read a short story by Nathaniel Hawthorne called "The Great Stone Face." In the story, a young boy named Ernest lives somewhere in New England, in a village in the shadow of a mountain whose side bears a striking resemblance to a human face. (Hawthorne's mountain was based on an actual mountain in New Hampshire.) Ernest grows up steeped in the legend of the Great Stone Face, a prophecy that one day the valley will produce a child who will become the greatest and noblest man of his time and whose face will exactly resemble the mountain's.

Like all the other residents of this valley, Ernest believes in the prophecy, but he finds himself disappointed time and again. Once, for example, a rumor circulates that a native of the valley who left years earlier and became a wealthy industrialist is the Great Stone Face. But when he returns to the valley to receive the welcome accorded a local hero, it becomes clear to everyone that there is no resemblance. This happens several more times with different people—a great statesman, a distinguished philosopher, and so on.

Leading the simplest of lives, Ernest comes to be regarded as a wise and good man. One day, after he has grown old, he addresses an assembled group—which includes a poet—in the main public square. Here's how the narrator describes the scene:

> The poet, as he listened, felt that the being and character of Ernest were a nobler strain of poetry than he had ever written. His eyes glistening with tears, he gazed reverentially at the venerable man, and said within himself that never was there an aspect so worthy of a prophet and a sage as that mild, sweet, thoughtful countenance, with the glory of white hair diffused about it. At a distance, but distinctly to be seen, high up in the golden light of the setting sun, appeared the Great Stone Face, with hoary mists around it, like the white hairs around the brow of Ernest. Its look of grand beneficence seemed to embrace the world.
>
> At that moment, in sympathy with a thought which he was about to utter, the face of Ernest assumed a grandeur of expression, so imbued with benevolence, that the poet, by an irresistible impulse, threw his arms aloft and shouted,—
>
> "Behold! Behold! Ernest is himself the likeness of the Great Stone Face!"
>
> Then all the people looked, and saw that what the deep-sighted poet said was true. The prophecy was fulfilled.[1]

Ernest, in other words, turned out to be the Great Stone Face. The man for whom he had been searching his entire life was none other than himself.

Something about this story captured my interest. At that tender age I had no idea what that something might be, and I'm sure I didn't think about it too much. Back then, it would have been an isolated case, a single data point. But as the years went by, I encountered some other stories that brought Ernest and his surprising discovery to mind.

For example, there was the movie *The Ten Commandments*, Cecil B. DeMille's classic, kitschy retelling of the story of Exodus. It usually came on television around Passover time, and I would watch it despite its length. I still do, despite—or perhaps because of—its kitschiness, which is best exemplified by the wraparound skirts and tunics that Vincent Price and Edward G. Robinson wear as they run around ancient Egypt.

The movie follows the biblical story of Moses in its broad outlines, but, being a Hollywood movie, naturally it takes some poetic license with the story. As in the Bible, Moses is found by the pharaoh's daughter in the ark of bulrushes, and even though she knows that he is the child of Hebrew slaves and would have been killed under her own father's order to slay all firstborn Hebrew sons, she raises him as her own. As a result, Moses grows up believing he is a prince of Egypt.

But then the screenwriters do some embellishing. As you may remember (or not), the Bible says nothing about how or when Moses discovers that he is not actually a prince of Egypt but the son of Hebrew slaves. As they would say on *Seinfeld*, the Bible yada-yadas over that part of the story. This being the case, the screenwriters were forced to fill in a major plot gap—and they did so in an extraordinarily clever way.

When Moses is grown, a rumor circulates within the royal court that a man has arrived in Egypt who will free the Hebrew slaves from bondage. As a powerful member of the royal family, Moses is tasked with finding this "deliverer." He begins his search, which ultimately leads him to discover his origins and realize that he himself is the deliverer for whom he has been searching. I was always intrigued by this way of telling the story—a search resulting in a discovery that the searcher is himself the person for whom he's searching. As with "The Great Stone Face," I didn't know exactly why I liked it; I just knew that I did.

I had a similar experience in high school, too, when I read Ray Bradbury's popular book *The Martian Chronicles*. In the final story, "The Million-Year Picnic," a family of Earth children living on Mars want to meet a Martian, so they beg their father to take them somewhere to see what they assume are little green men, or at least something strange and extra-worldly. He finally relents and takes them on a camping trip in the Martian landscape.

During the course of their journey, we learn that the family isn't just visiting Mars but has moved there permanently. The father brings the children down to a canal and tells them to look into the water: "'There they are,' said Dad, and he shifted Michael on his shoulder and pointed straight down. . . . The Martians were there—in the canals—reflected in the water. Timothy and Michael and Robert and Mom and Dad."[2]

We live in an age of self-discovery, self-exploration, and self-improvement. It sometimes seems as if everyone is on a quest to find themselves (or at least in therapy). One can hardly pick up a book or see a movie these days in which the main character is not on a quest of self-discovery of one kind or another—hitting the open road in an old car, say, to explore America and in the process discovering something about himself.

And yet, when I thought about these stories, it occurred to me that the most dramatic self-discoveries in literature, and perhaps in real life, too, are not made by people who are looking for themselves at all or who are engaged in a deliberate journey of self-exploration. They are, instead, made by people who are looking for *someone else*.

It's the difference between going up to a mirror to look at yourself and one of those moments when you think you see someone approaching and suddenly realize that, in fact, you're seeing *yourself* reflected in a store window or the like—a moment Sigmund Freud called "the uncanny."[3] Or imagine a situation in which you hear a voice, assume it belongs to someone else, and then suddenly realize it's yours—a moment memorably captured by Rudyard Kipling in "That Day," a poem told from the point of view of a man in battle:

> I 'eard the knives be'ind me, but I dursn't face my man,
> Nor I don't know where I went to, 'cause I didn't stop to see,

> Till I 'eard a beggar squealin' out for quarter as 'e ran,
> An' I thought I knew the voice an'—it was me![4]

Whether visual or aural, it's a shocking moment—a shock of *self-recognition.* A scene in *Alice's Adventures in Wonderland* provides another vivid example of this type of discovery. When Alice eats the magical cake, she grows ridiculously tall, which causes her to cry until she drinks the magical drink that shrinks her back to a decent size. But then she finds herself falling up to her chin in salt water. At first, she thinks she has fallen into the sea, until she realizes that she is swimming in a pool of the tears she shed when she was a giant.

At some point after encountering all of these stories—I don't remember exactly when—I realized I had a literary theme on my hands.

Then, in my senior year of high school, I had to read an ancient Greek play about a king who is told that he must find the man who killed his predecessor and discovers that he himself is that man. At that point, I decided I had stumbled across not just any old literary theme but a big one. This theme fascinated me for many years, and continues to do so.

WHO KILLED LAIUS REX?

The first genre that comes to mind when most people think about *Oedipus Rex* is Greek tragedy. But there's another genre to which *Oedipus Rex* also belongs, one with which it's usually not identified. And yet in fact, it's a genre that was more or less created by the play: the murder mystery. We don't normally think of it this way, but *Oedipus Rex* is actually a detective story, arguably the very first.[5]

When someone invents something new, you don't expect it to be the very best or most sophisticated version. The first motion picture is historic because it's the first, not because it's the greatest or is necessarily even any good. It's like Samuel Johnson's hypothetical dog that walks on its hind legs: It's enough that it walks on its hind legs; you don't ask if it walks well. But with *Oedipus Rex*, Sophocles both invented the detective genre *and* bent it at the same time, presenting a sophisticated twist on the detective format we've since come to know so well.

Here's what Sophocles did.

As I mentioned earlier, the backdrop of the play is that a horrible plague has descended on the city of Thebes, killing people and animals alike, drying up crops, bringing hell to the land. The people of Thebes, in the form of a chorus, approach Oedipus with a plea for help. You saved us once before, they remind the king, referring to his dealings with the Sphinx. Now save us again, they implore. Oedipus tells them that he is already on the case, having sent his brother-in-law, Creon, to consult the oracle of Apollo at Delphi. Creon is the brother of Jocasta—and, unbeknownst to Oedipus, his uncle. (One of the main characters in the play, Creon also features prominently in Sophocles's other two Theban plays, notably playing the heavy against Oedipus's daughter Antigone in the eponymous play chronicling her tragic death.)

Oedipus's promise of action is timely, for Creon has just returned to the city. He approaches Oedipus with interesting news. He says the oracle told him that the city is suffering from the plague because of the presence within its walls of a foul pollutant—the evildoer who killed Oedipus's predecessor, King Laius. As Creon explains: "Apollo commands us—he was quite clear—'Drive the corruption from the land, don't harbor it any longer, past all cure, don't nurse it in your soil—root it out!'"[6]

Oedipus had always known that his predecessor was dead but did not know the exact circumstances of his death. Creon fills him in, explaining that Laius had gone to consult the oracle about the Sphinx. He traveled with an entourage but was killed during an altercation on the road; only one member of the entourage survived the onslaught. After his return to Thebes, the survivor testified that a band of robbers attacked the king and his men. Oedipus asks why men from the city didn't track down the killer right after the murder, when the trail wasn't so cold. Creon explains that it was because of the Sphinx: With a monster at their doorstep, they were incapable of focusing on anything else.

Oedipus vows to find the guilty party or parties. Gently chastising the city, he proclaims that once more he, Oedipus, will bring everything to light, as he did in confronting the Sphinx those many years ago. He places a curse on the evildoer: "Whoever he is, a lone man unknown in his crime or one among many, let that man drag out his life in agony, step by painful step" (lines 280–83).

Oedipus wears a toga, not a trench coat. But the moment Creon returns with the news that they must find Laius's murderer, Oedipus is in full detective mode, doing all the things that we expect from modern-day detectives: He looks for clues, interviews potential witnesses, puts pieces together, and so on. He even says the kinds of things a detective says. "One thing could hold the key to it all" (line 136)—words that could easily have come from the mouth of Sherlock Holmes or any of the other great fictional detectives. So the play begins with a murder mystery that, if it were written by Agatha Christie, might have been called *Who Killed Laius Rex?* (True, we already know the answer, but that's the case in a lot of detective stories—think of *Columbo*, for example.)

At Creon's suggestion, Oedipus orders that Teiresias, the great blind seer of Greek mythology, be brought before him. According to the legend, he is blind because he made one god angry. In compensation for his blindness, another god gave him the gift of prophecy. Also, earlier in his life, Teiresias spent some time as a woman—another transformation resulting from divine wrath.[7]

Teiresias arrives and, under questioning from Oedipus, indicates that he can identify the killer but refuses to do. Understandably, this baffles and then enrages Oedipus, who in his anger accuses Teiresias of being part of a conspiracy of silence. This in turn infuriates Teiresias, who then blurts out that Oedipus himself is Laius's murderer.

At this point in the story, Oedipus has no basis on which to interpret the accusation as anything other than treachery and vengefulness, and so he accuses Teiresias of conspiring with Creon, as the latter had suggested the consultation with the seer in the first place. In his anger, Oedipus even attacks Teiresias's skills as a prophet, calling him a "pious fraud" and noting that it was he, not Teiresias, who solved the riddle of the Sphinx. He even threatens to have Teiresias whipped. Teiresias, in turn, lets fly all his prophetic fury, revealing everything—the murder, Oedipus's marriage to his own mother, *everything*—but at this point, Oedipus can only assume he's the victim of a vicious political calumny.

Oedipus has the seer removed from his presence and confronts Creon directly, accusing him of plotting with Teiresias. An ugly exchange ensues. Oedipus begins by cross-examining Creon on the suspicious nature of Teiresias's allegations. If he himself were really the killer, he asks, why had Teiresias never mentioned it before? Why hadn't Teiresias said anything until Creon proposed that he be questioned about the killing? Oedipus then accuses Creon of trying to usurp him. Creon responds that he has no reason to depose Oedipus; he already has what he wants in life. Oedipus is unconvinced, saying that Creon should be killed.

Jocasta now enters the scene, having heard that her husband and brother were fighting. The chorus steps in, begging Oedipus to drop his charge of treason against Creon. Oedipus agrees to this request, making clear that he does so only for the sake of the chorus, not for the sake of Creon. Creon exits, leaving Oedipus and Jocasta alone for the first and only time in the play. Jocasta asks Oedipus to explain what's happening. He does. What follows next is a dialogue that takes irony to a level that surely has never been exceeded in literature.

Jocasta tells Oedipus that he can't trust soothsayers like Teiresias, demonstrating her point by telling the story of how she and Laius were warned not to produce offspring. This must have been a false prophecy, she explains, because Laius was murdered by highwaymen, not his offspring, "at a spot where three roads meet." Laius couldn't have been killed by his offspring, she says, because his only son was killed when he was three days old: "My son—he wasn't three days old and the boy's father fastened his ankles, had a henchman fling him away on a barren, trackless mountain." And therefore, she concludes, the prophecy was worthless: "There, you see? Apollo brought neither thing to pass. My baby no more murdered his father than Laius suffered—his wildest fear—death at his own son's hands" (lines 790–96).

This is the pivot. There's much more play to go, including some additional stunning revelations. But by this point Oedipus has strong reason to believe that he is the man whom he's been searching for. Who killed Laius Rex? The conclusion, which is starting to seem inescapable, is that it was Oedipus himself. Who is the man lurking inside the city who has brought upon its people the scourge of the plague? Again, the answer is Oedipus.

Whenever I think about this idea, other stories come flooding back to mind: Ernest discovering that he himself is the Great Stone Face, Moses learning that he is the Hebrew deliverer for whom he has been searching, the Earth children realizing that they themselves are Martians. These stories share the same interesting pattern, but in the case of *Oedipus Rex* it shows up in one of the world's most important works of literature, not just a short story or a Cecil B. DeMille film. Discovering this theme in *Oedipus Rex*, above all the other stories, clinched it for me: This idea might be important.

THE MOONSTONE

Once I realized I had a theme on my hands—a theme that *Oedipus Rex* embodies—I needed a name for it. For years, I called it "the Accidental Self-Discoverer." This was meant to convey that the self-discovery was unintended, an accidental product of an entirely different exploration directed outward, without a hint of introspection.

Eventually, I decided that "Accidental Self-Discoverer" didn't quite work. It sounds as if I'm merely talking about someone who, in the course of doing something else, accidentally stumbles upon an undetected aspect of himself ("I really learned a lot about myself when I tried rock climbing for the first time"). The character I have in mind doesn't merely learn something *about* himself. In the course of searching for someone else, he opens a door and sees, standing on the other side of the threshold . . . himself.

"The Blind Detective" fits better, but I decided against that one because it suggests a detective who is literally blind, and there was such a TV show (*Longstreet*) in the seventies. I didn't want anyone thinking I was referring to that piece of kitsch.

How about "the Fake Detective"? After all, there's something kind of phony about the search, given what all of the characters engaged in it ultimately discover. But there already is a stock character who pretends to be searching for a villain, all the while knowing that he himself *is* the villain; he's merely *pretending* to be searching to throw everyone off the scent. One of my favorite examples is in the classic 1944 Billy Wilder film *Double Indemnity* (later remade as *Body Heat*), in which Fred MacMurray plays an insurance salesman who murders the husband of his lover and pretends to help the in-house detective, played by Edward G. Robinson, find the killer. But there are countless other models. Other great examples of Fake Detectives in film and literature include those in Nathaniel Hawthorne's *The Scarlet Letter* (Hester Prynne's lover is the minister Arthur Dimmesdale, who repeatedly exhorts his congregation to identify said lover), Edgar Allan Poe's story "Thou Art the Man" (the murderer pretends to find clues to the murder that implicate another person), Agatha Christie's *The Murder of Roger Ackroyd* (the murderer turns out to be the detective Hercule Poirot's sidekick, and is also the book's narrator!), and Heinrich von Kleist's 1808 comedy *The Broken Jug* (the villain is the judge presiding over the case). Eventually, I decided that Fake Detective doesn't work either, because the Oedipus-type protagonist is genuinely unaware he is the culprit. There's nothing fake about his search for the truth.

Ultimately, I decided to call this theme "the Circular Detective"—"circular" because the protagonist's search leads him back in a circle to himself, and "detective" because he's engaged in a sort of detective work while searching for the guilty party (or some other revelation). Most of the characters I have in mind aren't literal detectives. Ernest in "The Great Stone Face," Moses in *The Ten Commandments*, the Earth children in *The Martian Chronicles*—they aren't gumshoes or private eyes.

Some Circular Detectives *are* literal detectives, however. In my years of exploring this theme, I encountered a genre called the "metaphysical detective story." Literary critics have applied this term to contemporary detective stories by writers such as Paul Auster, Jorge Luis Borges, Thomas Pynchon, Don DeLillo, Umberto Eco, and Italo Calvino that, in one way or another, depart from the standard detective format.[8] In most of these stories, the detective wanders around aimlessly, never finding the answer to the mystery. They are very much in keeping with postmodernism's skepticism about objective truths. But in a few of the stories, the detective discovers, Oedipus-like, that *he* is actually the villain he's been searching for. The two leading examples of this are *Falling Angel* by William Hjortsberg (on which the 1987 movie *Angel Heart* is based) and the 1953 novel *The Erasers* by the French author Alain Robbe-Grillet. Both consciously echo *Oedipus Rex*.

In *Falling Angel*, the detective, Harry Angel, is hired to find a missing Frank Sinatra–like crooner named Johnny Favorite, who, when not busy singing, appears to have committed a series of unspeakable murders. Angel follows a trail of bloody clues until, eventually, he discovers that he himself is Favorite. As it turns out, Favorite sold his soul to the devil and then contracted amnesia, which is why he didn't know he was the person he was searching for.

The clever twist in *The Erasers* is that the crime isn't committed until the end of the story. In that novel, a police detective named Wallas is searching for the murderer of a man named Daniel Dupont. Unbeknownst to Wallas, however, Dupont is still alive. He wasn't killed by the assassin's bullet but merely suffered a flesh wound, and he is being hidden by friends who have put out the word that he's dead to protect him from future assassination attempts. Wallas obtains information leading him to believe that the assassin will return to Dupont's house to retrieve some important papers that, in the commotion of the kill, he had left behind. Wallas goes to Dupont's house and waits in the study for the assassin, his pistol cocked. Meanwhile, we learn that Dupont has decided to return to the house to retrieve the very same papers. You can see the end coming: Wallas shoots and kills Dupont, thereby committing the very murder he was sent to solve. In other words, in contrast to the usual detective story, the crime takes place *after* the investigation.[9] As we've already seen, the Circular Detective isn't always a murderer or undiscovered villain. Sometimes this character is a hero, as in "The Great Stone Face." In the 1999 movie *The Matrix*, the protagonist, Neo, is searching for a savior who is called "the One" (an anagram of "Neo") and eventually discovers that he is that savior. (*The Ten Commandments* is an interesting case because Moses is a combination of villain *and* hero. He begins by looking for a villain, but then, when he learns the truth, the villain becomes a hero, at least from Moses's point of view.)

For some Circular Detectives, the target is neither villain nor hero but victim. In *Sorry, Wrong Number*, a 1948 film noir classic, Barbara Stanwyck plays Leona Stevenson, a bedridden invalid heiress. Over the course of the movie, we learn that her husband, Henry (played by Burt Lancaster), married her strictly for her money and is waiting for the right opportunity to have her killed. One night, Leona is lying in bed, awaiting Henry's return home from work. He is quite late, and she tries to reach his office by phone. Trying to reach her husband's office, Leona overhears a conversation between two men plotting a murder. (This was a time when telephone lines could become "crossed," enabling callers to overhear another conversation without being heard.) She desperately tries to get the police to investigate, but without more detail, they can't do anything. Eventually, she discovers—sadly, too late to save herself—that she is the person whose murder they are plotting. Similarly, in Borges's great story "Death and the Compass," the detective turns out to be the fourth intended victim of the killer he has been tracking.

In some of these stories, such as *The Martian Chronicles*, the target isn't even a person, or at least isn't believed to be a person. This is the basis of one of the one of the best-selling novels of the 2000s, *The Da Vinci Code*. At the heart of the novel is a Circular Detective story: Throughout the book and the movie based on it, the protagonists, Robert Langdon and Sophie Neveu, are trying to find the Holy Grail. Like everyone else, they assume that the name refers to the cup from which Jesus drank wine at the Last Supper. As they discover in the end, however, the Holy Grail is not a cup at all: It is the bloodline of Christ, and, they learn, Sophie is one of his descendants. She discovers, in other words, that all along she has been searching for herself.

How can one be ignorant of the fact that one is searching for oneself? There are many ways. Some Circular Detectives are made ignorant by amnesia, as happens in *Falling Angel*. One of my favorite movies of recent years is 2001's *Memento,* which turns on the spotty recollections of the protagonist, Leonard, a man who suffers from anterograde amnesia, the type of amnesia with which one cannot form new memories. He searches in vain for his wife's murderer, without realizing that he himself killed her by giving her an overdose of the insulin she took for her diabetes. What we, and ultimately Leonard, learn is that his wife, taking advantage of his forgetfulness, had him give her the lethal injection because she could no longer bear to deal with his severe mental disorder. Precisely because of the disorder, Leonard forgets this fact and continues searching for her murderer as if it were someone else. A similar discovery is made by Leonardo DiCaprio's character in Martin Scorsese's 2010 film *Shutter Island.*

Another reason you might not know you're searching for yourself: You were drugged at the time of the inciting incident. This is what drives the plot of *The Moonstone*, published in 1868 by Wilkie Collins, a friend and protégé of Charles Dickens. It's considered the first detective novel in the English language, and so it is. (Edgar Allan Poe is credited with inventing the genre, but his works in the form were short stories.) The crime in *The Moonstone* is eventually solved not by the detective but by the protagonist. The plot revolves around the theft of a priceless gem from India called the Moonstone, which had been given to the protagonist's beloved for her birthday. In the end, the protagonist learns that he himself is the thief. It turns out that, as a prank, he was given a small dose of opium the night of the theft; he stole the stone while sleepwalking in his drugged state.

Hypnosis was the mechanism of obfuscation in Woody Allen's 2001 comedy, *The Curse of the Jade Scorpion.* Allen plays an insurance detective who is hypnotized by a criminal mastermind. Whenever he picks up a phone and hears a certain triggering word, he falls into a hypnotic trance, during which he robotically follows orders to steal valuable belongings from wealthy homes. During the day, he's the detective searching for the thief behind these burglaries, but he eventually discovers his other role.

The Curse of the Jade Scorpion illustrates how the Circular Detective theme shows up in every genre of storytelling—comedies as well as tragedies and suspense stories. I have found examples of it all over the place, in all forms of media, from movies and novels to plays and short stories. And its reach is even broader if you include the type of story in which the Circular Detective is a group rather than just a single individual; in other words, the scenario in which members of a group search for a villain without being aware that the villain is actually a fellow member. They assume that the miscreant is outside the group, not in it—one of *them* rather than one of *us*. From the point of view of the guilty member, this is a Fake Detective story, as in *Double Indemnity*. But if we shift the perspective to the other members of the group, you have a Circular Detective story, in which the surprise is that the evil lurks *within* rather than *without*. This is how *Double Indemnity* would appear if the movie's perspective shifted from Fred MacMurray's to Edward G. Robinson's.

THE WISEST MAN IN ATHENS

One day I was sitting in a temple service, flipping through the Torah. I opened it up at random and landed on the familiar story about Abraham heeding God's command to sacrifice his son Isaac—a story I had read or heard many times in the course of my life. But this time I noticed something I had never noticed before. A single phrase in the following passage jumped out at me:

> And Abraham took the wood of the burnt offering, and laid it upon Isaac his son; and he took the fire in his hand, and a knife; and they went both of them together. And Isaac spake unto Abraham his father, and said, My father: and he said, Here am I, my son. And [Isaac] said, Behold the fire and the wood: *but*

> *where is the lamb for a burnt offering?* And Abraham said, My son, God will provide himself a lamb for a burnt offering: so they went both of them together.[10]

Where is the lamb, indeed? I chanced on one of the most famous passages in the entire Bible, and there it was—a Circular Detective story. Isaac asks where the lamb is, and a few moments later he discovers, like the woman in *Sorry, Wrong Number*, that he himself is the lamb.

When this passage is discussed, the focus is almost always on the horrible sacrifice Abraham is prepared to make. The story is about his devotion to God and God's reaction. But if you shift perspectives and look at events from Isaac's point of view, you have a very different story: the story of a son suddenly discovering that his father is prepared to slaughter him, that he is the sacrificial lamb they have traveled all this way to offer God.

I was struck by the fact that Isaac's question is even there in the first place. Isaac's inquiry is superfluous to the overall message of the story; the passage would raise the same exact questions about the relationship between Abraham and God with or without it. The passage skips over many details, and the absence of a question from Isaac to his father about the lamb wouldn't be missed. Yet the anonymous writer (or writers) of this dramatic scene chose to put it in there. That reinforced for me once again the irresistibility of this theme.

Here's another example from the ancient world. In *The Apology*, published at the turn of the fourth century BC, Plato recounts Socrates's trial for corrupting the youth of Athens. In his closing statement to the jury, Socrates tells the story of how he came to be the Socrates we think of today—the great questioner who, through subtle and skillful interrogation, exposes the flaws and fallacies in his opponent's arguments.

As a young man, Socrates explains, he learned from a friend that when he asked the Delphic oracle if anyone was wiser than Socrates, the oracle answered in the negative. This puzzled Socrates greatly, for he knew he had no wisdom. Having no wisdom, how could he be considered the wisest of men? He decided that he would try to find a man wiser than himself, proving the oracle wrong.

And so, like Ernest in "The Great Stone Face," Socrates sought out men with reputations for great wisdom and engaged them in dialogue. But, also like Ernest, each time he interacted with them he was disappointed, for he would discover upon questioning that, though each man thought he knew a great deal, he actually knew nothing. Socrates's interactions annoyed the powerful of Athens and earned him many enemies. But each time he left one of these men, he thought to himself:

> Well, although I do not suppose that either of us knows anything really beautiful and good, I am better off than he is—for he knows nothing, and thinks that he knows. I neither know nor think that I know. In this latter particular, then, I seem to have slightly the advantage of him.[11]

He did this time and again, until at last he concluded that the oracle was right. He really was the wisest man in Athens—not because he knew more than the others but because he knew that he knew nothing.

> [T]he result of my mission was just this: I found that the men most in repute were all but the most foolish. . . . I will tell you the tale of my wanderings and of the "Herculean" labors, as I may call them, which I endured only to find at last the oracle irrefutable.[12]

Notice the parallels with *Oedipus Rex*: In both *The Apology* and *Oedipus Rex*, a search is triggered by a pronouncement by the Delphic oracle. In both, the search involves a series of interviews. And in both stories, the hero lands himself in an inordinate amount of trouble in the course of making his discovery (Socrates, under sentence of death, drinks the hemlock; Oedipus blinds himself and is forced out of town).

Nobody knows if Socrates (or Plato) fabricated the oracle part of the story, or the story as a whole. I suspect so; the story seems too clever. It also seems too much like *Oedipus Rex*, with which both men, whose paths crossed in the decades just after the play's initial performance, were presumably familiar. But whether it was true or not, Socrates (or Plato) chose to tell the story in this way. The storyteller could have left out the part about the oracle and the search for the wisest man in Athens and still made the same point about the importance of questioning your own beliefs and so on—but he didn't. He chose the oracle as a vehicle through which to tell the story.

The more examples of the theme of the Circular Detective I came across, the more I became convinced that it lay at the heart of what makes *Oedipus Rex* so extraordinarily powerful. And my conviction became even stronger when, one day, I realized that there's another example of the Circular Detective theme contained within the broader Oedipus myth itself.

A GREAT FORESHADOWING

If it's not the most famous riddle of all time, it's definitely up there: "What creature walks on four legs in the morning, two legs in the afternoon, and three in the evening?" I heard it when I was young, long before I had ever heard of Oedipus. When my daughter was eight or nine, she told my wife and me over dinner one night that she had learned a riddle at school: "What creature walks on four legs . . ." She asked for our response with the delight of a young person who thinks he or she knows something a grown-up doesn't. I, for one, was thrilled to discover that kids are still learning the riddle. Feigning ignorance, we let her tell us the answer.

Solving the Sphinx's riddle was Oedipus's signal accomplishment. It's referenced many times in the course of the play. "He solved the famous riddle with his brilliance," the chorus declares at the end, acknowledging his former greatness. When Oedipus is called on to solve the mystery of who killed Laius, he declares, "Then once more I must turn what is dark to light"—with "once more" referring to the time he solved the Sphinx's riddle.[13] In the scene with Teiresias, he challenges Teiresias's powers of prophecy by noting that it was he, Oedipus, and not the blind seer who saved the people from the Sphinx.The Sphinx episode is central to Oedipus's life story; it's his claim to fame. And how appropriate, too, for the riddle applies with special force to Oedipus. After all, he himself exemplifies the three stages of life to a heightened degree: He was more helpless as an infant than most, due to the binding of his feet; in the prime of his life he achieved power few men ever hold, because he was a king; and he was feebler than most old men owing to his blindness.[14] Oedipus without the Sphinx wouldn't be Oedipus. The image of the confident hero standing in front of the Sphinx, on the cusp of solving her riddle, is one of the most enduring depictions of contemplation in Western art, along with Auguste Rodin's sculpture *The Thinker* and various depictions of Shakespeare's Hamlet holding the skull of Yorick as he contemplates mortality.

One day, years ago, I had an epiphany. I realized that the riddle of the Sphinx was integral to the story of *Oedipus Rex* in another way: The riddle is itself a Circular Detective story. Think about it: The Sphinx asks you to identify a creature. At first you don't know what the creature is—then you suddenly realize, "Oh my god! It's man. Which means that it's *me. I'm* the creature being described." Like the Earth children in *The Martian Chronicles*, your attention is focused on an alien creature, something to which presumably you bear no resemblance. You wonder who or what it is, what it looks like. And then all of a sudden, you find the answer: It's you.

This must be one of the most powerful instances of foreshadowing in all of literature. In the backstory, Oedipus was given a riddle in which he had to figure out who or what something was, only to realize it was himself—and that's precisely what happens in the drama unfolding before us. He is given a second riddle: Who killed Laius? Once again, eventually he realizes the answer is *himself.* As with Chekhov's gun, which is shown in an early scene and must go off in a later one, the Sphinx's riddle, which Oedipus himself invokes at the beginning of the play, returns with a vengeance. Later in the play, he discovers that *he* is that mysterious, alien creature—Laius's killer. The riddle was not just a riddle; it was also a prophecy.

I was excited when I made this connection, and for a while I felt that thrilling sense of discovery. Eventually, I learned that I wasn't the only person to have noticed this relationship between the Sphinx episode and Sophocles's play. As it turned out, several scholars had made the same observation.[15] In fact, the German Romantic thinker August Wilhelm Schlegel (1767–1845) had, as far back as 1808, noticed the massive irony in the fact that "to the very Oedipus who solved the riddle of the Sphinx relating to human life, his own life should remain so long an inextricable riddle . . ."[16]

Looking back, I realize the foolish grandiosity of thinking that such a thing would have gone unnoticed for 2,500 years! After getting over my initial disappointment at having been scooped, I took the fact that others saw in the Sphinx's riddle a foreshadowing of the play's plot as a sort of confirmation that in focusing on the Circular Detective theme, I was on the right track in my effort to solve the Riddle of Oedipus.

Plainly there is something irresistible about this theme, I decided, which is why it shows up so often and in such a variety of creative works. So, for many years, I was convinced that it was the key to understanding *Oedipus Rex*. The play is not just another example of the theme in action; it is *the* example par excellence; Oedipus is the archetype of the strange kind of investigator I decided to call the Circular Detective. But at a certain point, I realized that I had ignored the really important question: What's so interesting about the Circular Detective theme, anyway, and why does it appear in so many places?

Chapter Two

Know Thyself

If you lived in ancient Greece, you might have had occasion to consult an oracle about something important, like whether to get married to a certain woman or whether to go to war. Oracles were big business in the ancient world. There were oracles all over the place, and they made a lot of money from the donations left by those seeking oracular wisdom. If you wanted to get the very best advice, you'd seek out the one at Delphi, which had the greatest reputation and popularity of all oracles. Delphi is about two hours by bus from Athens. You can visit it today—as my wife and I did on our honeymoon.

If you traveled to Delphi in ancient times, you would have had to wait your turn, for it was a busy place. When your turn came, you would have walked into the temple of Apollo. Once inside, you would have left your donation (the bigger the donation, the better the advice) and approached the priestesses of Apollo, the earthly representatives through whom the god spoke and made his oracular pronouncements. And then you would have left.[1]

But on your way into the temple, you would have noticed a large inscription in the entrance to the inner shrine, perhaps the most famous phrase coined in the ancient world: "Gnothi seauton." In English, it means "Know thyself."

We hear that phrase all the time. Today, we tend to think of it as a command to get in touch with ourselves and our feelings—a kind of New Age injunction. According to scholars, it meant something quite different to the ancients. To them it meant something like, "Know your limitations in relation to the gods and stay within those limits. Don't get too big for your britches. See what happened to Icarus, who flew too close to the sun? You don't want to end up like poor Marsyas, who challenged Apollo in a musical contest, lost, and was flayed alive as punishment."[2] Each age interprets this phrase differently.

For me, the commandment to "know thyself" is inseparable from the myth of Oedipus and the Circular Detective theme. The phrase is never spoken in the play, not even once—and yet, like the Sphinx's riddle, its presence suffuses every single moment of the play. It is inseparable from the oracle, and the oracle is inseparable from Oedipus. The oracle is what triggers the entire chain of events of Oedipus's horrible fate, first by causing Laius and Jocasta to cast out the infant Oedipus from Thebes and then by causing Oedipus to leave Corinth and head right into disaster. This, of course, all occurs before the play actually begins. But when the play starts, it is the oracle that sets everything in motion. Its message, carried back by Creon, unleashes the play's drama and revelations. The oracle is everywhere.

The Delphic oracle plays a role in many myths and works from ancient Greece—for example, Herodotus's *Histories*. But nowhere does it loom larger than in *Oedipus Rex*, hovering over the story like a brooding presence; it's practically a character. What an extraordinary irony this is—for Oedipus, a man whose entire life was shaped by the Delphic oracle, the source of one of the world's most timeless phrases about self-knowledge, is the most famously self-ignorant character in all of literature, a man who brought horrors upon himself precisely because he didn't have the first clue as to who he was. The irony here matches the one noted by Schlegel regarding the Sphinx's riddle.

As I noted at the end of chapter 1, once I had collected a critical mass of examples of the theme of the Circular Detective, I posed this question to myself: What's so compelling about the theme, of which *Oedipus Rex* is the greatest exemplar? It took a little while, but it eventually occurred to me that "Know thyself" probably has a lot to do with it. In his prediscovery phase, the Circular Detective (Oedipus or any other) is missing some very basic information about himself. That's what makes him a Circular Detective—he is a living, breathing violation of the Delphic command.

But what applies to the Circular Detective applies to us as well—*all* of us. We're all guilty, to some extent, of failing to comply with the Delphic command. Some of us are more oblivious than others, but I think it would be hard to find someone who isn't at least a little self-ignorant. That, I decided, is what makes the Circular Detective theme so intriguing. We keep coming back to this theme time and again because it embodies and reflects that fundamental fact of human nature. The Circular Detective theme is a deliciously good parable of self-ignorance, a syndrome afflicting all of us to some extent, even the most self-aware.

"THE MAN THAT HATH DONE THIS THING SHALL SURELY DIE"

I'm not a professional psychologist or neuroscientist, but I spend a lot of time following developments in the field, and it has been my observation that if there's one thing we've learned from modern psychology and brain science, it's that we don't know ourselves very well. I don't mean mankind as a whole; from a physiological, anatomical, and evolutionary standpoint, we've learned a huge amount in just the last few decades about the human brain and how the mind works, and we learn more every day. Rather, I mean each of us as individuals remain ignorant about ourselves. And the more we learn, the more we become aware of our individual self-ignorance. Few people in literature or real life have been as spectacularly self-ignorant as Oedipus, but each of us partakes in his condition to some degree.

Self-ignorance is not a unitary phenomenon; it assumes many different forms. For example, at the simplest level, there's ignorance about one's own abilities. Sometimes you're better at something than you think you are—though usually it's the opposite.

One reason we may be blind to our own limitations is that the limitations themselves may reduce our ability to spot them, just as your need to wear eyeglasses makes it harder for you to find your eyeglasses when you misplace them. This form of blindness is known today as the Dunning-Kruger effect, after the authors of several studies on the subject. As they put it in one of their articles: "The skills that engender competence in a particular domain are often the very same skills necessary to evaluate competence in that domain—one's own or anyone else's."[3] The Dunning-Kruger effect applies primarily to cognitive skills like logical reasoning, writing ability, and sense of humor. The Civil War veteran and writer Ambrose Bierce put it more wittily when he defined "mind" as a "mysterious form of matter secreted by the brain [whose] chief activity consists in the endeavor to ascertain its own nature, the futility of the attempt being due to the fact that it has nothing but itself to know itself with."[4]

At any rate, this is one of the things we mean when we speak of self-ignorance. There's also self-ignorance in the sense of obliviousness to how one comes across to others, which psychologists call the "persona problem"—the gap between how someone is perceived and how he perceives himself.

Those are fairly obvious forms of self-ignorance. But in actuality, our ignorance of ourselves goes much deeper than that. In fairly fundamental ways, we are all "strangers to ourselves," to invoke the title of a pathbreaking book on the subject by University of Virginia psychologist Timothy Wilson.

At first, this might seem counterintuitive. After all, we have direct access to our own inner thoughts.[5] Despite that front-row seat, though, we still don't know ourselves very well. That's because consciousness is, in the words of Harvard psychology professor Steven Pinker, "the tip of an iceberg of mental computation."[6] You may think you're the boss of you, but in reality you're just along for the ride, as if you were sitting on top of a horse, to use a metaphor of the psychologist Jonathan Haidt.[7] Scores of social-psychology experiments from the last several decades have suggested myriad ways in which we are influenced by factors outside our conscious awareness—experiments in which, for example, subjects who are standing next to hand sanitizers are momentarily likelier to express politically conservative views than control subjects, or subjects who are smelling delicious baked goods are likelier to be kind to strangers.[8]

Much of the time, we don't even know what we want in life, or why we do what we do. That's why, quite often, others know what we want better than we know it ourselves, which in turn is why (among countless other examples) the smart real-estate agent ignores what homebuyers *say* they are looking for but pays close attention to their reactions to actual homes.[9]

The notion that we're not really in charge, of course, did not start with modern psychology and neuroscience. And contrary to popular belief, the idea of the unconscious didn't even start with Freud.[10] (The cognitive neuroscientist Stanislas Dehaene has written that the solid parts of Freud on the unconscious weren't original, and the original parts weren't solid.)[11] Pick up almost any great nineteenth-century novel, and you'll find suggestions of unconscious motivations at work. "I doubt whether the wisest of us know what our own motives are," wrote William Makepeace Thackeray in the nineteenth century, "and whether some of the actions of which we are the very proudest will not surprise us when we trace them, as we shall someday, to their source."[12] In the eighteenth century, Immanuel Kant wrote, "We can never, even by the strictest examination, get completely behind the secret springs of action."[13]

But modern science keeps advancing knowledge about our ignorance—and the results aren't always pretty. As many laboratory tests have shown, our conscious selves are usually the last to get the memo about a decision made by our unconscious selves. Brain-imaging studies show that a test subject performs an action before becoming consciously aware of it.[14] In fact, a number of neuroscientists have argued that the main role of consciousness is to concoct after-the-fact reasons for our actions. Each of us is like the leaf Ambrose Bierce describes in *The Devil's Dictionary*, which is under the illusion it's in charge:

> A leaf was riven from a tree,
> "I mean to fall to earth," said he.
> The west wind rising, made him veer.
> "Eastward," said he, "I now shall steer."
> The east wind rose with greater force.
> Said he: "'Twere wise to change my course."
> With equal power they contend.
> He said: "My judgment I suspend."
> Down died the winds; the leaf, elate,
> Cried: "I've decided to fall straight."[15]

Now, as the psychologist Paul Bloom recently cautioned, we shouldn't become so enamored of neuroscience findings from brain imaging and the like, and social-psychology experiments involving hand sanitizers, that we jump to the conclusion that *everything* we do is the product of unconscious factors. We're also influenced by *rational* factors, and probably a lot more so than all those fun experiments involving undergraduate psychology students would suggest. To go back to Pinker's iceberg analogy, surely *some* of the iceberg sticks out of the water.[16] But no one, including Paul Bloom, denies that much of it is under the water. The debate is over the ratio, not over whether we're ignorant of a pretty big percentage of our true motivations.

One form of self-ignorance is particularly relevant to the Circular Detective theme: the inability to see ourselves in a clear moral light. From an evolutionary point of view, it can be quite useful to assume that you're the one wearing the white hat and that, in spite of your actual behavior, your essence is goodness. It helps in climbing up the greasy pole of success. That's why so few people, if in fact any, think of themselves as evil. As Pinker writes:

> In cartoons and movies, the villains are mustache-twirling degenerates, cackling with glee at their badness. In real life, villains are convinced of their rectitude. Many biographers of evil men start out assuming that their subjects are cynical opportunists and reluctantly discover that they are ideologues and moralists. If Hitler was an actor, concluded one, he was an actor who believed in the part.[17]

From an evolutionary point of view, our number one job is to look out for, well, number one. This self-love that philosophers and moralists have talked about for centuries is grounded in evolutionary logic. According to Pinker, "Our brains were shaped for fitness, not for truth. Sometimes the truth is adaptive, but sometimes it is not."[18] Our self-love enables us to advance our favorite cause—ourselves. Seeing the evil in our own ways may be a great thing to do from a moral point of view, but from an evolutionary point of view, it generally gets in the way. We see ourselves, in psychologist Jonathan Haidt's phrase, through a rose-colored mirror.[19]

Our slowness in recognizing our own evil ways is matched only by the speed with which we condemn others, often for faults we ourselves possess or for conduct we have committed. As the writer Robert Wright commented, "The keen sensitivity with which people detect the flaws of their rivals is one of nature's wonders."[20] But when it comes to noticing our own moral shortcomings, we're bumblers. Some neuroscientists call this the "holier-than-thou effect."[21] Others call it the "moralization gap."[22] But these are just new names for a phenomenon that has been known for a very long time. The Buddha put it this way: "The fault of others is easily perceived, but that of one's self is difficult to perceive."[23]

There is a whole vintage of sayings on this topic. Mark Twain drily noted that "nothing so needs reforming as other people's habits."[24] It's always the other guy who's evil, not me, it seems—a state of mind characterized by Timothy Wilson as "the psychological immune system."[25] He explains:

> One of the most enduring lessons from social psychology is that . . . people go to great lengths to view the world in a way that maintains a sense of well-being. We are masterly spin doctors, rationalizers, and justifiers of threatening information. . . . Just as we possess a potent physical immune system that protects us from threats to our physical well-being, so do we possess a potent psychological immune system that protects us from threats to our psychological well-being. When it comes to maintaining a sense of well-being, each of us is the ultimate spin doctor.[26]

August Wilhelm Schlegel's brief summation of the plot of *Oedipus Rex* makes this point nicely, too; he calls it "a striking picture of the arrogant pretension of human wisdom, which is ever right enough in its general principles, but does not enable the possessor to make the proper application to himself."[27]

The Bible furnishes a beautiful illustration of this phenomenon in a story about another king of ancient legend—in this case, David. After King David has seduced Uriah's wife, Bathsheba, and sent him off to die in battle, God sends the prophet Nathan to pay David a visit. Nathan tells David that in a certain city in the kingdom, there are two men, one rich and the other poor. The rich man has many sheep; the poor man, only one lamb. Yet when the rich man needed a lamb to serve a houseguest, he took the poor man's only lamb. The story continues:

> And David's anger was greatly kindled against the man; and he said to Nathan, As the Lord liveth, the man that hath done this thing shall surely die.
>
> And he shall restore the lamb fourfold, because he did this thing, and because he had no pity.
>
> And Nathan said to David, Thou art the man.[28]

Nathan then explains that he was sent by God and that the story was a parable of David's own conduct toward Uriah. David realizes the size of his own sins and seeks God's forgiveness.

The search for the culprit in this story lasts only a moment—long enough for Nathan to spring the trap. But it's a Circular Detective situation, for David, like Oedipus, fails to understand that *he* is "the man that hath done this thing." It's a brilliant lesson in how to shake someone out of his moral blindness. Nathan doesn't grab David by the tunic and shout in his face, "You terrible man! You did a horrible thing! You stole another man's wife when you had many and he had only one!" He works by indirection, drawing King David's attention to another person—an unnamed stranger—and thereby getting David himself to issue the condemnation, as surely as Oedipus condemns Laius's killer to "drag out his life in agony, step by painful step." And David, just like Oedipus, finds himself in the remarkable position of being the object of his own curse.

My point is not that the two kings' respective actions were morally equivalent. David failed to appreciate the moral significance of his conduct, but he understood the brute fact of what he had done; Oedipus, in contrast, was simply ignorant of the brute facts. My point is that the story of Oedipus—the Circular Detective par excellence—is an unmatched parable of self-ignorance, an unforgettable reminder that we don't know ourselves very well.

"THE PLAY'S THE THING"

Imagine you recently committed a crime. Afterward, it just so happens that you decide to watch a play. It's a new play, and you know nothing about it. The curtain rises, the actors come out on stage, and the play begins. You enjoy it at first, but then something strange happens: You start to notice that the actors are reenacting a crime you recently committed. At first, you think it's a strange coincidence. But as it goes on, the performers include more and more details that capture exactly what you did. You panic. *Why is this is happening?* Do the creators of the play know about your crime? Are they watching you right now? Are the police there, ready to arrest you as soon as the play ends? You jump out of your seat and hurry to the exit.

I just described the scene in *Hamlet* in which King Claudius finds himself watching a performance reenacting his murder of his brother, Hamlet's father (the previous king). The performance was devised by Hamlet; looking for a way to prove his uncle's guilt, he concocts a plan whereby the actors in a traveling troupe reenact Claudius's crime. "The play's the thing wherein to catch the conscience of the king," says Hamlet.[29] Everything proceeds exactly as planned. When the actors play out a poisoning scene, Claudius loses control of himself and has to leave the room, deepening Hamlet's conviction that he is guilty.

We tend to look at this scene from Hamlet's point of view, since he is the protagonist and is watching Claudius carefully. But if you undertake one of those shifts in perspective discussed in the previous chapter and put yourself in Claudius's place, you will have the same shock of self-recognition that lies at the heart of the Circular Detective theme. This happens when you see something or someone in the outer world, wonder what or who it is, and then experience the distinct shock of realizing it's all about you. You see firetrucks racing by you in your car, think little of it, and then later learn, to your horror, that it was your own house on fire.

There's a great example of this phenomenon at work in Herodotus's *Histories*. In the book, Herodotus tells a story about the Persian king Cyrus after he captured Croesus, the deposed king of Lydia. After this happens, Cyrus's men begin to ravage and plunder Sardis, the wealthy capital of Lydia. Croesus, feigning ignorance, asks Cyrus what his men are doing. "Plundering your city," replies Cyrus. "No," responds Croesus. "They are plundering *your* city!" Cyrus, in other words, has not yet appreciated the fact that, having conquered Sardis, it is now his city that is being robbed of its wealth.[30]

Here we have yet another form of self-ignorance. You think you are safe. You think you are the objective observer, outside of the Plexiglas box in which the experimental mice are running around. What you haven't yet realized is that you, too, are a mouse. You're not behind the impregnable wall of a tower. You think you're the hunter, but you are in fact the hunted, the observer observed. This is the essence of the Circular Detective theme and of *Oedipus Rex* in particular.

Looking back, I realize that I've been intrigued by this idea for a long time. When I was in high school, I wrote a short story called "In the Coffee Express." The protagonist, who narrates the story, is a writer sitting in a coffee shop observing the world, perhaps waiting for inspiration. He sees someone at another table who, like him, is sitting with pen and paper. Then he notices something interesting—that the person he's observing is observing someone else. It goes on like this, through several people, until the narrator realizes that at the end of the chain is himself.

The Circular Detective, when he discovers the truth, realizes that while the whole time he thought he had been an objective observer, in fact it was the detective himself who was under the microscope. He has a sense of having been tricked, just as Claudius was tricked by Hamlet and King David by Nathan.

ONE ANSWER TO ALL RIDDLES

Not all the messages that come out of a Circular Detective story are quite so negative. I detect one more message within the genre, and it's a fairly upbeat one: Don't wait for someone else to rescue or help you. Do it yourself, for you have all the powers you need. In other words, it's a message of self-reliance. Look to yourself first, since the chances are good that you already have the answer to whatever question you're asking or the ability to accomplish the task at hand. It's not that you *always* have the answer, but you are a great place to start.

When it comes to this message, I can't help thinking of *The Wizard of Oz*. In her journey through Oz, Dorothy is seeking the answer to a question—how to get back home to Kansas. At the end of her journey, however, she discovers that she herself has the answer, in the form of the ruby slippers. Satisfyingly, each of her three sidekicks—the Tin Man, the Scarecrow, and the Cowardly Lion—discovers that he, too, already has what he desires, whether it's brains, a heart, or courage.

One time, while reading one of the Harry Potter books to my kids, I ran across another striking example of this idea. It's in *Harry Potter and the Prisoner of Azkaban*. Stick with me—it's a little complicated because it involves time travel. Late in the book, Harry travels back in time to a moment several days earlier when he was about to be destroyed by Dementors—ghoulish creatures that obliterate their victims by sucking out their souls. Harry was spared that fate at the last instant only because an unseen benefactor rescued him by scaring off the creatures with his magic wand. Now, as a time traveler, Harry is trying to find out who saved him. As the critical moment arrives, however, Harry realizes no one else is coming and that the only person who can save Harry-from-the-past is *himself*, Harry-from-the-future. He proceeds to do precisely that, becoming the person he has been searching for. In the process, he recognizes that he doesn't need anyone else, because his powers are greater than he realized.

Interestingly, in his version of the Oedipus story, André Gide takes this idea of self-reliance to the extreme through a speech he puts into Oedipus's mouth. Offering advice to his sons, Oedipus asserts:

> You must understand, my boys, that each one of us encounters at the beginning of his journey a monster that confronts him with the riddle that may prevent him from going farther. And although to each one of us, my children, the Sphinx may put a different question, you must persuade yourselves that the answer is always the same. Yes, there is only this one same answer to those many and various questions; and that this one answer is: Man; and that this one man, for each and all of us, is: Oneself. [31]

This takes the idea to an absurd, almost solipsistic, extreme. But isn't this, in a way, a lesson learned by all of us as we mature—that we have to rely first and foremost on ourselves? That doesn't mean we can't call on others for help; no man is an island. But shouldn't we at least try to be as self-reliant as possible?

In a sense, this message reflects the much broader shift in history from a god-centered view of the world, in which everything is about God, or the gods, to a man-centered view, in which we create our own world, our own values, and our own destinies. Stop blaming the gods, Gide's Oedipus seems to be saying—blame yourself. Stop looking to God for meaning; look to yourself.[32]

I'm not suggesting that we must always go it alone. One does not have to be Robinson Crusoe, completely resourceful and dependent on no one else, to practice sensible self-reliance. We would be foolish *not* to take advantage of the infinitely valuable resources around us in the form of other people. But self-help is the place to start. Troubleshooting guides for electronic appliances sensibly ask us to first check the obvious things, like whether the power plug has come out of the outlet. If there were an instruction manual for life, the troubleshooting guide at the back could give worse advice than "See if you already have the answer."

These are the messages I have gleaned from the theme of the Circular Detective. The more I contemplated it, the more meaningful it became—and, in turn, the more important it seemed in understanding the Oedipus mystique.

Accordingly, for a long time, I thought that the Circular Detective theme was the key to *Oedipus Rex*. When I looked at the play through the lens of this theme, every aspect of the story seemed to reflect it in one way or another. Here is a man who, everywhere he turns, encounters himself, in one form or another. He kills a man who's his father. He marries a woman who's his mother. The Sphinx poses a riddle, the answer to which is himself. Everything seemed to fit, like the pieces of a jigsaw puzzle.

Eventually, though, I realized that the figure of the Circular Detective does not hold the complete answer to the Riddle of Oedipus, only a partial one. I still think it is a fascinating tool with which to analyze the play, but I came to believe that there is much more to *Oedipus Rex*.

During my Circular Detective phase, I had begun consuming the massive Oedipus literature. And what I found was a remarkable story in its own right.

Chapter Three

From Aristotle to Freud and Beyond

Oedipus Rex has had a long and fascinating afterlife. The list of people who have written about and commented on the play is practically a who's who of Western intellectual history. In fact, it's almost easier to list those who *didn't* have something to say about it. Philosophers, psychologists, and others have found Oedipus an irresistible subject of analysis, resulting in a true cacophony of interpretations. The editor of a collection of essays about the play spoke the truth when he asserted that there was a "seemingly hopeless controversy" as to its meaning.

Like so much else in the history of ideas, it all started with Aristotle.

THE MODEL TRAGEDY

Aristotle (384–322 BC) presented his views on Oedipus in his *Poetics*, a book that essentially invented literary criticism, just as his other writings invented fields such as logic and biology. Today, we don't put much stock in Aristotle's theories on bodies in motion or spontaneous generation—those went out of style after the Middle Ages, when he was known as "the master of those who know."

But we still take seriously his views on literature and drama, and they continue to influence modern writers and thinkers.

Even if you've never read *Poetics*, you're still under its influence. When you talk about catharsis or say that someone has a tragic flaw, or talk about a story exhibiting the three unities (time, place, and action), you're communicating ideas from *Poetics*. Those are all key concepts from the book.

In *Poetics*, which was written roughly one hundred years after *Oedipus Rex* was first performed, Aristotle argued that a tragedy's power came from provoking—through pity ("eleos") and fear ("phobos")—a catharsis. He borrowed the term from medicine; a cathartic is a purgative drug or device. Catharsis has been variously defined in English as purification, purgation, relief, or emotional release. The core of the concept seems to be that when you experience strong feelings of pity and fear while watching a tragic play, you acquire some kind of emotional benefit, one that's analogous to getting it all out from a good long cry or going into the woods and howling at the top of your lungs.

In laying out the criteria for a good tragedy, Aristotle draws on *Oedipus Rex* over and over. In fact, at times it looks as though he built his entire definition around the play, like someone shooting the side of a barn and then drawing circles around the hole to make a bull's-eye. He argues, for example, that the ideal tragedy involves the combination of "peripatea" (reversal) and "anagnorisis" (recognition), and he uses *Oedipus Rex* as his chief example of both concepts. To illustrate the concept of reversal, he writes: "For example, in the *Oedipus* someone came to give Oedipus good news and free him from his fear with regard to his mother, but by disclosing Oedipus' identity he brought about the opposite result"—a reference to the scene where the messenger from Corinth tells Oedipus not to worry about incest, because the queen of Corinth is not his true mother.[1]

Oedipus Rex is the model tragedy, Aristotle argues, because recognition ("a change from ignorance to knowledge") is most powerful when it "occurs simultaneously with a reversal."[2] This is exactly what takes place in *Oedipus Rex*, according to Aristotle. He acknowledges that "there are indeed other kinds of recognition" and offers a couple of examples of them. "But," he affirms, "the one that has most to do with the plot and the most to do with the action is the one I have mentioned [namely, the *Oedipus Rex*–type plot]. For a recognition and reversal of that kind will involve *pity or fear*."[3] The combination in Oedipus is so powerful, he is saying, that even without seeing the play performed, "anyone who hears the events which occur *shudders and feels pity* at what happens; this is how someone would react on hearing the plot of the *Oedipus*."[4]

By the end of his discussion of tragedy, one thing is absolutely clear: Aristotle *loved Oedipus Rex*. He couldn't seem to say enough good things about it. And remember: This is the world's foremost advocate for a happy medium! For Aristotle, *Oedipus Rex* is not merely a handy example to illustrate principles he derived from scratch; as classical scholar Bernard Knox put it, the play "is the basis of the definition."[5]

Poetics is not the world's easiest treatise to understand. But it has had enormous influence. In the words of the contemporary classicist Frederick Ahl, "Many assumptions we have inherited about myth, about tragedy, about Sophocles, and about *Oedipus* derive, ultimately, from Aristotle."[6]

One assumption, by the way, that is *thought* to come from Aristotle but doesn't is the popular notion that Oedipus has a "tragic flaw." Oedipus, goes the cliché, is a man who, but for some flaw of character, wouldn't have suffered his terrible fate. The notion of a tragic flaw is often applied to politicians like Lyndon Johnson, Richard Nixon, Bill Clinton, and others—men who, in one view, fell from great power or lost their chance at greatness due to a character flaw such as paranoia or dishonesty or sexual promiscuity. The concept supposedly comes from the term "hamartia," which Aristotle uses several times in *Poetics*. But scholars, who agree on virtually nothing else about *Oedipus Rex*, are in near-total accord that the concept of the tragic flaw is a mistranslation of "hamartia," at least as applied to Oedipus, and that by "hamartia" Aristotle meant nothing more than some kind of factual error—say, a misidentification of a person—not a character flaw or moral failing.[7]

FROM FRENCH ENLIGHTENMENT TO GERMAN ROMANTICISM

In the first century AD, Seneca, the Roman Stoic philosopher and writer, wrote a version of the Oedipus myth modeled on the Sophocles version. He added a few sensationalistic touches of his own: He has Teiresias conduct a séance to call forth the ghost of Laius, and he has Jocasta kill herself onstage for all to see. He also took great relish in describing the symptoms of the plague in gory detail ("blood oozing from the nose," etc.), much like a Centers for Disease Control and Prevention report on Ebola. (One commentator referred to Seneca's "unconquerable bad taste.")[8] Because Seneca's version was in Latin, which was far more accessible than Greek throughout the Middle Ages, it was better known at that time than the Sophocles one.[9] But with the rediscovery of the Greek classics during the Renaissance, the Sophocles version soon became the canonical one, and it has remained so ever since.[10]

Not that there weren't attempts to knock it off its pedestal. The French of the seventeenth and eighteenth centuries in particular—the period of the great French playwrights such as Molière, Jean Racine, and Pierre Corneille—hoped to oust it to make way for their own versions. (Recall from the introduction that at least seventeen adaptations were authored in France in the eighteenth century.)

The most famous critic of *Oedipus Rex* was Voltaire (1694–1778). When he was twenty-three, he wrote his first play, a version of the Oedipus story that did well and launched his career as a playwright. He made a number of changes to the Sophocles play, including adding a subplot about Jocasta having another lover, and he had the action begin soon after Oedipus's marriage to Jocasta, to smooth over the implausibility that Oedipus was ignorant of how and where Laius died. Like the Seneca version, Voltaire's was largely derivative of Sophocles's, and in my opinion, any veering from the Sophocles version was to its detriment; to paraphrase Stanislas Dehaene on Freud in chapter two, the good parts were not original and the original parts were not good.

In any event, when Voltaire's play was published, he wrote a series of essays in which he explained what, in his view, was wrong with the Sophocles version and why his was a big improvement. Voltaire was one of the great wits of all time and, unsurprisingly, his takedown of the ancient version is hilarious. He walks through the play scene by scene, pointing out all the places Oedipus should have figured out the truth but didn't.[11] At each point along the way, Voltaire argues, the play should be over; Sophocles was just dragging things out. (And, he says, given Oedipus's slow-wittedness, it's a good thing for the Thebans that the Sphinx's riddle was as easy as it was!)[12] Voltaire was particularly apoplectic over the fact that Oedipus went all those years in Thebes without learning the circumstances of Laius's death. "I confess that I do not know any term to express such an absurdity," he wrote in exasperation.[13]

For Voltaire, all of this added up to a very bad play that should have been replaced with modern versions such as the one by the seventeenth-century playwright Corneille and, naturally, his own. He didn't blame the Athenians for loving it, as the art form was in its infancy at that time. But by the advanced and sophisticated eighteenth century, he felt it was time to put childish Greek tragedies away. Of course, Voltaire's own play is full of improbabilities that were pointed out by critics even in his own day.[14]

Even though he called the Sophocles play ridiculous and found Sophocles's Oedipus comically dim, Voltaire was quite obviously fascinated by the myth; otherwise he wouldn't have written his own version. But today, Voltaire's *Oedipe* is mostly forgotten.[15] Sophocles withstood Voltaire's onslaught and won, and he has continued winning ever since.

Of course, Voltaire wasn't the last person to find parts of Sophocles's version implausible from a strictly realistic point of view. Modern critics aren't oblivious to the ways in which the story violates what Voltaire called "the principle of verisimilitude"—for example, the fact that Oedipus and Jocasta don't work out the whole thing years earlier (she didn't notice the scars on his feet?). But unlike Voltaire, they understand that Sophocles was adapting a *myth*, and since when are myths supposed to be true to life? Most modern critics view these plausibility issues within the context of overall admiration for the play as a work of art.

Voltaire's attack on the Sophocles version is a product of his age, in both senses. He was twenty-three when he wrote it, and smart young people love goring sacred cows. Plus, this was the Enlightenment, the age in which reason was king and anything contrary to it dismissed as backward, dangerous superstition. Voltaire was Mr. Enlightenment himself, and his approach to *Oedipus Rex* reflects this world view. How else to explain the fact that he found it absurd and a fatal flaw that the man who could solve the riddle of the Sphinx "does not understand the clearest things [about his own life]"?[16] Here is one of the great ironists of the eighteenth century missing one of the central ironies of the play.

It's no coincidence that the Romantics, the generation that came after the Enlightenment and formed their views in reaction to it, took an entirely different approach to *Oedipus Rex*. The Romantics, especially the Germans—Gotthold Lessing, Friedrich Hölderlin, Schlegel, Goethe, Heinrich von Kleist, Schiller, and many other great figures of the era—absolutely adored Sophocles's play and placed it on a pedestal, where it has remained to this day. They took critics like Voltaire to task for their failure to appreciate Sophocles's genius and for applying an overly literal analysis. As Schlegel explained, "[T]he ancients did not produce their works of art for calculating and prosaic understandings."[17] *Oedipus Rex* loomed so large among these writers and thinkers that one scholar has called the Romantic period "the Age of Oedipus."[18]

Some of the great German philosophers were also fascinated by *Oedipus Rex* and considered it full of profound meaning, and, not incidentally, support for their philosophical positions. For Hegel (1770–1831), *Oedipus Rex* represented one of the big turning points in history, one that became a cornerstone of the Hegelian world view: the shift from innocent, Edenic happiness to an existence based on knowledge.[19] Similarly, Nietzsche (1844–1900), following in the Romantic tradition of viewing reason with suspicion, saw Oedipus's defeat of the Sphinx as an allegory of man's conquest of nature, a "victory" for which man has paid a steep price. Oedipus's use of reason to defeat the Sphinx led him into big trouble, argued Nietzsche. "Oedipus, the murderer of his father, the husband of his mother, the solver of the riddle of the Sphinx! What does the mysterious triad of these fateful deeds tell us?"[20] Nietzsche's answer, contained in the famous passage below, is that he who conquers nature by solving her riddle will be fated to commit unnatural acts:

> The same man who solves the riddle of nature—the Sphinx of two species—also must break the most sacred natural orders by murdering his father and marrying his mother. Indeed, the myth seems to wish to whisper to us that wisdom . . . is an unnatural abomination; that he who by means of his knowledge plunges

> nature into the abyss of destruction must also suffer the dissolution of nature in his own person.[21]

The German philosopher Martin Heidegger (1889–1976) also saw in Oedipus a symbolic vindication of his own philosophical gestalt, which is all about the distinction between appearance and reality. For Heidegger, *Oedipus Rex* was a great symbol of that duality, for on the surface Oedipus was a wise and benevolent king, but in reality he was "the murderer of his father and desecrator of his mother."[22]

HE LOVED HIS MOTHER

This brings us to Sigmund Freud (1856–1939), whose views on the Oedipus myth had a bigger impact on Oedipus scholarship and commentary in the twentieth century than anyone else's. I'm referring, of course, to his theory that boys want to kill their fathers and get them out of the way so they can have their mothers all to themselves—the Oedipus complex.

The Oedipus complex was one of the biggest ideas of twentieth-century psychology, a central plank in Freudian psychology, which itself dominated a good chunk of twentieth-century psychotherapy.[23] As one prominent observer of the psychiatric scene put it, it was central to "[t]he entire massive apparatus of counseling, social work, developmental psychology—therapy in every form."[24] Just think, for example, of the stereotypical psychiatrist stroking his beard and asking the patient to talk about his relationship with his mother.

The Oedipus complex is deeply embedded in popular culture, and it's the source of much humor. In Woody Allen's "Oedipus Wrecks," the protagonist's mother becomes a giant figure in the sky who hovers over New York City, tormenting and embarrassing him night and day. "*Oedipus* won't bomb if he winds up with Mom," sing those bemoaning the overseriousness of Broadway shows in the "Keep It Gay" number in Mel Brooks's *The Producers.* (If you look up "Oedipus complex" in the *Oxford English Dictionary*, you'll find the following example: "'I have to tell you, madam,' the psychiatrist said, 'that your son is suffering from an Oedipus complex.' 'What does it matter,' she replied, 'so long as he loves his mum.'")[25] One of my favorite Tom Lehrer songs is about the Oedipus complex:

> From the Bible to popular song,
> There's one theme that we find right along.
> Of all ideals they hail as good,
> The most sublime is motherhood.
>
> There was a man, oh, who it seems,
> Once carried this ideal to extremes.
> He loved his mother and she loved him,
> And yet his story is rather grim.
>
> There once lived a man named Oedipus Rex.
> You may have heard about his odd complex.
> His name appears in Freud's index
> 'Cause he loved his mother.
>
> His rivals used to say quite a bit,
> That as a monarch he was most unfit.
> But still in all they had to admit
> That he loved his mother.[26]

Freud wasn't the first person to claim that boys want to kill their fathers so they can marry their mothers. To give one example, the French philosophe Denis Diderot (1713–1784) has one of the characters in his play *Rameau's Nephew* describe the mind of the infant in the following terms: "If the little savage were left to himself, preserving all his foolishness and adding to the small sense of a child in the cradle the violent passions of a man of thirty, he would strangle his father and lie with his mother."[27] There's also evidence that the concept may have occurred to some in the ancient world:

Artemidorus, author of a five-book treatise on dreams, wrote about mother-son incest dreams.[28]

But, as he did with the unconscious (see chapter 2), Freud took a fuzzy idea and ran with it. The Oedipus complex plays a fundamental role in Freudian psychology because to Freud it was the key to the unconscious. He also coined the term. He introduced the Oedipus complex in 1899 in his landmark book *The Interpretation of Dreams* (though he first used the actual term in a later paper, in 1910).[29] In a section on "typical dreams," Freud argued that "being in love with one parent and hating the other are among the essential constituents of the stock of psychical impulses which is formed" in childhood—a phenomenon true of everyone, he insisted, not just neurotics.[30]

Everyone has heard of Freud and the Oedipus complex. In fact, today, the Oedipus complex may be better known than the work of literature from which it derives its name. As a result, in the popular imagination, Oedipus is probably more closely linked with Freud than with Sophocles.

What is *not* widely known is that Freud didn't simply invoke Oedipus to give the complex a memorable name, in the way, for example, that the Greek myth of Narcissus is used to describe self-infatuation. In *The Interpretation of Dreams*, Freud expressly presented the complex as an answer to the Riddle of Oedipus—a full-throated theory as to the meaning of *Oedipus Rex*:

> This discovery [of the Oedipus complex] is confirmed by a legend that has come down to us from classical antiquity: *a legend whose profound and universal power to move can only be understood* if the hypothesis I have put forward in regard to the psychology of children has an equally universal validity. What I have in mind is the legend of King Oedipus and Sophocles' drama which bears his name.[31]

But why exactly does the hypothesis of the Oedipus complex explain the legend's "profound and universal power to move"? Freud answered this question in the following passage:

> His destiny moves us only because it might have been ours—because the oracle laid the same curse upon us before our birth as upon him. It is the fate of all of us, perhaps, to direct our first sexual impulse toward our mother and our first hatred and our first murderous wish against our father. Our dreams convince us that this is so. King Oedipus, who slew his father Laius and married his mother Jocasta, merely shows us the fulfillment of our own childhood wishes. But, more fortunate than he, we have meanwhile succeeded, in so far as we have not become psychoneurotics, in detaching our sexual impulses from our mothers and in forgetting our jealousy of our fathers. Here is one in whom these primeval wishes of our childhood have been fulfilled, and we shrink back from him with the whole force of the repression by which those wishes have since that time been held down within us. While the poet, as he unravels the past, brings to light the guilt of Oedipus, he is at the same time compelling us to recognize our own inner minds, in which some same impulses, though suppressed, are still to be found.[32]

In bolstering his case, Freud pointed to the fact that Jocasta, in trying to calm Oedipus's fears about marrying his mother, tells him his fears are normal because "many a man before you, in his dreams, has shared his mother's bed" (lines 1074–75). This, Freud argued, constitutes "an unmistakable indication in the text of Sophocles' tragedy itself that the legend of Oedipus sprang from some primeval dream-material which had as its content the distressing disturbance of a child's relation to his parents owing to the first stirrings of sexuality."[33] He added that "today, just as then, many men dream of having sexual relations with their mothers, and speak of the fact with indignation and astonishment."[34] For Freud, this passage is "clearly the key to the tragedy."[35]

Oedipus Rex certainly wasn't the only piece of literature to be subjected to the Freudian approach. Even Freud himself applied his theory of the complex to works other than *Oedipus Rex*. In a lengthy footnote in *The Interpretation of Dreams*, Freud claimed to have cracked one of the other great unsolved riddles of literature—the reason for Hamlet's dithering (the basis of the phrase "Hamlet-like"). The solution to the so-called "Hamlet problem," said Freud, lies in the Oedipus complex: Hamlet couldn't bring himself to kill his uncle because his uncle had done what he himself had wanted to do—namely, kill his father and marry his mother.[36] One of Freud's disciples, Ernest Jones (1879–1958), later expanded this argument into a full-length book called *Hamlet and Oedipus*, which forever linked these two preeminent masterpieces.

Freudians saw the Oedipus complex everywhere. Another Freud disciple, Otto Rank (1884–1939), applied the Freudian approach to world folk literature.[37] Psychoanalyst Erich Wellisch (1898–1954) devoted an entire book, *Isaac and Oedipus*, to analyzing the story of Abraham and Isaac through the lens of the Oedipus complex.[38] Another psychoanalyst claimed to find the Oedipus complex in every part of Greek mythology, not just the Oedipus myth.[39] And another even claimed to see an Oedipus complex in the life of Jesus.[40] As one observer of the scene put it, critics "have seen the Oedipus complex at work in every imaginable place in literature—from the ancients to the moderns and everyone in between."[41] Of course, they made the task easier for themselves by broadening the definition of the Oedipus complex to include any sort of intra-familial sexual relationship. In his analysis, for example, Rank did not limit himself to the classic Oedipus complex—the triangular father-son-mother relationship—but searched also for tales of father-daughter and brother-sister incest. Like Freud, he viewed the latter as a displacement of the boy's desire for his mother onto his sister.[42]

But Oedipus himself long remained a central focus for Freud and his followers. Freud didn't just offer his interpretation of Oedipus and move on. He remained fascinated not just by the psychological phenomenon but by the myth and the play that gave it a name throughout his entire life. In his study, he kept a statue of the Sphinx. When friends struck a coin in honor of his fiftieth birthday, the image they placed on it was that of Oedipus and the Sphinx.[43] Freud thought he had solved the Riddle of Oedipus. And he found in Oedipus a model for how to conduct psychoanalysis.

For Freud's followers, Oedipus long remained fertile soil in which to plant Freudian theories. Some even argued that Oedipus himself had an Oedipus complex.[44] (This is strange, given that the complex is supposed to be about the childhood urge to commit the Oedipal acts, not the actual completion of those acts.)[45] Freud himself never made such an argument; he claimed not that Oedipus had his complex but that *we* do, and that's why we are so drawn to the story of a man who carried out our repressed fantasies.[46]

Nevertheless, Freudians have seen penises and vaginas everywhere in the story. Take Oedipus's swollen foot (the vestige of his feet having been pinned together when he was a newborn). Since, according to Freudians, the foot is a phallic symbol, Oedipus's swollen foot is an obvious symbol of an engorged penis. Freud acolyte Sándor Ferenczi (1873–1933) was the first to make that linkage; he was also the first to interpret Oedipus's self-blinding as a symbolic castration.[47] Another Freud confidant, Karl Abraham (1877–1925), interpreted the narrow pass where Oedipus encountered Laius as a symbol of female genitalia.[48]

It seemed that one twentieth-century psychologist after another was able to find rich sexual meaning in every part of the story. One, for example, found sexuality in Oedipus's conduct even after he learned that Jocasta was his mother. In an analysis that could pass for a clever parody of a Freudian interpretation, he argued that "the climax of the play is a fantasy of sexual intercourse" and that even the act of storming Jocasta's bedroom "lends itself to an obvious sexual interpretation":

> Oedipus, having arrived in the outer room, demands to find his way into his mother's inner room. He wants to find "this mother's womb," and he asks for a "sword." Having procured his "sword," he bursts through the barriers into the inner chamber. That Oedipus—whose name, as I have said, suggests a crippled man—must ask for a "sword" at the same time as he is asking for the whereabouts of his mother's "inner" room, suggests that unconsciously he does not view himself as a complete man.[49]

To the psychologist Géza Róheim (1891–1953), the Sphinx—the being with the indefinite number of legs—replicates a child's perspective of parents having sexual intercourse, with limbs all tangled together.[50] Another Freudian saw Creon as having an incestuous lust for his sister Jocasta.[51]

GREATER FREUDLANDIA

Freud opened up the sluices to a flood of psychological theorizing about Oedipus that drew on various Freudian and non-Freudian concepts.

Carl Jung (1875–1961), a onetime Freud disciple who later broke away, had his own distinctive take on the Oedipus myth, focusing primarily on the Sphinx. For Jung, the Sphinx was the "Terrible Mother" sent by the "mother-goddess." And according to Jung, Oedipus had not actually conquered the Sphinx—he *thought* he had conquered the Sphinx by solving her "childishly simple riddle," but he was wrong. All those "tragic consequences . . . could easily have been avoided if only Oedipus had been sufficiently intimidated by the frightening appearance of the 'terrible' or 'devouring' Mother whom Sphinx personified. . . . Little did he know that the riddle of the Sphinx can never be solved merely by the wit of man."[52]

While they had Oedipus on the couch, commentators with a psychological bent diagnosed Oedipus with one mental malady after another. One post-Freudian critic, for example, applied the Freudian concept of "condensation" (the fusing of different emotions or ideas into one fraught symbol) to him.[53] Another critic devoted a whole book to breaking down Oedipus's personality into four levels—the good king, the hypermasculine, the little girl, and the infant.[54] Still another critic saw in Oedipus's supposed recklessness at the crossroad and in his encounter with the Sphinx signs of a depressive indifference to life and death.[55]

But the most popular diagnosis was repression, the granddaddy of all psychoanalytic theories. A number of commentators have argued that what may have started out as Oedipus's recklessness ended up as repressed knowledge of his horrible misdeeds and that on some unconscious level, Oedipus knew all along that he was guilty of patricide and incest. This is a departure from the conventional view, which is that Oedipus starts off happy and ends up miserable (as Euripides put it in his lost *Antigone*, "A happy man was Oedipus at first; then he became the wretchedest of men").[56] Proponents of the repression theory, on the other hand, believe that there was no golden period of blissful ignorance; according to them, Oedipus was a miserable, deeply conflicted man from the first, unable to consciously accept such an ugly reality—and then he became even more miserable.

Advocates of this theory see Oedipus as a man who has worked hard to put out of his mind some very unpleasant things that have confronted him in his life. For example, in *The Unspoken Motive: A Guide to Psychoanalytic Literary Criticism*, Morton Kaplan and Robert Kloss compare Oedipus to "the neurotic who resists the truth in analysis" by ignoring "thought[s] too painful to acknowledge."[57] A drunkard told him he is not the son of Polybus and Merope, the rulers of Corinth, but he must have repressed that memory when he visited the oracle that told him he would kill his father and marry his mother. He must have buried the memory of the oracle when he encountered Laius on the road and again when he was presented with an older woman as his bride.

This theory has been hard to resist. Every few years, some new scholar comes along and, with an air of amazing discovery, argues that *Oedipus Rex* is *really* about the way Oedipus represses the truth, as if previous generations of Oedipus scholars had repressed knowledge of the repression. As recently as 2007, one scholar wrote that "Oedipus takes so long to learn the truth about himself because, like Jocasta, at some level he already knows what it is; and knowing it already . . . he'll do everything he can to hide it from himself."[58]

But another scholar went even further, arguing that Oedipus didn't merely have a troubled subconscious: He was *consciously* guilty. British classical scholar Philip Vellacott (1907–1997) argued that Oedipus knew he was guilty of patricide and incest and that Sophocles wrote the play for the purpose of shocking the audience with that revelation.[59]

In fact, Vellacott speculated, based on the scars on his feet, that Oedipus might have suspected that he was a foundling from his earliest days.[60] Once the seed of doubt was planted in Oedipus's mind, Vellacott reasoned, he must have been aware of the danger of his conduct at the crossroad. Furthermore, when Oedipus finally entered Thebes, everyone must have been talking about the murder of their king, and so "it is certain that within an hour of entering Thebes Oedipus knew that he had killed [Laius]."[61]

Other psychologizers have zoomed in on the infanticide in the story, arguing in effect that when we talk about Oedipus's fraught relationship with his father, we shouldn't forget that Oedipus didn't start it. James Hillman, the prominent Jungian psychologist, mythologist, and author of the best-selling work *The Soul's Code*, chastised Freudians for ignoring the infanticide in the story and argued that it is much more about a father killing his son than about a son killing his father. After all, the patricide came about only because of the infanticide.[62] As the psychiatrist Kenneth Robbins has noted, this focus on infanticide is consistent with the broader Theban saga, which was marked by violence *toward* children, not *by* them.[63]

Some have gone back even further than the attempted infanticide to what might be called the "way backstory," mining myths about Laius's youthful misconduct for revealing clues. According to some versions of the myth, as a young man, Laius abducted and raped a boy named Chrysippus, the son of King Pelops. After Chrysippus committed suicide, Pelops placed a curse on Laius and all his descendants as retribution.[64] In the view of commentators who emphasize this part of the mythology, this deep past holds the key to understanding everything else in the Oedipus story. (In some versions, Laius's crime is also the reason the Sphinx comes to torment Thebes.)[65]

The Hungarian-French psychoanalyst George Devereux (1908–1985) came up with a strange theory that posited that the conflict between Laius and Oedipus was due to the fact that Oedipus, like his father, was homosexual—and father and son were competing over Chrysippus.[66] Their encounter at the crossroad, Devereux argues, is a symbolic fight over Chrysippus (so much for the vagina theory!), and Oedipus's relationship with Jocasta should be viewed "primarily as a symbolically homosexual and only epiphenomenally as a heterosexual act, Oedipus' true love-hate object being the now feminized homosexual ogre Laius."[67]

The contemporary French psychoanalyst Marie Balmary has also brought the Laius backstory to the foreground, writing, "The original fault in this story is therefore committed not by Oedipus . . . but by Laius."[68] Balmary further argues that this reading of Oedipus "corresponds to the great mythical and religious explanations of human existence: an original fault, the punishment of the guilty party and the transmission of this punishment through generations."[69]

For Balmary, in fact, the Laius backstory provides a clue not just as to the meaning of *Oedipus Rex* but also as to Freud's own psychological state and why he was so fascinated by the Oedipus myth to begin with. There has long been a rich tradition of psychoanalyzing Freud because, as the psychiatrist and writer Irvin Yalom put it, "[W]hen one considers a theory that purports to lay bare the deepest levels of behavior and motivation, and when the data supporting that theory emanate, in large part, from the self-analysis of one man, then it becomes not a luxury but a necessity to study that man as deeply as possible."[70]

In that spirit, several scholars have psychoanalyzed Freud himself to understand his lifelong interest in Oedipus. They have produced some fascinating theories suggesting that his interpretation based on the Oedipus complex was actually an unconscious cover for something else. This is the focus of Balmary's book, which is entitled *Psychoanalyzing Psychoanalysis: Freud and the Hidden Fault of the Father*. Balmary shows that the developer of the concept of repression had himself repressed some unsavory facts about his father, Jakob Freud. Reconstructing Jakob's marriages, she concludes that he may have driven his second wife, Rebecca, to suicide by leaving her for a much younger woman, Amalia (Freud's mother), whom he had impregnated, just as Laius's rape of Chrysippus had led to the latter's suicide. Balmary argues that this repression on the subject of his own father is reflected in Freud's reading of *Oedipus Rex* and in particular the way he ignores Laius's sins. Under Balmary's reading, "It is no longer Freud who explains everything through Oedipus; it is Oedipus who questions Freud."[71]

John Murray Cuddihy (1922–2011) developed an even more intricate theory of why Freud was unconsciously fascinated by the Oedipus myth.[72] When Freud was a young boy, Cuddihy wrote, Jakob told him a story about how, many years earlier, he had been accosted on the street by an anti-Semite who knocked his hat off his head, and how Jakob had meekly retrieved his hat from the mud without responding to the bully. Upon hearing the story, Freud felt deep shame about his father's passivity—a shame he never overcame, as reflected in the fact that he wrote about the incident several times in his adulthood. Cuddihy's theory is that when Freud encountered the Oedipus story, he must have been struck by the parallel between his father's story and the incident at the crossroad. In both stories, two men encounter each other on the street; one man considers himself the social superior of the other (the anti-Semite in the Jakob Freud story, Laius in the crossroad incident) and assaults the other, in both cases striking the head (knocking Jakob's hat off, smashing Oedipus on the head with his goad). Yet, while Jakob did nothing, Oedipus acted courageously. As Cuddihy puts it, "Oedipus *does* what the young Freud *wished* his father had done. It is a forbidden wish, one that Freud cannot admit into consciousness except in 'sublimated' form."[73] This, Cuddihy argues, is the *real* reason Freud was captivated by the story of Oedipus. Further, Cuddihy believes that Freud was unaware that this was the basis of his fascination with Oedipus—in other words, it was outside of Freud's conscious awareness. In support of that contention, Cuddihy notes that Freud, despite having written extensively about the myth, never once described the critical crossroad incident—a suspicious silence.

One benefit of this theory, according to Cuddihy, is that it accounts for an otherwise baffling exchange between Freud and Karl Abraham, who, as I mentioned above, interpreted the narrow crossroad as a vagina. When Abraham sent Freud a draft of his paper on Oedipus, Freud's primary response was that Abraham better recheck his assumption that the crossroad was narrow. For Abraham, the narrower the crossroad, the more suggestive it was of Jocasta's vagina (which Laius and Oedipus were symbolically fighting over, under Abraham's theory). Freud was evidently uncomfortable with the idea of a narrow crossroad. Why? Why on earth would Freud, or anyone for that matter, care about the width of the crossroad? Well, according to Cuddihy, if the crossroad was wide, then Oedipus could easily have stepped out of the way, letting Laius and his men pass; and if he could easily have stepped out of the way but didn't, that shows even more courage than if the road had been tight.[74] (As I said, it's an intricate argument!)

NATURE, KINGS, PHARAOHS, AND HEROES

Of course, modern and contemporary students of the Oedipus myth were interested in many other aspects of the story, not just psychological interpretations. Throughout the twentieth century, there was an enormous amount of scholarship focused on a variety of other issues that had nothing to do with the Oedipus complex. Some scholars searched the deep past for the sources of the Oedipus myth to better understand its meaning. But they looked in different places.

Some mythologists searched for the myth's origins in nature. Under one theory, for example, Oedipus is the sun. He slays Laius, who symbolizes darkness, and marries Jocasta, violet-tinted twilight. Or, alternatively, Oedipus is a personification of light whose blinding at the end of the play symbolizes the disappearance of the sun at the end of each day.[75]

Others searched for links to the myth in historical figures and events from eras long before Sophocles. An early twentieth-century scholar named H. J. Rose thought the myth derived from stories about real-life Mycenaean kings.[76] The English novelist and poet Robert Graves, a serious student of mythology, suggested in a 1955 book the possibility that the incest and patricide elements are add-ons to a very old story about a thirteenth-century-BC invader of Thebes who suppressed the Minoan civilization.[77]

My candidate for most creative historical analysis is that of Immanuel Velikovsky (1895–1979), who is best known for some strange theories, mostly rejected by the scientific community, about planetary activities affecting the course of ancient history. Velikovsky thought he could trace the myth directly back to the Egyptian pharaoh Akhenaten, an important and transformational pharaoh who broke away from the empire's polytheistic belief system to follow something resembling monotheism.[78] In arguing his case, Velikovsky relies on several supposed parallels between the two figures: Like Oedipus, Akhenaten may have spent part of his childhood away from his birth home. Akhenaten destroyed memorials to his father, Amenhotep III, which Velikovsky considers a symbolic version of patricide. He also is depicted in several surviving drawings as having swollen thighs, which could easily be transformed into swollen feet, according to Velikovsky, because there is no distinction in Egyptian between "foot" and "leg."

Velikovsky also relies on the fact that incest was common among Egyptian royalty, and he thought he detected evidence that Akhenaten had had a child with his mother. Other coincidences: Akhenaten was deposed; the Egyptian capital at the time of Akhenaten was called Thebes; and there was a big emphasis on burial issues in the Theban saga, despite that fact that burial was considered a more important issue in Egypt than in Greece. (In *Oedipus Rex*, Oedipus is concerned about Jocasta's burial, and the entire plot of *Oedipus at Colonus* is about where Oedipus can die in peace. In *Antigone*, the eponymous heroine—Oedipus's daughter—is killed for having tried to bury her brothers with dignity.)

Another area of scholarly interest concerns the relationship between the patricide/incest story and the Sphinx episode. Oedipus is a mythological figure who killed his father and married his mother. He's also a mythological figure who vanquished the Sphinx by answering her riddle. But did the same person commit both of these acts? In other words, was the Sphinx affair always part of a larger story about a man who commits patricide and incest? The question arises because, when you think about it, they are two very different kinds of stories. Scholars have taken both sides of this debate, with some arguing that the Sphinx episode was always integral to the basic myth while others argue that it was a late add-on.[79] Advocates of the latter argument point to the fact that in Hesiod's telling of the myth it is Heracles, not Oedipus, who fights and kills the Sphinx.[80]

Many students of mythology have striven to place the Oedipus myth in the context of hero stories in general, and not just from Greek mythology but from all over. For some, Oedipus is not just a great mythological hero but the *greatest* hero—the mythical figure who brings together the largest number of attributes of the heroic archetype.

Today, the idea of the "hero's journey" is most closely associated with the scholar Joseph Campbell, who in his 1949 book *The Hero with a Thousand Faces* showed how certain basic mythological patterns about heroes extend across diverse cultures and mythologies. But Campbell wasn't the first person to look for recurrent themes in hero stories.

In 1909, Freud's disciple Otto Rank (who, as I mentioned above, wrote about the incest theme in world literature) published a now classic work titled *The Myth of the Birth of the Hero*. In it, Rank identifies a recurring hero saga that has shown up time and time again throughout history; the leading examples of this saga include Cyrus, Romulus, Jesus, Lohengrin, Siegfried, Heracles, Tristan, Gilgamesh, Paris, Sargon, Moses, and, of course, Oedipus. The life story of Oedipus bears a striking resemblance to what Rank calls "the standard saga."[81]

Then in 1936, a British mythologist named FitzRoy Richard Somerset, or Lord Raglan, published *The Hero: A Study in Tradition, Myth and Drama*, which built on Rank's work. Raglan identified twenty-two key traits common to the great mythological heroes.[82] The list includes descriptions such as "(6) At birth an attempt is made, usually by his father or his maternal grandfather, to kill him, but (7) He is spirited away, and (8) reared by foster-parents in a far country." Many of these read like a summary of the Oedipus myth. What really caught my eye is that, according to Raglan, Oedipus is the highest scorer among heroes in possessing traits on the list, claiming twenty-one of those twenty-two.[83] (In case you're wondering, Moses came in second place, scoring twenty out of twenty-two.)

A more recent student of hero mythology has argued that, to the contrary, Oedipus is a perversion of the standard hero model. Jean-Joseph Goux, a French philosopher-psychoanalyst, devotes an entire book, *Oedipus, Philosopher*, to arguing that the Oedipus myth is about what he calls "deviant initiation."[84] Like the conventional hero, Oedipus was sent away as an infant or young boy and then at some point left his childhood home to go seek his fortune. So far, so good. But that, according to Goux, is where the similarity ends. For while the conventional he-man hero gets an assignment from a king to slay a monster and then goes and slays it, not so Oedipus. "In place of such noble deeds . . . Oedipus is condemned to a sordid and dishonoring combat in which he beats an old man to death with a stick."[85] And then, when he does encounter a monster, what does he do? He does not slay it in a proper heroic way. Instead, he gets the monster to kill herself by answering a riddle. In Goux's view, this makes Oedipus's the story of initiatory failures "par excellence."[86]

This is what we have, then: Some scholars consider Oedipus the greatest of mythological heroes, while others consider him a kind of negative hero. It's yet another illustration of the diversity of views on the subject of Oedipus—and we're not done yet.

FROM HERO TO SCAPEGOAT

In the twentieth century, anthropologists got very interested in *Oedipus Rex*, for a variety of reasons. For some, it represented a window into certain aspects of the ancient mind-set. For example, Sir James George Frazer (1854–1941), the great Scottish anthropologist and author of the voluminous study of religion and mythology *The Golden Bough*, viewed the Oedipus myth as a reflection of "the wasting effect of incest."[87] Other anthropologists have seen *Oedipus Rex* as a reflection of ancient rituals like ostracism and scapegoating—practices performed for the supposed good of society.

The anthropological approach is far removed from the mythological perspective of Raglan and Rank. To the anthropologist, Oedipus is not a mythological hero; he's a victim—a handy scapegoat to cure whatever ills society is facing.[88]

The leading proponent of the scapegoat theory was anthropologist René Girard (1923–2015), who argued that the treatment of Oedipus merely reflects the way premodern societies tried to limit the violence that would otherwise break out all over the place. According to Girard, "The entire investigation is a feverish hunt for a scapegoat, which finally turns against the very man who first loosed the hounds."[89] Girard argued that *Oedipus Rex* speaks to the long-suppressed memory of the violence that characterized primitive societies—and that still lies just beneath the veneer of peace and order in "civilized" societies such as ancient Greece. The real suppression in *Oedipus Rex*, according to Girard, relates not to "the desire for patricide or incest [the Oedipus complex] but the violence that lurked behind these all-too-visible motifs, the menace of total destruction that was diverted and concealed by means of the surrogate victim."[90]

The dialogue throughout the play makes this theme plain, argued Girard, who was amazed that attentive readers overlooked it. He points, for example, to Oedipus's response to the chorus after he accedes to their request to let Creon go. As if he had read Girard's writings on rivalry, Oedipus tells the chorus that by letting Creon go he has written his own death sentence: "Well then, let him depart—though his departure means my certain death, or else my ignominious expulsion from Thebes." This, says Girard, does not indicate Oedipus's blindness to his situation (unawareness that he's the guilty one)—it shows his clear-eyed vision about the rivalrous, zero-sum nature of male relations.

Another French anthropologist, Jean-Pierre Vernant (1914–2007), tied Oedipus to the human sacrifice ritual, which was still practiced by the Greeks into the fifth century BC, contemporary with Sophocles's play. It occurred during an annual religious ritual called the "pharmakos," in which "pharmakois" were paraded through the streets of the city, beaten, and then expelled or killed.[91] The goal was to cleanse the city of undesirables. The most famous "pharmakoi" in Greek lore history was Aesop, who is believed to have been sacrificed on account of his lameness. According to Vernant, the same treatment was given to Oedipus, who had some disability—however minor—based on the early injury to his foot. (In an odd stretch, Vernant also mentioned the fact that Laius was supposedly left-handed.)

If you study the Oedipus literature long enough, sooner or later you'll see references to a Claude Lévi-Strauss interpretation of the Oedipus myth.[92] Lévi-Strauss (1908–2009) was one of the giants of twentieth-century anthropology, credited with developing the so-called "structural approach" to the study of myth as a way of understanding the mind-sets of primitive societies. In a nutshell, his structural methodology involves taking myths, rituals, and other social phenomena and looking for pairs of opposites—e.g., raw vs. cooked, fresh vs. rotten, parched vs. moist. Lévi-Strauss did indeed apply this methodology to the Theban saga, but to call it an "interpretation" of that myth is a stretch. All he did was pull out several elements of the saga and line them up as opposites on a couple of different scales. Most notably, he saw several elements of the saga as constituting what he called "undervaluation of kin relationships" and others as "overvaluation of kin relationships." Thus, for example, the killing of Laius by Oedipus fell on the *undervaluation* end of the spectrum, as did the fratricide between Oedipus's sons, Eteocles and Polyneices; incest between Oedipus and Jocasta, on the other hand, landed on the *overvaluation* end.[93]

At first, I wondered if I was missing something profound here, but eventually I concluded that there was no there there. In the first place, this so-called analysis extended to the entire Theban saga all the way back to Cadmus, not just the Oedipus myth, so it can't really be called an "interpretation" of the latter. But more importantly, Lévi-Strauss expressly stated that he was using the Theban saga as a mere illustration of his methodology, and an illustration that was, in his own words, "probably not legitimate"![94] (In another one of his writings, he compared *Oedipus Rex* with a nineteenth-century comedy about the search for a straw hat eaten by a horse (don't ask), again to illustrate his point that myths should be analyzed based not on their content but on their "structure," and again he asked the reader not to take him too seriously.)[95] In light of his express disavowal of his own analysis, I wasn't sure why others had decided to take it seriously as an interpretation of Oedipus. The emperor himself said he was naked; I don't know why they thought he was clothed.

GOD AND ATHENS

While anthropologists and mythologists were busy probing the deep past and wider world for clues to the meaning of *Oedipus Rex*, classicists spent much of their time exploring the narrower Athenian context, trying to understand specifically what Sophocles had in mind in writing his masterpiece and exactly how the play was viewed and understood by his contemporaries. Of course, classicists haven't limited themselves entirely to those concerns—they have engaged the psychoanalysts and anthropologists on a variety of disputes—but the classicist's comparative advantage lies in his deep knowledge of ancient Greek language, history, and literature.

Classicists have produced a staggering body of commentary on *Oedipus Rex*. I've read a pretty big chunk of it (so you don't have to!). In fact, given the sheer volume, sometimes it feels as though *all* classicists have written about the play. The breadth of the scholarship is truly mammoth. (One bibliography lists more than five hundred books and articles.)[96]

Much of it has focused on understanding Sophocles's intentions, an approach that's analogous to the way legal scholars try to understand the Founders' intent when interpreting the US Constitution. Apparently, Sophocles held various priesthoods, and in the view of some scholars, writing *Oedipus Rex* was his reaction to the loosening of religious scruples in Periclean Athens.[97] The Athens of the Golden Age of Pericles, when *Oedipus Rex* was written, was in a period of religious laxity.

C. M. Bowra (1898–1971), one of the twentieth century's leading classicists, wrote that *Oedipus Rex* "shows the power of the gods at every important turn in its development and leaves no doubt about the poet's theological intention."[98] Another prominent classicist, T. B. L. Webster (1905–1974), thought that Sophocles was trying to "support . . . the traditional religion against contemporary attacks" by, among other things, restoring faith in divine oracles, which had lost credibility due to a proliferation of fake oracles. "In this atmosphere Sophocles wrote [*Oedipus Rex*] to defend what was for him . . . one of the basic facts of religion," Webster argued.[99]

Some have pushed this argument even further, arguing that Oedipus was punished for his disrespectful attitude toward the gods, but most scholars have rejected this view on the grounds that, by and large, Oedipus shows sufficient reverence to the gods. "By no

Athenian standards whatsoever are the king and queen godless or sinful in their religious attitude," one scholar explained.[100]

According to the Irish scholar E. R. Dodds (1893–1979), the play makes it clear that even if the gods are unjust, we still have an obligation to worship them; the Greek world saw no inconsistency between the two ideas.[101] The gods may well have been unjust and even cruel—and that's just the way things were. As one scholar put it, *Oedipus Rex* can be seen as embodying the line from *King Lear*: "As flies to wanton boys, so we to the gods. They kill us for their sport."[102]

So religion was one thing on Sophocles's mind. But that wasn't all. For example, there's the fact that a year or so before the play was performed, Athens suffered a great plague that killed about a quarter of its population.[103] According to Harvard classicist Charles Segal (1936–2002), "*Oedipus* [*Rex*] is almost certainly a response to events of this period."[104]

One of the victims of the plague was Pericles, the political figure most closely associated with the Golden Age of Athens. This was the age when the Parthenon was built at the Acropolis and Athens reached its peak as a naval and political power in the Aegean region. Pericles was born in 494 BC and thus was a contemporary of Sophocles; in fact, they were friends. This has led some scholars to see a lot of Pericles in the character of Oedipus.[105]

To other *Oedipus Rex* specialists, the play is a reflection of its time in a broader sense. In 1957, the great American classicist Bernard Knox (1914–2010) published *Oedipus at Thebes*, one of the most impressive close readings of the play. He argued that, far from being about the gods, the play is the *least* theological and "most relentlessly secular" of Sophocles's works.[106] Instead, Knox explained, "Oedipus, in his capacities and failings, his virtues and his defects, is a microcosm of the people of Periclean Athens."[107]

Knox concedes that the parallels between Oedipus and Pericles are "striking and not to be lightly dismissed."[108] For one thing,

Pericles, like Oedipus, was under a hereditary curse (in Pericles's case, because of a sacrilegious murder committed by one of his ancestors). And like Oedipus, Pericles was called "the first of men." But according to Knox, "these similarities are only incidental details of a basic pattern which suggests a comparison of Oedipus not to any individual Athenian but to Athens itself."[109] In the course of his book, Knox walks through the many ways in which Oedipus the man is a mirror of Athens and would have struck the contemporary Athenian audience as such, both in good ways and bad.

ENDLESS CONTROVERSY

Classical scholars have argued over virtually every single aspect of the play. At times, it feels as though they can't agree on *anything*.

Take Oedipus's character and conduct. It's hard to find a single issue on which scholars have not engaged in heated debate, reaching diametrically opposed views. Was Oedipus rash in running away from Corinth after receiving the prophecy? Should he have considered that the old man in the chariot was his father? Did he act in self-defense? Did he suspect all along that Jocasta was his mother? (Or, in other words, what did Oedipus know and when did he know it?) Is he too quick to anger? Does he exhibit hubris during the play (that is, is he an arrogant SOB)? Is he smart or dumb? Is he a good questioner or a sloppy one? On and on it goes. And that list doesn't touch on deeper philosophical questions about fate, God, society, life, justice. As this chapter has shown, no one has been able to agree on what exactly the play *means*.

That is, if it even *has* any meaning. There's even been a debate about *that*. Just as some literary critics are fond of arguing that Moby Dick is just a whale, so some Oedipus commentators argue that *Oedipus Rex* has no meaning whatsoever, that it just *is* (a position not to be confused with the argument that its meaning is "Life is meaningless").

The debate is endless. (Again, for a more comprehensive look at the biggest debates about the play, see the table in the appendix.) Nothing about the story, it seems, is sacred. In the last few decades, in the most astonishing controversy of all, scholars have even begun debating whether Oedipus committed the "Oedipal" acts! One scholar, for example, argued that perhaps it was the *chorus*, not Oedipus, who killed Laius.[110] (I guess this is the ancient Greek equivalent of "The butler did it.")

The theory that Oedipus was innocent has been most prominently developed by the American classicist Frederick Ahl, who—in what must be one of the most stunning revisions in the history of literary criticism—wrote an entire book arguing that Oedipus didn't commit the acts for which his name is a byword but was, instead, framed.[111] According to Ahl, Creon and Teiresias conspire to frame Oedipus because Creon wants to be king and Teiresias is jealous of Oedipus's victory over the Sphinx. What's more, Oedipus allows himself to be framed because he had not an Oedipus complex but a good old-fashioned Freudian guilt complex.

If you go through the play without preconceptions, Ahl argues, you will see that the conclusion that Laius and Jocasta were Oedipus's parents is "based entirely on his own testimony against himself and unsupported hearsay."[112] What exactly is the evidence proving Oedipus's guilt? Some very unreliable sources, Ahl argues: the drunk at the party in Corinth, the always duplicitous oracle at Delphi, the old man who claimed to be a messenger from Corinth, and the old man who claimed to be the servant to Laius and Jocasta who saved Oedipus from death by exposure.

To bolster his argument, Ahl performed an experiment in which he presented his students with the basic Oedipus story but changed all the names of the characters and the locations.[113] When presented with this disguised version of the story, the students thought that the play was about someone being framed for a crime he didn't commit, Ahl reports. All in all, Ahl argues, "There is much to suggest that [Oedipus] is misled by his own fears, his faulty inquiries, and the ambiguous statements and complex motives of his interlocutors."[114]

For Ahl, Sophocles was a trickster, sprinkling hidden clues throughout the play for the clever reader to find, like Dan Brown's Leonardo da Vinci in *The Da Vinci Code*, who placed clues in *The Last Supper*. Why would Sophocles write such a play? Maybe, according to Ahl, he did it as a way of "stimulating and maintaining audience interest in a story whose general outline is already known"; what better way to capture this interest than by "some surprising 'twist' in the mythical 'plot' variations"? Perhaps, in other words, *Oedipus Rex* was an early example of experimental theater. Whatever the reason, Ahl argues, we, like Oedipus, have been duped. Unwittingly, we have been "climb[ing] over all the obstacles of missing evidence, answers that do not match questions, and irrational arguments . . ."[115]

The Ahl thesis is echoed by critics of the deconstructionist school, which sees everything as radically ambiguous and doubts the existence of any objective truth. (When Jacques Derrida, the founder of deconstructionism, died in 2004, the *Onion* cleverly captured the essence of this mode of thought with the headline "Jacques Derrida 'Dies.'")[116] For the deconstructionist, *Oedipus Rex* is about the inability to ever achieve certainty about anything. In fact, Oedipus fails to achieve true knowledge *even after the revelation*. The revelation merely replaces one version of "truth" with another, and we, the reader or audience, are just as fooled as the characters.[117]

In essence, the deconstructionists try to turn Oedipus into one of those postmodern "metaphysical" detectives who never learns the truth about anything but instead wanders around a maze, never finding the center, because, in the words of one scholar, "there is no center to the maze."[118] Instead of there being a solution to the mystery, there is (to invoke the title of one of the books analyzing the genre) only a "mystery to a solution."[119]

This, in summary, is the range of views I encountered when I set about reading the Oedipus literature. And what an extraordinarily disparate range of views it is.

Oedipus has been like a cultural Rorschach blot. Freudians saw it through a Freudian lens, Jung through a Jungian lens, Claude Lévi-Strauss through the lens of his structuralism. There are Marxist interpretations of Oedipus—feminist ones, too. In *The Castration of Oedipus: Feminism, Psychoanalysis, and the Will to Power*, scholars J. C. Smith and Carla J. Ferstman argue that Oedipus suffered because he "clings to the certainty of science" and "surrendered the possibilities of life to the patriarchal institutions that make claim to certainty . . ."[120] And new interpretations are generated all the time.

The history of Oedipus commentary and scholarship presents an interesting story in its own right. Because of the number and variety of thinkers who have weighed in, the literature is practically a microcosm of Western intellectual history. Take the Freudian analyses, for example. One can learn a lot about Freudian psychology from studying the Freudian commentary on *Oedipus Rex*.

Much of the literature is useful; some of it is quite bizarre. Collectively, it's fascinating. But ultimately, devouring reams of studies and theories about *Oedipus Rex* is not how I came to understand the meaning of the play. I came to understand its meaning—or more accurately, meanings—by living my life and spending many years reflecting on what happens in the play itself rather than what others have said about it. This chapter was about the views of others. Now I turn to what *I* think it really means.

Chapter Four

Borne Back Ceaselessly

Sometimes in life we miss the most obvious things, the big, honking clues hiding right in front of our eyes. Sometimes we miss the obvious course of action we should take. Or we fail to see a solution that was there all along. It could be as simple as failing to see that the object that we're searching for is right there, staring at us—hidden in plain sight, as in Edgar Allan Poe's great story "The Purloined Letter." Oedipus missed the big, obvious thing about his own life. And after many years of thinking that the answer to the Riddle of Oedipus lies in the Circular Detective theme, eventually I realized that I had missed something very big and obvious about *Oedipus Rex*. That something is, well, what happens after the first third of the play.

You'll recall that to soothe Oedipus after his fights with Teiresias and Creon, Jocasta tells him to ignore prophecies, because Laius was told he'd be killed by his son but in fact the king was killed "by strangers, thieves, at a place where three roads meet" (lines 789–90). The speech stuns Oedipus. Her reference to the place where three roads meet brings back to mind the man he killed on the way to Thebes—a killing that also occurred at a crossroad where three roads meet. He begins to think that perhaps Teiresias was telling the truth and that he really is the murderer, a feeling that is only reinforced by further details furnished by Jocasta in the following pivotal dialogue:

> Oedipus: Strange, hearing you just now . . . my mind wandered, my thoughts racing back and forth.
>
> Jocasta: What do you mean? Why so anxious, startled?
>
> Oedipus: I thought I heard you say that Laius was cut down at a place where three roads meet.
>
> Jocasta: That was the story. . . .
>
> Oedipus: Where did this thing happen? Be precise.
>
> Jocasta: A place called Phocis, where two branching roads, one from Daulia, one from Delphi, come together.
>
> Oedipus: When? How long ago?
>
> Jocasta: The heralds no sooner reported Laius dead than you appeared and they hailed you king of Thebes.
>
> Oedipus: My god, my god—what you have planned to do to me? (lines 801–13)

Not much doubt is left there. And doubt is further put to flight when Jocasta describes Laius's appearance:

> Jocasta: He was swarthy, and the gray had just begun to streak his temples, and his build . . . wasn't far from yours.
>
> Oedipus: Oh no no, I think I've just called down a dreadful curse upon myself—I simply didn't know!
>
> Jocasta: What are you saying? I shudder to look at you.

Oedipus: I have a terrible fear the blind seer can see. I'll know in a moment. One thing more— . . . Did he go with a light or heavy escort, several men-at-arms, like a lord, a king?

Jocasta: There were five in the party, a herald among them, and a single wagon carrying Laius.

Oedipus: Ai—now I can see it all, as clear as day. (lines 818–31)

Oedipus asks her how she knows what took place. She was told by a servant, she says, the sole survivor. Where is he? asks Oedipus. Well, says Jocasta, when he returned to Thebes and found Oedipus on the throne in place of Laius, he begged her to send him to a distant pasture far from the city. Oedipus says he wants to see this man—who, unbeknownst to Oedipus, is the same man who had carried him away from the palace as an infant all those years ago. Oedipus's only hope now is that this man will stick to his story, which is that Laius was killed by more than one man. "So, if he still holds to the same number, I cannot be the killer," he tells Jocasta. "One can't equal many. But if he refers to one man, one alone, clearly the scales come down on me: I am guilty" (lines 933–34).

Oedipus is smart enough to know his hope is hanging by a slender thread. What they hear from the Theban shepherd will either confirm that he's the killer or disprove his fear as no more than a horrible series of coincidences. Either way, he's no longer capable of being shocked. He has already had the shock of his life.

In a sense, I was shocked, too, when I realized that I had missed this obvious fact. For many years I thought the Circular Detective theme was the answer to the Riddle of Oedipus. But over time, this unifying theory stopped working, and eventually I was forced to acknowledge to myself that I was wrong and that what happens in the rest of the play is even more important. I was forced to accept this conclusion because there is no getting around the fact that by the end of the dialogue with Jocasta, which is roughly only one third of the way through the play, *the story of Oedipus as a Circular Detective has effectively ended.*

STUNNING NEWS FROM CORINTH

When a palace servant announces the arrival of a messenger from Corinth, an almost entirely new play begins. Oedipus is still a detective of sorts, but he is no longer investigating a murder, and *Oedipus Rex* is no longer a murder mystery.

The messenger from Corinth, an old man, has come with news that Polybus, the king of Corinth, has died, and that the people of Corinth are calling for Oedipus to come and be their king. Oedipus is relieved at the news, because it means he no longer need fear the dreadful prophecy that he will kill his father. At this point in the play, the news is especially important to Oedipus, who realizes that because of his self-curse he may very well have to leave Thebes. (Corinth would be the logical place to go.) So much for the gods and their prophecies, he declares blasphemously. No more listening to prophecies or scanning the sky for birds. So relieved is he by the news that he even suggests the possibility that Polybus died pining for him, implying that maybe this is what the oracle meant when it predicted he would "kill" his father: "[H]e's dead . . . and here I am in Thebes, I never put hand to sword—unless some longing for me wasted him away, then in a sense you'd say I caused his death" (lines 1058–61).

But then he remembers the second part of the prophecy—the incest. Hearing this concern, the messenger then lowers the boom, delivering the news that turns everything on its head: No, he explains, you need not worry about that, since Merope, the queen of Corinth, is not your real mother anyway, nor was Polybus your real father. In fact, the messenger himself gave the infant Oedipus to them.

Where did you find me, then? Oedipus asks, stunned by this turn of events—the second time that an attempt to comfort him produces the opposite effect. The messenger says he was found on the woody flanks of Mount Cithaeron, which, as Oedipus notes, is close to Thebes. The messenger explains that he was a shepherd then, tending his flocks on the mountain slopes. And how exactly did you find me? Oedipus asks. Pointing to Oedipus's ankles, he says that they tell the story; they're even the source of his name.

Who did this to me? Oedipus demands to know. But the old messenger doesn't know; he received the infant from another person. *Who?* Another shepherd, who worked for King Laius. Oedipus asks the chorus if they know the man the messenger is referring to. The chorus answers that it is the very man who has already been sent for: the sole surviving witness to the incident at the crossroad.

Jocasta now knows what is coming, and she begs Oedipus to leave the matter alone. But Oedipus is determined to learn the mystery of his own origin. She pleads with him that he will be doomed if he proceeds. "May you never come to know yourself," she cries. Undeterred, Oedipus instructs a servant to hurry and fetch the shepherd. Jocasta leaves the stage, but not before calling him a "man of agony."

With the arrival of the Corinthian messenger, in other words, the play's central mystery has shifted from *Who killed Laius?* to *Who am I?* The play is no longer about the killing of an old king: It's about the attempted murder of a newborn prince many years earlier. And Oedipus has gone from being a Circular Detective to a modern self-searcher. His plight now is existential.

For a long time, I didn't appreciate how remarkable this transformation is. Enlightenment came over many years, as I absorbed a lot more life and literature. It started by asking questions about something that we see in stories all the time and yet take for granted: backstories. What role do they play? How do they function? What are the different kinds? In answering these questions, I received a lot of assistance from one of the great American playwrights, Arthur Miller.

RETURN OF THE REPRESSED

In a sense, every work of literature, play, or movie has a backstory. Outside of the Bible, which literally begins with the beginning, or a novel (if there is one) that starts with the Big Bang, there is always some background to every story. Even if the story commences with the protagonist's birth (the title of chapter 1 of Charles Dickens's *David Copperfield*: "I Am Born"), there is obviously stuff that happened earlier, and it influences the narrative. But backstories are more important to some narratives than to others.

In some, the backstory is just useful context meant to set things up; for example, we're told that the protagonist had a rich uncle who died before the story starts, leaving our hero with a large inheritance. The purpose of the backstory here is to explain why he's independently wealthy, no more, no less. In other stories, past events are an essential part of the narrative because the author chose to begin in the middle of things—"in medias res," as it's called. In the *Odyssey*, we learn about Odysseus's big adventures with the Cyclops and Circe and the rest when Odysseus recounts the events over dinner. That's because Homer chose to start the story later in time. If certain events are told through flashback, then voilà, there's a backstory.

But there's a certain type of story in which the backstory plays a special role and in which the backstory itself is the entire focus of the story. It provides much more than just useful context or flashback. Rather, the backstory provides an entire framework for the story; the events of the past have an overwhelming influence on the events of the present. This kind of story looks backward rather than forward.

A straightforward detective story would be an example of this, because by definition the detective is delving into a crime that has already occurred. But what I really have in mind is a story in which the protagonist is not merely delving into the past, like a detective, but is *haunted* by it. The backstory is a brooding presence in such narratives, almost like another character; it dominates the action. The past exercises a kind of gravitational pull on the characters, sucking them back to an earlier time.

Take, for example, a revenge story. The whole plot is driven by the protagonist's haunted desire to get revenge; his grievances from the past dominate the action. (Alexandre Dumas's *The Count of Monte Cristo* and Aeschylus's *The Oresteia* are two famous models.) Or think about stories where the protagonist is haunted by his wartime experiences or a sense of guilt about something terrible he's done.

A good recent example of the guilt scenario is the movie *Manchester by the Sea*. Casey Affleck's character, Lee Chandler, is haunted by the knowledge that through his negligence he caused his children to die in a house fire, and the movie is about how he can't stop punishing himself for his role in their deaths. In such a story, it doesn't matter when the narrative begins. It could be told in flashback, or it could start earlier in time, before the haunting event. Either way, the protagonist remains haunted.

To be clear, I'm not talking about any old narrative in which the protagonist is given a haunting backstory. That type of thing has become fairly obligatory in recent times; everyone is supposed to be haunted or else he's not deep. As Calvin Trillin put it: "Memoir in America is an atrocity arms race."[1] In some stories, you get the feeling a dark, guilty past was put there because the author felt aesthetically obligated to do so, regardless of its role in the plot. What I'm talking about instead is a story in which, as in *Manchester by the Sea*, the backstory is central.

All the characters in *Manchester by the Sea*, know about the fire, and they know why Lee has withdrawn from the world. In that sense, the backstory is not a secret. It's unknown to the *audience* until about a third of the way through the movie, when we learn through flashbacks about the fire. After the flashback, everything becomes clear. But the backstory is not a secret to the characters, and no one, including Lee, has tried to suppress the memory; in fact, Lee suffers precisely because he can't get over the past. The drama is in seeing him struggle to come to terms with the past and regain some semblance of a life.

But there is another kind of narrative in which the haunting backstory *has* been repressed and at least some of the characters are in the dark, while others try to keep the truth hidden and buried. Arthur Miller helped me appreciate this type of backstory, which he called "the return of the repressed."[2] It marks several of his plays. Most people will probably recognize it in *Death of a Salesman*, when Willy Loman's son discovers his father's affair. But Miller used that phrase specifically in regard to *All My Sons*, the play that made him famous in 1947.

The play revolves around Joe Keller, a businessman who owns a factory that, during the war, produced machine parts for military aircraft. In 1943, the factory shipped a batch of defective parts, leading to the deaths of twenty-one American servicemen after their planes went down in the Pacific. At the resulting trial, Joe and his partner, Steve Deever, were found guilty, but Joe was released from prison when he successfully appealed the verdict based on the alibi that he had been home with the flu the day the bad parts were shipped. This is all backstory.

When the play begins, it is the summer of 1946. Steve is still in prison, but Joe is a free man. He lives at home with his wife, Kate, and still owns and runs the factory, though now he works with his son Chris, who has returned home from the war. Chris was overseas when the crime took place and, knowing nothing other than the official court outcome, believes his father innocent. Joe and Kate's other son, Larry, never returned from the war and is officially missing in action. Apart from Larry's absence, their lives seem to have regained a semblance of normalcy—that is, until the arrival on the scene of Steve's daughter, Ann. She was engaged to Larry before he went to war but is now involved in a postwar romance with Chris. Ever since Chris returned from the war, he and Ann have been corresponding, and having arrived back in town, she is now a visitor in the Kellers' home.

Ann's presence is unsettling for two reasons. One is that it forces Kate, who alone has been clinging to the hope that Larry is still alive, to confront the fact that he will never return. The other is that it dredges up memories of the horrible crime they are all doing their best to forget.

One person who won't let any of them forget is Ann's brother, George, now a successful attorney in New York who has just visited their father, Steve, in prison for the first time since his conviction. Based on his conversation with his dad, George has become convinced that Joe is the guilty partner after all and was merely better at squirming out of trouble. George arrives at the Kellers' home and tries to tear his sister away from Chris, but Kate manages to soothe him. He has always respected Kate, and he feels at peace in Joe and Kate's home. Joe hits the mark when he reminds George of other times when his father tried to blame others for his own mistakes. Reevaluating things, George even agrees to stay for dinner.

Over dinner, George compliments Joe on how well he looks, which leads Kate to make the fatal slip. After Joe says, "I ain't got time to get sick," Kate comments, "He hasn't been laid up in fifteen years." Recognizing the danger of what she has just said, Joe quickly jumps in with "except my flu during the war."[3] But it's too late; the damage has already been done. George begins hammering on Kate's slip. This eventually leads to Chris finally realizing that his father is guilty, which in turns leads to the unfolding of some other long-buried secrets that even Joe wasn't aware of. The play builds toward its inevitable tragic ending.

All My Sons has two protagonists—the father, Joe, and the son, Chris. It is as much about Chris's slow realization that his father is guilty of a horrible crime as it is about Joe's failed effort to repress the past. Joe knows what he did. He has done his best to bury it from the view of others and has struggled mightily to rationalize his crime. But he is fully awake to the facts (although there's something critical he is *not* aware of, which I'll discuss in the next chapter). Chris, on the other hand, is in the dark. Yet both men are haunted by the same event from the past, Chris every bit as much as Joe—Chris just doesn't yet know it. He thereby represents the kind of character who is ignorant about the past, a past that will eventually surface and bring his world crashing down around him.

Though he coined the term "return of the repressed," Miller obviously wasn't the first to tell a story in which the protagonist makes a remarkable, life-shattering discovery about his past. The concept was even given a name, back in the early nineteenth century: the "well-made play." The French used this term to describe a certain format, originated by the French playwright Eugène Scribe, in which there is always some revelation at the end that had been a secret to the protagonist.

But because of its brilliance, *All My Sons*, more than any other single modern work, opened my eyes to how powerful this type of story can be. And with my eyes thus opened, I had a firmer grasp on what was so thrilling about the story of a man who in the course of one day goes from supreme leader of his people to blind beggar, all because of something that happened deep in his past, at the very dawn of his life.

THE MOTHER OF ALL BACKSTORIES

Oedipus Rex practically invented the backstory.[4] As we move through the play, we travel further and further into the past. It's like the multilayered site of an archaeological excavation; the deeper the layer unearthed, the older the civilization. And each layer contains a secret.

The play begins with the most recent layer—the plague that has descended on Thebes—and proceeds backward into the backstory, piece by piece. There is a secret behind the plague that had to be pried out of the oracle, we learn. The next layer down, in chronological time, is Oedipus's conquest of the Sphinx, which Oedipus mentions right after learning about the oracle's message ("Then once more I must bring what is dark to light").[5] The Sphinx had a secret that had to be guessed on pain of death.

Then we move further back in time, to the period before the Sphinx episode. We learn about the incident at the crossroad, which is discussed at the beginning of the dialogue with Jocasta. The secret of the crossroad incident (apart, of course, from the even more explosive secret of who Laius is in relation to Oedipus) is that Oedipus is the very killer for whom he's searching. Aside from Teiresias, who knows all, only one person alive knows *that* secret: the Theban messenger, who has repressed it for many years.

Later, in the dialogue with Jocasta—and therefore later in time onstage—we journey even further back in time, to Oedipus's consultation with the oracle about his parentage. The secret there is that he was given a misleading answer, a fact that won't be known until all is revealed. The priestesses of Delphi, like the Sphinx, guard their secrets jealously.

Then the Corinthian messenger arrives onstage, and we are transported still further back in time, to Oedipus's childhood. The next two scenes—the dialogues with the Corinthian messenger (who was a shepherd back in the day) and with the Theban shepherd (who was a servant to Laius back in the day)—reconstruct, *in reverse order*, what happened to Oedipus as infant, tracing the chain of parental custody to its very beginning.

We learn about the handoff from the Corinthian messenger to Polybus and Merope, Oedipus's Corinthian parents. Then we learn about the handoff from the Theban shepherd to the Corinthian. The Theban, now an old man, approaches Oedipus with great reluctance. The original reason for calling the old Theban shepherd—to question him about the murder of Laius at the crossroad—is entirely forgotten. All the focus now is on what happened with the infant Oedipus. With help from the Corinthian messenger, Oedipus confirms that the Theban is in fact the man who gave the Corinthian the infant Oedipus.

The Theban reluctantly admits that he knows the messenger but snaps at him to shut his mouth. He knows the horrible implications of what he has to say and doesn't want to say it, for he doesn't want to expose Oedipus to the world as the pollutant, just as all those years ago he didn't want to expose the infant Oedipus to the lethal elements on the mountain. But Oedipus won't take no for an answer; the old man is forced to spill the secret he has harbored these many years.

In doing so, he has taken us all the way down to the lowest layer of the excavation. This is the dialogue that, all those years ago, gave me the visceral sensation of barreling down the hill of a roller coaster—or, perhaps, falling into a deep hole. To this day, it remains the most intense stretch of dialogue I have ever encountered:

Oedipus: Did you give him that child?

Theban Shepherd: I did . . . I wish to god I'd died that day. . . .

Oedipus: Where did you get it? Your house? Someone else's?

Theban Shepherd: It wasn't mine, no, I got it from . . . someone.

Oedipus: Which one of them? [*Looking at the citizens*] Whose house?

Theban Shepherd: No—god's sake, master, no more questions!

Oedipus: You're a dead man if I have to ask again.

Theban Shepherd: Then—the child came from the house . . . of Laius.

Oedipus: A slave? Or born of his own blood?

Theban Shepherd: Oh no, I'm right at the edge, the horrible truth—I've got to say it!

Oedipus: And I'm at the edge of hearing horrors, yes, but I must hear!

Theban Shepherd: All right! His son, they said it was—his son! But the one inside, your wife, she'd tell it best.

Oedipus: My wife—she gave it to you?

Theban Shepherd: Yes, yes, my king.

Oedipus: Why, what for?

Theban Shepherd: To kill it.

Oedipus: Her own child, how could she?

Theban Shepherd: She was afraid—frightening prophecies.

Oedipus: What?

Theban Shepherd: They said—he'd kill his parents.

> Oedipus: But you gave him to this old man [the Corinthian]—why?
>
> Theban Shepherd: I pitied the little baby, master, hoped he'd take him off to his own country, far away, but he saved him for this, this fate. If you are the man he says you are, you were born for pain. (lines 1271–1305)

The truth, long repressed, has returned, and with a fury that is nearly indescribable: "Oh god—all come true, all burst to light! O light—now let me look my last on you! I stand revealed at last—cursed in my birth, cursed in marriage, cursed in the lives I cut down with these hands!" (lines 1306–10).

Having finally reached the deepest layer of the excavation, Oedipus rushes into the palace and bursts into Jocasta's bedroom, the room in which he was born and from which he was taken to be killed. And in that room, he now blinds himself, becoming as helpless as when he was a newborn infant straight out of Jocasta's womb.

HOPE FOR THE PAST

I've spent a lot of time over the years thinking about why this scene has had such an impact on me. I may never know for sure—one can never be certain what goes on even inside oneself (see chapter 2). But I have developed a theory. As paradoxical as it may sound, I believe my fascination with Oedipus's excavation of his past arises not from fear or horror but from fantasy. For poor Oedipus, the discovery was a nightmare, but for me as a reader, at the heart of this nightmare lies the fantasy that buried deep within my past sits the secret of my life, and this secret will somehow set me free.

We normally associate hope and fear with the future, but I think we have hopes about the past, too—hopes about what we might *learn* about the past. And when we contemplate our deep past—our childhood especially—there's a strong dose of hope in the mix, I think. We hope, even if only subconsciously, that uncovering a secret from the past will make everything better. Not all buried secrets produce nightmares.

Here's an example. In the novel *Fifth Business*, by the Canadian Robertson Davies, the protagonist has never recovered from the guilt he feels about an episode from his childhood, an innocent snowball fight with a friend. The friend throws a snowball at the narrator, who ducks, and the snowball accidentally hits his neighbor's wife. The snowball has an impact he never expected: It knocks down the neighbor's wife, and she never fully regains her mental faculties after her fall. He spends the rest of his life plagued by guilt and dealing with the consequences of his decision to duck. And then, toward the end of the novel, his friend reveals the terrible secret that he has harbored all these years: He put a rock in the snowball.

For a brief moment, even Oedipus harbors the fantasy that learning about his past will be a happy discovery. After learning that he is not the son of Polybus and Merope, and while waiting for the Theban witness to arrive, Oedipus and the chorus express their hope that the secret they will learn about Oedipus's birth will be wonderful—that, say, he is the son of a god. At that same moment, though, Jocasta knows the horrible truth and begs Oedipus not to pursue his search, saying, "May you never fathom who you are!" (line 1173). As she leaves the stage, Oedipus exults, declaring, "I count myself the son of Chance" (line 1187). It never occurs to him that the news might be catastrophic; the worst he imagines is that he'll learn he was lowly born. The important thing, to him, is to find out the truth of his origins.

In a sense, this validates the Freudian theory (call it the Freudian fantasy) that beneath every hysterical neurosis there lies a hidden secret that can be brought into the open—with, conveniently, the aid of a skilled psychoanalyst. (This is not to be confused with

Freud's theory of "family romance," which is about children fantasizing that they come from nobler stock than they actually do.) Freud himself compared the exploration within *Oedipus Rex* to psychoanalysis.[6]

How often this kind of curative awakening actually happens is a question of intense debate in the psychiatric profession. Rooting around in the patient's deep past is certainly a less popular technique today than it was in the heyday of Freudianism, the 1950s and 1960s. Mental health professionals today are likelier to make jokes about improper toilet training than to actually search for signs of it (or for signs of an Oedipus complex, but we'll come back to that in the next chapter). Primal-scream therapy, in which a patient releases the supposed horrors of their deep childhood via screaming, is long past its heyday, too.

Today, many if not most therapists believe that you don't have to go fishing around in the patient's deep unconscious to cure him. Albert Ellis, the founder of cognitive-behavioral therapy, believed that a patient could improve without necessarily discovering the source or root cause of the symptom."[7] He need not, in other words, return to the beginning to cure himself of his mental suffering. But the Freudian fantasy is alive and well, as reflected in the many movie scenes where the protagonist, in his therapist's office, recovers a long-lost childhood secret, a process that always results in a dramatic epiphany—for example, in the movie *The Prince of Tides*, based on the novel by Pat Conroy.

Whether this ever happens in real life, it remains a powerful fantasy. There is something romantic and thrilling about the idea that everyone has deeply hidden secrets, and if you rummage around in your past long enough, you might uncover some of yours—clues as to the true meaning of your life. It may be that in most cases, there's nothing to find, no secret of your childhood that, if unveiled, would explain everything about you and lift your misery. In my own case, I think I have spent far too much time hunting around my past for clues. But the appeal of the fantasy is strong.

I think that some people, like some stories, are more backward-focused than others. If so, I definitely fall in the retrospective camp. I waste inordinate amounts of time ruminating about the past, wondering what might be back there that I haven't yet discovered. (It doesn't even have to be anything dramatic.) But I've always been drawn to the idea that our origins hold many answers, or, as James Baldwin put it:

> We cannot escape our origins,
> however hard we might try,
> those origins contain the key
> —could we but find it—
> to all that we later become.[8]

A few years ago, my mother, cleaning out her garage, found a box of miscellany from my childhood that had survived the years: report cards, letters, and the like. Rummaging through the box, I found nothing terribly interesting until I came across a diary I had kept in my early teens. I started reading it and was stunned by the overlap between what occupied my mind then and what still occupied me many years later, as an adult. You could say that I came from him. But where did *he* come from? To find out, I'd have to go even further back in time, but I don't know how to do this—and even if I could, I probably still wouldn't learn the answer.

To some extent, this fantasy may also be about reclaiming something from the past, as this passage from *The Great Gatsby* suggests:

> He talked a lot about the past, and I gathered that he wanted to recover something, some idea of himself perhaps, that had gone into loving Daisy. His life had been confused and disordered since then, but if he could once return to a certain starting place and go over it all slowly, he could find out what that thing was.[9]

Like Jay Gatsby, many of us secretly harbor a fantasy of being able to return to the past for the sake of fixing things we got wrong. For few of us, alas, have gotten our lives completely right. Many of us wish for a do-over, a second chance to right those mistakes, which are legion. I know I do.

Of course, not every return to the past is voluntary. Sometimes the repressed truth returns without any invitation, of its own accord, and whether we like it or not, we get dragged into the past. That's the point of the famous final sentence of *The Great Gatsby*: "So we beat on, boats against the current, borne back ceaselessly into the past."[10] Oedipus was eager to get to the truth, and in that sense his exploration was voluntary, like the way I hungrily read that old diary my mom had preserved. But from another perspective we can say that, like Gatsby, he was carried ceaselessly into the past. The truth of the past was also eager to get to *him*.

And what was that truth? By the end of the dialogue with the Theban shepherd, Oedipus digs his way to the very bottom of the excavation, and he now knows everything. He knows who he is: the son of Laius and Jocasta.

We may think of this as one discovery, one revelation, and so it is, but it has several distinct, critical implications. The most obvious one is that the man he killed all those years ago was his own father, and the woman to whom he is now married and with whom he has had children is his mother. But there are two other related but separate implications: He learns that the terrifying prophecies he received from the oracle, which he thought he had escaped, were true all along. He also learns that he is, in fact, a native Theban. Each of these implications has its own profound significance, its own color and character. In the next three chapters, I consider each one in turn. I start with the patricide and incest.

Chapter Five

"The Lives I Cut Down with These Hands"

In 1986, two French movies came to America and did surprisingly well in American theaters: *Jean de Florette* and its sequel, *Manon of the Spring*. They were set in the Provence region of France, in the years after World War I. The main character in the story, César (played by Yves Montand), is an old bachelor who, to his regret, never had any children. He and his nephew, Ugolin, his only surviving relation, own a farm together, and they want to expand by buying an adjoining piece of land. Water is everything in this dry part of France, and César happens to know of a spring underneath the property that has been clogged with rubble for many years. The neighbor won't sell to César, and when the neighbor dies a year later, the land goes to his sister, Florette, whom César had been in love with in their youth. Florette herself dies soon after, and the land then descends to her son, Jean (Gérard Depardieu), who has a young wife and daughter.

Jean is a tax collector, but with the inheritance, he decides he wants to take up farming. Accordingly, he, too, refuses to sell the land to César. To ensure that Jean will fail, thus enabling them to buy the land on the cheap, César and Ugolin secretly fill the spring's source with concrete and cover it over with earth. Without a good source of water, farming is a struggle for Jean, who already suffers from a physical deformity—he has a hunchback. He destroys his health by transporting water from a spring much farther away and eventually dies while trying to build a well. By stopping up the spring, César and Ugolin have effectively killed him. After Jean's death, César and Ugolin buy the land from Jean's young widow. They remove the concrete from the spring, and the farm flourishes.

Years pass. An old woman who knew both César and Florette, Jean's mother, moves back to a nearby village. Through her, César learns the truth about his past: After César went to Africa for military service, Florette learned that she was pregnant with his child. She wrote to him, but he never received the letter in Africa. She then tried to abort it but ended up moving to another town and marrying another man before the baby was born, so everyone thought it was the blacksmith's child. That baby was Jean. César, a man who has always wanted a child, realizes therefore that by concealing the spring, he drove to his death the only one he ever had.

To César, Jean de Florette was a stranger, which is why he didn't care what happened to him. But his factual assumption was incorrect. Likewise, to Oedipus, Laius was a stranger—but he, too, was wrong. They both learned a bitter lesson.

As I mentioned in the introduction to the book, *Oedipus Rex* has struck a number of different chords in me over the years. For example, the Circular Detective theme set me on a path of exploring the psychology of self-ignorance (see chapter 2). The middle third of the play, in which Oedipus explores his past, pointed me in another direction—the psychological power of a backstory (see chapter 4). In each case, I was aided by other works of fiction—for example, the way Arthur Miller's *All My Sons* helped me appreciate why Oedipus's exploration of his past is so spellbinding.

But there are important aspects of the play I haven't yet discussed, ones that touch other nerves. As I mentioned at the end of the last chapter, Oedipus's discovery of his identity has several distinct implications. The first one that comes to our minds, because it's the most shocking, is that he has committed patricide and incest—discovering *who he is* opens his eyes to the horror of *what he has done*. This aspect of the play has had a profound moral significance for me, and that's what I discuss in *this* chapter. In other words, I have come to view this aspect of the play—the patricide and incest—through a primarily *moral* lens, and the sad tale of César and Jean de Florette, and similar stories I'll discuss here, helped me get there.

I recognize that there is, of course, a whole other way of viewing the patricide and incest—through a Freudian rather than a moral lens. Freud and his followers attached a very different significance to Oedipus's signature crimes from what I see in it. Though I disagree with the Freudian approach, it's too important to ignore, so I discuss it later in the chapter, too. But first, let's discuss morality.

THE EXPANDING CIRCLE

Homo sapiens is not naturally inclined to care about strangers. As the psychologist Paul Bloom puts it, "We are constituted to favor our friends and family over strangers, to care more about people from our own group than people from different, perhaps opposing, groups."[1] By instinct, we have a limited and confined sense of morality. We divide the world into two camps: those to whom we owe kindness and consideration and those to whom we owe nothing. The latter is the Other and therefore less than human. Innately, our sense of moral obligation extends to those with whom we have a close genetic or personal relationship—our kith and kin—and for good genetic reasons.

But over time, our moral sense breaks out of its initial confinement. In his classic work *The Expanding Circle*, Peter Singer shows how we eventually come to recognize obligations toward others outside the narrow circle of kinfolk and begin to appreciate that the stranger is human like us, capable of feeling and suffering, of having the same thoughts and aspirations as we have.[2] He shows, in other words, how we reach a point where we agree with the Roman playwright Terence when he said, "I am human, and therefore nothing human is foreign to me." The psychologist Steven Pinker sums up Singer's work in the following terms: "Our moral sense, though shaped by evolution to overvalue self, kin and clan, can propel us on a path of moral progress, as our reasoning forces us to generalize it to larger and larger circles of sentient beings."[3]

There are various ways to remind ourselves that nothing human is foreign to us. One is to remember that we've been in the same boat as another person. There's a brief but wonderful moment in *Homage to Catalonia*, George Orwell's memoir of the Spanish Civil War, that illustrates this principle and how it can be upheld even in the most trying of circumstances. Orwell is about to shoot an enemy soldier when he notices that the man is trying to hold up his pants because he has no belt. This little gesture forces Orwell to realize his shared humanity with the man, and he holds his fire.

This is essentially the same message reflected in one of the greatest moral statements in the Bible: "Thou shalt neither vex a stranger, nor oppress him: for ye were strangers in the land of Egypt."[4] That's from Exodus. Leviticus and Deuteronomy go even further, exhorting us not just to refrain from harming the stranger but to *love* him.[5] In fact, Leviticus commands us to love the stranger *as ourselves*. The common denominator of all three is the reminder that, in effect, "Hey, you've all been in that same situation." And there's at least one other person from the ancient world who was fully alive to this message: Sophocles, for in *Oedipus at Colonus* he puts virtually identical words into the mouth of Theseus, the mythical king of Athens. In his speech welcoming the dying Oedipus to Colonus, Theseus says: "I too was reared like thee in exile and in foreign lands . . . therefore no alien in adversity shall seek in vain my succor nor shalt thou."

Whenever I find myself starting to become hardened to the suffering of others in the world, I find the strongest antidote is to remind myself that that suffering person we're seeing on television or reading about in the newspapers is someone's son or daughter, or father or mother, or brother or sister. This is why a news story about human suffering becomes more poignant when it shows a mother or father crying over the victim's casket or transmits the look of pain in a child's or spouse's face.

Now think about the story of someone who learns after the fact that the person he killed was his *own* father, or son, or brother, or mother, or daughter, or sister. How better to convey the message that the person you've harmed has people who love him and will be grieved by his actions? You yourself, you learn, are one of those very people! It's like a voice screaming out, "You fool! You thought you could treat this person as though he were of no moral worth! Have you forgotten that everyone is loved by someone else?! Your punishment will make sure that you never, ever forget this. The harm done to the person you forsook will bring great pain to *you*!"

It's a powerful theme that has been repeated many times since *Oedipus Rex*. You can find every permutation imaginable: children unknowingly killing their fathers (Oedipus, of course) and their mothers (Hans Christian Andersen's story "The Neighbors"), grandchildren killing their grandparents (the myth of Perseus), husbands killing their wives (*Sweeney Todd*), mothers killing their daughters (*Lucrèce Borgia*), and fathers killing their daughters (*Rigoletto*). And, as portrayed in *Jean de Florette*, there is the story of fathers unknowingly killing their sons. The tragedy of Rostam and Sohrab from the *Shahnameh* is another heartbreaking example of that last one.[6]

But Oedipus is the paradigm of this theme, the ur-example. There's no way to think about it without calling Oedipus to mind. His unknowing patricide is the source of inspiration for later storytellers. You can tell this from allusions to Oedipus in the stories that grapple with this theme. The creators of *Jean de Florette* made no effort to conceal their debt to the story of Oedipus; the old woman from whom César learns the truth is blind and named Delphine! And there's another modern work of storytelling art whose author acknowledged the role of Oedipus in inspiring him. It's the same one that gave me so much help in understanding the power of a haunting backstory: *All My Sons*.

"THERE'S A UNIVERSE OF PEOPLE OUTSIDE"

As we discussed in the previous chapter, in *All My Sons*, the Keller patriarch, Joe, always knew he was guilty of selling defective parts. Until the end of the story, he already knew he had done a terrible thing, but he didn't know the full story. It's the rest of the play—what I didn't describe in the previous chapter—that makes *All My Sons* a modern-day *Oedipus Rex*.

In Joe's eyes, his conduct is excusable because he acted to save the business he was building for his sons. He's able to live with the knowledge that his actions contributed to the deaths of twenty-one airmen because the men he killed were strangers. It would be different, of course, if his son Larry had been killed because of one of the defective parts, but he feels certain that that was not the case, since Larry flew a different type of plane. Joe insists on that. The audience is not so sure—throughout the play, we're kept wondering what really happened, why Larry never returned from the war. That's the play's central mystery.

After Chris learns the truth about his father's guilt, he runs from the house in agony. That ends act 2. Act 3 takes place in the middle of the night. Joe and Kate are waiting up to see whether Chris returns. Ann, who also knows the truth now, enters the house and assures Joe and Kate that she has no intention of turning Joe in. But she insists that Kate accept that Larry is dead and let Chris know that she accepts his brother's death. When Kate resists, Ann tells her that she knows for certain that Larry is dead—but she insists Joe leave the room before she will say anything more. She then shows Kate a letter from Larry she has kept in her purse for the last three years.

At first, we don't know what the letter says because Kate reads it to herself. But we know it must be something powerful, for it has a devastating impact on her. Chris returns to the house, still reeling from his discovery that Joe was guilty and trying to figure out how to convey to Joe the magnitude of what he has done. For even after Joe confessed his guilt to Chris, he still insisted that what he did was ultimately right because of what it meant for the family. Then Kate shows Chris the letter, and Chris now knows what to do.

Joe reenters the room and continues to protest that he was no worse than other war profiteers. Then Chris reads the letter to him, written the day Larry died.

> My dear Ann: It is impossible to put down the things I feel. But I've got to tell you something. Yesterday they flew in a load of papers from the States and I read about Dad and your father being convicted. I can't express myself. I can't tell you how I feel—I can't bear to live any more. Last night I circled the base for twenty minutes before I could bring myself in. How could he have done that? Every day three or four men never come back and he sits there doing business. . . . I don't know how to tell you what I feel . . . I can't face anybody . . . I'm going out on a mission in a few minutes. They'll probably report me missing. If they do, I want you to know that you mustn't wait for me. I tell you, Ann, if I had him here now I could kill him—[7]

Joe is now a broken man. After a moment's pause, he tells Chris to take him to the police. The dialogue from which the play derives its title then ensues:

> Joe: Get the car, I'll put on my jacket.
>
> Kate: Why are you going? You'll sleep, why are you going?
>
> Joe: I can't sleep here. I'll feel better if I go.
>
> Kate: You're so foolish. Larry was your son too, wasn't he? You know he'd never tell you to do this.
>
> Joe: [*Looking at the letter in his hand*] Then what is this if it isn't telling me? Sure, he was my son. *But I think to him they were all my sons. And I guess they were, I guess they were*. I'll be right down.[8]

Joe goes into the house. A few moments later we hear a shot from inside, and the play ends.

So Joe does discover, in the end, that he killed his own son, though not in the way we expect in these Oedipus-inspired stories. Miller cunningly plays on our expectations that we're going to learn that Larry flew a P-40, the plane that Joe and Steve, Kate's father, supplied (defective) parts for. When Ann shows Kate the letter, we suspect that that's what the letter says. Miller is careful not to suggest otherwise. It isn't until the very end that we learn what actually happened—that Larry didn't die in a defective plane; he committed suicide. But Joe caused his death as much as if he had flown in a compromised P-40.

If Joe had learned that Larry died from flying in a defective plane, he would have been shattered. His life would have come to an end. But he would have drawn a limited lesson rather than the broad lesson Miller is trying to teach us in this magnificent play. He would have blamed himself for inadvertently killing his own son, but nothing more. He could have continued to rationalize his actions as being the best for his family. Miller's switch forces Joe, and us, to focus instead on the broader issue: Joe's unforgiveable treatment of the other men, the men he didn't know, men who were strangers to him.

The grandeur of the play consists in watching Joe Keller travel the moral journey that mankind has made from a narrow to a wide circle of obligation. His mental model at the beginning is one in which strangers—people outside his narrow circle of friends and family—matter very little. Family and kinship is really all that counts. As he explains to Kate at the beginning of act 3, as they are awaiting Chris's return:

> Kate: There's something bigger than the family to [Chris].
>
> Joe: Nothin' is bigger.
>
> Kate: There is to him.
>
> Joe: There's nothing he could do that I wouldn't forgive. Because he's my son. Because I'm his father and he's my son.
>
> Kate: Joe, I tell you . . .
>
> Joe: Nothin's bigger than that. And you're going to tell him, you understand? I'm his father and he's my son, and if there's something bigger than that I'll put a bullet in my head.[9]

He does put a bullet in his head, but only after he has shed his moral blindness. He learns in the end that he was wrong, that there *is* something bigger. He learns that Chris was right when he said, "There's a universe of people outside and you're responsible to it, and unless you know that you threw away your son because that's why he died."[10]

It's not that you have to treat everyone identically, regardless of family connection. We don't need to take literally Leviticus's admonition to love the stranger as much as we love ourselves, or be like the Dalai Lama, who has said that no one in the world is of higher worth to him than anyone else in the world.[11] As long as we don't all end up becoming Hatfields and McCoys, it's healthy and sensible for us to be fiercely loyal to our families. In fact, as Paul Bloom puts it, "Any creature that *didn't* have special sentiments toward those that shared its genes . . . would get its ass kicked from a Darwinian perspective."[12] But just as we should never forget who is in our family, we should also never forget that everyone else is a member of someone's family, and they matter to each other. And Oedipus is the poster child for failing to see one person's connection to another person.

In a sense this is unfair to Oedipus, because his conduct at the crossroad is not on the same moral plane as that of, say, César in *Jean de Florette*, who knew that he was driving Jean to despair by depriving him of his water, which eventually led to his death, or Joe Keller, who shipped defective plane parts that he knew could, if used, make the planes unsafe, killing many men. Oedipus didn't ask for or start the trouble, and he didn't hit the road for the purpose of killing random strangers. Remember, too, that his next act was to rescue Thebes, a city whose people he didn't know, in an act of bravery he didn't need to undertake.

Some commentators have argued that Oedipus acted quite badly at the crossroad. Personally, I think the debate about his crossroad conduct borders on silly because it tries to extract too much from too little information. Here's the sum total of what we know about the crossroad incident, which comes from Oedipus's speech to Jocasta:

> Making my way toward this triple crossroad I began to see a herald, then a brace of colts drawing a wagon, and mounted on the bench a man, just as you've described, coming face-to-face,

> and the one in the lead and the old man himself were about to thrust me off the road—brute force—and the one shouldering me aside, the driver, I strike him in anger!—and the old man, watching me coming up along his wheels—he brings down his prod, two prongs straight at my head! I paid him back with interest! Short work, by god—with one blow of the staff in this right hand I knock him out of his high seat, roll him out of the wagon, sprawling headlong—I killed them all—every mother's son! (lines 884–98)

With my lawyer's eye, I view the account as too threadbare to point definitively to one interpretation or another. Some have relied on the phrase "I strike him in anger" to argue that Oedipus used unnecessary force. But anger and self-defense are not inconsistent with each other; if people are trying to harm you, you'll probably get very angry at them, but that doesn't mean you weren't acting in self-defense if you strike them. At worst, an argument could be made that his anger got the better of him and he used disproportionate force. But that's not equivalent to having a malignant heart bent on harming one's fellow man.

In any event, fairly or not, Oedipus will always be remembered as the man who unintentionally killed his own father. And his example provides an unparalleled vehicle for delivering a powerful moral message. It even illustrates an interesting legal point. This scenario, in fact, is often used in law-school classes to illustrate the case of someone who commits a certain act—in Oedipus's case, patricide—without having the requisite mens rea (culpable mental state) to be considered legally guilty.

All of that said, there's a whole different way of viewing Oedipus's patricide and incest that eschews all moral lessons. And that, of course, is the Freudian argument that we discussed in chapter 3. As we saw there, the Oedipus complex was always a central part of Freud's psychological theories, and the concept has been enormously influential, even up to the present time. As we also saw, Freud didn't just invoke the myth as a catchy name for his theory.

He explicitly argued that the Oedipus complex is the answer to the Riddle of Oedipus. The story of Oedipus moves us, Freud argued, because "the oracle laid the same curse upon us before our birth as upon [Oedipus]—to direct our first sexual impulse toward our mother and our first hatred and our first murderous wish against our father."[13]

If Freud was right, then a lot of what I'm saying about the things that move me about *Oedipus Rex* may be delusional. A Freudian would argue that I may *think* I'm moved by the Circular Detective theme and the backstory and all the psychological and philosophical issues I've been discussing, but in fact what really moves me is my Oedipus complex, and that I should make a beeline to the nearest Freudian psychoanalyst, who will then set me straight as to the real reason for my fascination with this ancient masterpiece. So over the years, I've had to answer this question: Was Freud right?

GENETICS 101

I've always been fascinated by Freud. He's not taken nearly as seriously today as he used to be—a fact reflected in book titles of recent decades like *Decline and Fall of the Freudian Empire* and *Why Freud Was Wrong*. As the science journalist Daniel Goleman put it:

> As far as the systematic, scientific theory of neurosis is concerned, and such deductions from such a theory as might lead to improved methods of treatment, the Freudian theory is as dead as that attributing neurotic symptoms to demonological influences, and his method of therapy is following exorcism into oblivion.[14]

But few deny that he was a powerful and seminal thinker, and most today agree that, though he got a lot of things wrong, there are large kernels of truth in his overall system—for example, the idea of the unconscious and the opposing forces within the mind.[15] Plus, he's a great writer, and it's easy to fall under his spell, as I do from time to time.

But what about *Oedipus Rex*—was he right about why we are so drawn to it? Over time, what I've concluded is that whatever the merits of the rest of his theories, Freud's argument about *Oedipus Rex* is just plain wrong.

The first and most obvious objection is that it excludes half the population. As my wife has said about Freud's argument that Oedipus's fate is "the fate of all of us": "What do you mean, 'us'?!" I've never seen any evidence that women find the play less fascinating than men do. My wife has assured me that's not the case (though unlike me, she hasn't spent a lifetime obsessing over it!). Since even under Freud women don't have an Oedipus complex, his theory has a big gaping hole.

Another big objection is that, as others before me have said, the theory fails to distinguish between the myth and Sophocles's interpretation of it in *Oedipus Rex*. There's nothing in Freud's theory that doesn't apply to any other version of the myth—say, Seneca's or Voltaire's. After all, they all involve incest and patricide; that's just part of the basic myth, which Sophocles didn't invent.[16] Yet nobody cares much about those versions today; they're largely forgotten except by specialists. It's because of Sophocles's play that we care about the Oedipus myth, not the other way around. Without Sophocles, Oedipus would be one more mythological character in literature and the general culture.

But the most devastating objection to the Oedipus complex theory is that . . . there is no such thing as an Oedipus complex.

During much of the twentieth century, belief in the Oedipus complex was an article of faith among psychologists and many others. Debate about it generally revolved around the *extent* to which it was present around the world, not its existence. Some prominent anthropologists, such as Bronisław Malinowski and Karen Horney, argued that it didn't apply to all, or even many, primitive societies but only modern capitalistic societies, which breed Oedipal tendencies in children through tyrannical and narcissistic behavior. But almost everyone assumed that the Oedipus complex was a real thing.

Today, that's not necessarily the case. Popular belief in the complex is still widespread, and remains engrained in the psychological profession—especially, of course, among die-hard Freudians. But Freud's idea has been met with an increasing amount of skepticism, particularly from those whose views on human nature derive from someone who died before Freud even conceived of the Oedipus complex—Charles Darwin.

For the evolutionary psychologist—the branch of psychology that applies Darwinist principles to human behavior—the operative question is always how this or that behavior is likely to affect the individual's or the group's evolutionary fitness. In other words, how will doing something, or refraining from doing something, help you survive, find a suitable mate, and produce healthy offspring? Evolutionary psychology has something to say about many areas of human behavior, but one major focus in the field has been intra-family relations—marriage, mating, sibling rivalry, and parent-child relations. And according to the perspective of evolutionary psychologists, the Oedipus complex makes no sense.

Their argument starts with the fact that incest is bad from the genetic point of view, because genetically it increases the risk of passing along harmful traits, and for this reason we're almost certainly hardwired *against* incest, not *for* it.[17] The Oedipus complex starts to look even more dubious when the issue is fully considered from the evolutionary point of view. As the evolutionary psychologist Michelle Scalise Sugiyama explains:

> From a biological perspective, childhood feelings of sexual desire for one parent and murderous jealousy toward the other are implausible: there is no need driving their emergence. The evolution of oedipal desires would be a waste of energy because a

> child is incapable of carrying them out. Even if this were possible, such desires would be counter-productive: on the one hand, copulation before sexual maturity is fruitless, and, on the other, killing one of its providers would at best sharply decrease a child's quality of life and at worst drastically reduce its chances of survival. . . . In sum, the oedipal complex postulates the existence of psychological mechanisms that are not only unnecessary but would be deleterious to the individual possessing them.[18]

That's the basic logic of the case against the Oedipus complex. And the logic is backed up by the fact that, as Sugiyama notes, "incest among humans is statistically rare and mother-son incest the rarest of all."[19] And what's the evidence on the other side? Not very much. Today, the water for the Freudian theory is carried mostly by folklorists who have purported to find evidence for the complex in Oedipus-like folktales from around the world, the logic being that where such stories are told, the Oedipus complex must be present. If you can find oedipal stories told everywhere, across all culture, then the complex must be universal.[20] In the thrall of such reasoning, folklorists have scoured the globe in search of oedipal tales, and those who searched found. The title of one representative book authored by two folklorists says it all: *Oedipus Ubiquitous*.[21] But their evidence never blew me away. For example, they cite a story from the Ozark Mountains. A brother and sister have sex with each other. When they're finished, the following dialogue takes place:

> "My god, Jenny," says Jack. "I never had it so good in my whole life! Why, you're lots better than Maw!" The girl just wiggled her ass, and started to tickle Jack's balls some more. "Yeah," she giggled, "that's what Paw always says."[22]

In advancing this story as evidence of the Oedipus complex, I think they take too seriously what is obviously a joke playing on the stereotype of the incestuous redneck, and they offer no evidence that this joke reflects an underlying reality (evidence that most jokes based on stereotype similarly lack). These same scholars also ask us to accept the presence of an Oedipus complex in the story of Aladdin, from *The Thousand and One Nights* (better known as *Arabian Nights*). Their evidence? Someone *pretending* to be Aladdin's *uncle* is vying with Aladdin for the affection of Aladdin's *wife*. Again, these scholars fail to explain how this proves that in reality, sons want to have sex with their mothers.

The anthropologist Melford Spiro (1920–2014) made the strained (and strange) argument that the insult "You're a motherfucker" suggests the existence of a desire to sleep with one's mother, for "if the accused is so strongly offended and provoked by such an accusation, it is perhaps plausible to infer that it touches a raw nerve, so that (psychodynamically viewed) the intensity of his reaction conceals the intensity of his desire to commit the very deed which the insult accuses him of committing."[23] It apparently didn't occur to him that we simply find the suggestion offensive (to the extent that we even think about it in a literal sense anymore) or that the phrase might refer to other people's mothers.

If this is the best evidence in favor of the Oedipus complex, then I gladly side with the skeptics.

This isn't to say that the bond between mother and child isn't hugely important; rather, it's simply not sexual. It's also not to deny that there's plenty of father/son conflict in the world. It's just that the conflict is not about sexual access to the mother.[24]

For these reasons, Freud's attempted answer to the Riddle of Oedipus doesn't ring true for me. Even less plausible are the various Freud-inspired sexual readings of the play under which Oedipus himself actually has an Oedipus complex and the play is fraught with sexual meaning. In my view, these readings are silly. They're like the joke told by the anthropologist Mark Anspach about the man who was administered a Rorschach test by a psychiatrist. In one blot after another he saw something sexual—breasts, genitals, intercourse, and so on. At the conclusion of the test, the doctor said to the man, "Sir, I'm afraid to tell you that you have a serious sexual obsession." The man responded: "What do you mean, *I* have a sexual obsession? You're the one drawing all the dirty pictures!"[25]

It's titillating to talk about swollen phalluses and vaginas, and in the early years of the twentieth century, it must have been liberating to apply sexual interpretations to things that previously had been covered up under the Victorian veil of prudery.[26] But I don't think Sophocles was drawing dirty pictures. And when you think about it, did he really have to sex up the story to be able to hold our interest? Oedipus has a swollen foot because he was the victim of attempted infanticide—isn't that scandalous enough? Oedipus destroys the Sphinx when he solves her riddle about feet and destroys himself when he solves the riddle of his own feet—that is, what the scars are from.[27] Isn't that far more interesting than a clichéd analogy to an erect penis? At the crossroad, Oedipus killed the man he later learned was his father. That's an extraordinary act, with enough devastating consequences on its own; I don't see what's gained by describing the crossroad as a woman's vagina. And does the act of someone blinding himself after his world has collapsed have to be compared with self-castration to be powerful?

The strict Freudian might say that all of my objections merely demonstrate how repressed I am. One Freud-inspired critic mocked the classicist E. R. Dodds for being insufficiently attuned to sexual issues in the play: "It is much nicer to think of ourselves as hunting bravely for our true identities than as trying to cope with ancient sexual troubles [whatever those are]."[28] But even Mr. Sex himself famously said that sometimes a cigar is just a cigar. Just so here, sometimes a swollen foot caused by attempted infanticide is just a swollen foot caused by attempted infanticide.

Of course, the idea of the Oedipus complex has been so watered down in common parlance, and even in psychological circles, that it has come to refer to any sort of dysfunction in a male's relationship with his mother, such as any sort of overdependence or smothering. The previously mentioned Woody Allen film *Oedipus Wrecks*, which depicts an obnoxious mother haunting the protagonist as a giant figure in the sky, comes to mind as an example of this broader interpretation.

THE ZEUS COMPLEX

The Oedipus complex has been watered down in another important respect. While Freud spoke of "our first sexual impulse toward our mother and our first hatred and our first murderous wish against our father," the complex is often used to refer to *any* father/son conflict, not just conflict related to the mother's attention. In this interpretation, the mother/incest side of the triangle drops away, and we're left with a complex composed of nothing more than hostility to the father—a "skinny" Oedipus complex. It's not your grandmother's Oedipus complex, but it's extremely influential and has become an important part of the Oedipus literature.

The leading advocate for applying the skinny version of the Oedipus complex to *Oedipus Rex* was the German-American psychoanalyst Erich Fromm (1900–1980), who argued that the play is about father-son conflict, not mother-son incest. Fromm based his argument on two facts. First, the play contains no indication that Oedipus is attracted to Jocasta; she simply came with the throne. Fromm asks, "Should we believe that a myth, the central theme of which constitutes an incestuous relationship between mother and son, would entirely omit the element of attraction between the two?"[29] Second, the other two plays in the Oedipus cycle involve father-son conflict: In *Oedipus at Colonus*, Oedipus curses Polyneices (his son), and in *Antigone*, Haemon rebels against his father, Creon. There is no hint of incest in either of these plays (unless Haemon's interest in his cousin Antigone is considered incest, which legally, morally, and medically it often is not). Therefore,

Fromm argues, "If we interpret King Oedipus in light of the whole trilogy, the assumption seems plausible that the real issue in [*Oedipus Rex*], too, is the conflict between father and son and not the problem of incest."[30]

I don't buy it. Fromm was right in jettisoning the incest aspect of the Freudian theory, for the reasons discussed above, but I believe he's wrong in thinking that *Oedipus Rex* is about father/son conflict. It's simply not there in the play. For one thing, where's the evidence of hostility toward the father? Far from exulting in triumph over having dispatched his father and taken his throne, Oedipus feels nothing but intense horror at what he has done once he understands it fully. His stated reason for blinding himself is to avoid having to look his father in the eyes when he joins him in the underworld ("How could I look my father in the eyes?" [line 1501]). He certainly feels no vindication or sense of liberation.

In fact, if Oedipus directs anger toward any parent in the play, that parent is Jocasta. After rushing into the palace, Oedipus asks for a sword right before bursting into Jocasta's room. Scholars have debated the significance of the sword-grabbing, but it wouldn't be implausible to interpret this as an indication that he intends to kill her, for he has just learned about the attempted infanticide.[31] (It may also be worth noting that Jocasta is the only parent mentioned by the Theban in connection with that horrible act.) Further, even if you believe, as some do, that Oedipus was too quick to anger at the crossroad, how can that constitute rebellion against his father if he didn't know their relationship at the time of the slaying?

True, as Fromm notes, the other two Theban plays involve father/son conflict. But recall from earlier in this book that the three were written many years apart, and each one is very different from the others in focus and theme. They are sometimes called a "trilogy," but just for convenience: They were not created as a true trilogy, as were, say, the three plays in Aeschylus's *Oresteia*, which were created with each other and performed together. So reading

Oedipus Rex in light of the other two plays is problematic. Just because something is important in the other two doesn't necessarily mean it's important in *Oedipus Rex.*

In rejecting Fromm's theory, I am, of course, not denying that the father-son relationship is extremely complicated and freighted with all manner of psychological baggage. I loved my father deeply, but we had lots of disagreements and fought frequently. The father/son relationship is nothing if not complicated, but it's about a lot more than conflict; it's not a zero-sum game but a mixture of competition and cooperation. My son's success in life gives me nothing but joy; it adds to my life, never subtracts. The same was true of my father: I believe he never felt anything but pride in regard to any of my achievements.

Apparently, Sophocles and his son had a complicated relationship, too, based on two data points. On the one hand, his son Iophon was also a playwright, and there's a suggestion in *The Frogs* of Aristophanes that Sophocles helped him with his plays. On the other hand, when Sophocles was very old, Iophon went to court to have him declared incompetent and therefore ineligible to manage his property.[32] (The court sided with Sophocles, based in part on the fact that he had just written *Oedipus at Colonus*, the writing of one of the world's greatest literary masterpieces being a pretty good sign of mental competence!)

So yes, father/son relationships are complicated and contain plenty of conflict. But does that mean that a man watching *Oedipus Rex* will secretly be pleased by the discovery of patricide in the play? If anything, I would think it's the opposite. Maybe there are some men out there who would cheer on an act of patricide, but based on the father/son relationships I'm familiar with, including my own, these men must be a rarity. Eight years after my father's death, I still have strong feelings about him, recognizing that much of the fighting between us was unnecessary and could have been avoided if I had been more patient and diplomatic—if I had been, in other words, wiser than I was. The sight of Oedipus learning that he has killed his own father triggers in me a sense of lingering guilt about those times I could have been kinder to mine.

If you want a symbol for the desire to destroy one's father, *Oedipus Rex* is not your play, and Oedipus is not your man. Why not Zeus? According to Greek mythology, he not only killed his father, Cronus, he also castrated him. What's more, Cronus had previously killed and castrated *his* father, Uranus. And those were all intentional, premeditated acts. You can't get much more "Oedipal" (heavy on the scare quotes) than that. In fact, it would be more fitting to call this supposed phenomenon the "Zeus complex." As well, Hera, Zeus's wife, was also his sister, so you've got incest—real, deliberate incest—in the story, too![33]

There is, by the way, an even skinnier version of the Oedipus complex—rebellion against *any* father figure, not just one's literal father. In this narrower version, every older male, especially one in a position of authority, becomes a stand-in for the biological father: For example, Freud himself has been described as having an "Oedipal" relationship to intellectual precursors such as Nietzsche.[34]

This broader conception of the complex has also made its way into the Oedipus literature. In an intriguing essay called "The Four Fathers," the literary scholar James Schroeter argues that each of the four principal male figures in the play—Teiresias, Creon, the Corinthian messenger, and the Theban shepherd—is a stand-in for Laius, and what we are seeing on stage is essentially a reenactment of the murder of Laius in the form of a rebellion against each of these men.[35] Schroeter bases his argument on the fact that each is old enough to be Oedipus's father and that each performs a specifically paternal function in Oedipus's life: Teiresias fosters Oedipus's psychic good, by having kept the truth a secret; Creon his political good, by allowing him to rule; the Corinthian messenger his social good, by having brought him to the king and queen of Corinth; and the Theban shepherd his biological good, by saving him from death as an infant. And how does Oedipus repay these paternal acts? By committing "some violent or destructive act against each of his fathers, exhibiting a pattern similar to that in the antecedent action at the crossroads, when he had unwittingly murdered his real father, Laius."[36] Schroeter also argues that each of the men represents a different stage in the development of man, and that Oedipus is in a sense a composite of the four.[37]

I think it's a clever reading, and Schroeter is onto something in noting the interesting fact that, aside from Jocasta and Oedipus, the main characters in the play are all older men and that, as I discussed in the previous chapter, the progression of the play from Teiresias through Creon and the Corinthian messenger to the Theban shepherd represents in effect a voyage back in time, a "recovery of increasingly earlier and therefore more deeply buried memories, exactly as in a psychoanalysis."[38] But it's inaccurate to say that those conflicts reflect a rebellious nature on Oedipus's part. Each one arises for very specific reasons that have nothing to do with the fact that his antagonists are all older men. Teiresias, for example, triggers Oedipus's rage by at first refusing to answer his question and then accusing him of horrible deeds. And in no respect can the Corinthian messenger and the Theban shepherd be considered authority figures—socially, they are far beneath Oedipus, who has complete power over them. More importantly, whatever conflict he had with those four doesn't change the fact that Oedipus feels guilty and horrified after discovering what he did to his own father. Ultimately, therefore, I wasn't persuaded that the Oedipus complex, however fat or skinny, is a useful lens through which to view the play.

In fiction, the killing of family members generally takes one of two forms. One is intentional killing, in which the character knows that the person he or she is killing is a family member. Many great works of literature fit this model, including Greek literature: Agamemnon sacrifices his daughter Iphigenia, and his wife, Clytemnestra, kills him in revenge, and then their son, Orestes, kills her for killing his father; Medea kills her own children to get back at Jason; and so on. The other kind is unintentional—as in *Jean de Florette*, in which the family relationship is unknown. It's a very different act. There are likewise many examples of unintentional family murder in literature, of which *Oedipus Rex* is the most famous.

But think about it: If Freud and Fromm were right, then it wouldn't matter if Oedipus knew or didn't know that these were his parents. In other words, as far as their theories are concerned, a story about a man who unknowingly kills his father and marries his mother would have the same psychological effect on us as a story about a man who intentionally commits those acts. That makes no sense to me. *Oedipus Rex* is a play about a man who killed a man and married a woman and only many years later learned that they were his father and mother. This particularly horrible discovery is absolutely critical to the power of the play. To describe it in any other way is to miss what makes it what it is, which is why I dislike the use of "Oedipal" to describe any and every instance of incest or intra-family conflict.

There's an interesting irony in all this discussion about Freud: Apart from its preoccupation with the Oedipus complex, Freudian theory actually has some useful concepts for analyzing *Oedipus Rex*. Take, for example, repression. As I mentioned in chapter 3, some commentators have usefully drawn on that concept in analyzing Oedipus's character and state of knowledge. Or think about the concept of the divided self, the battle between the different parts of the psyche. Freud once referred to the "strange state of mind in which one knows and does not know a thing at the same time."[39]

But he himself did not apply those concepts to *Oedipus Rex*. Freud thought Hamlet was repressed, not Oedipus. In *Oedipus Rex*, according to Freud, "The child's wishful fantasy that underlies it is brought into the open and realized as it would be in a dream," while in *Hamlet*, that childish wish "remains repressed; and—just as in the case of a neurosis—we only learn of its existence from its inhibiting consequences."[40] Some of Oedipus's unintentionally truthful remarks can also be thought of as Freudian slips—for example, his using the singular "robber" after Creon, relaying the oracle's message, refers to the plural "robbers."[41]

But outside of the Oedipus complex, Freud didn't use any of the other tools in his toolkit to analyze the play.[42] Freud also didn't have anything to say about the other two major discoveries made by Oedipus—that the prophecies had come true and that he in fact was a native of Thebes—which are the subject of the next two chapters.

Chapter Six

"Cursed in My Birth"

If you had to read *Oedipus Rex* in high school, chances are excellent that your teacher stood in front of the class and referred to it as a "tragedy of fate." That assertion is probably the single most popular cliché about it. In fact, not only is the play widely viewed as a tragedy of fate, it's considered the *premier* tragedy of fate.[1]

I've never been particularly fond of the concept of fate, especially when it's used in connection with an event that hasn't yet happened. When it comes to a possible event in the future, use of the word "fate" suggests that there's nothing that can be done, when in some circumstances, that might not be true. As the Serenity Prayer reminds us, the key is knowing what we can change and what we can't.

But plainly, something about *Oedipus Rex* has caused (and continues to cause) people to think about it as a tragedy of fate. Some classical scholars are no less attracted to this idea than high school teachers. Here's a typical statement about the play, from a modern scholar: "[T]here is no doubt that the whole narrative of Oedipus has one main point: the fate was bestowed upon him at birth."[2] And so I have long pondered the question: Is *Oedipus Rex* a tragedy of fate, and if so, what exactly does that mean?

This touches on the second implication of Oedipus's discovery—namely, that the oracle's prophecies had come true. Focusing on this fulfillment-of-the-prophecy aspect of the story led me to a whole different set of issues from the ones I've already discussed in this book, starting with a fairly fundamental question: What do we even mean by "fate"?

A ROLL OF THE DICE OR A FALL OF THE DOMINOES?

People talk about "fate" in several distinct ways. Sometimes it's used synonymously with luck, chance, or circumstance. If a plane crashes into a house, killing a whole family, or someone is hit by a bus, we might say it was fate that this happened, in the same way we would say that they suffered bad luck or were victims of circumstance. Used in this way, fate conjures up the image of a roll of the dice, the spinning of a roulette wheel—an unpredictable outcome over which we have no control.

Some scholars view *Oedipus Rex* in precisely this light: a warning that bad things can happen to anyone at any time. Martha Nussbaum puts it this way: "[I]f someone who enjoys the extreme of control, prosperity, and in general good fortune [as Oedipus] can be so brought low by events and circumstances beyond his control, then no human life seems safe from this possibility."[3] It's this view of Oedipus that led the Greek Stoics to hold up Oedipus as Exhibit A in support of their argument that we should never hold the things of this world too dear, for they can vanish at any time.[4]

I don't find *Oedipus Rex* a particularly good illustration of this conception of fate. What happened to Oedipus was not a bolt out of the blue, like a plane crashing into a house. It feels much more like something that had been building for a long time. Sure, the manifestation of his bad luck was sudden, but the pipeline of his misfortune was long, stretching all the way back to his beginnings. Oedipus certainly demonstrates that bad things *can* happen to people—even good people—but that banal observation applies to countless people in countless other stories.

A second interpretation of fate may be closer to the mark and better capture that sense of a long pipeline in *Oedipus Rex*: fate as inexorability. Here, the operative metaphor is not a roll of the dice or a bolt out of the blue but instead a chain of falling dominoes: Once a certain event happens, everything else follows with unstoppable inevitability. This meaning of "fate" carries the connotation that no matter which path you take, you will end up in the same place; no matter which door you open, you will get the same booby prize.

From one perspective, Oedipus's life story does seem to resemble a row of dominoes. One thing seems inexorably linked to another: His parents are told that their son, if allowed to live, will kill his father and marry his mother, so they cast him out; having been cast out, he doesn't know his parents, and therefore they are strangers to him when they meet; because he was adopted, one day he wonders about his origins, which in turn leads him to the oracle; and so on, down the line, as one domino falls after another.

This is how the French writer and artist Jean Cocteau viewed Oedipus in *The Infernal Machine*, his version of the Oedipus story. "Watch now, spectator," the play begins. "Before you is a fully wound machine. Slowly its spring will unwind the entire span of a human life. It is one of the most perfect machines devised by the infernal gods for the mathematical annihilation of a mortal."[5]

But on closer inspection, I'm not sure this sense of fate really fits Oedipus, either. When he received the prophecy, he faced a choice between two paths—one leading back to Corinth and safety, the other toward Thebes and doom. He took one road and, as the poet Robert Frost would put it, that made all the difference. If he had taken the other road, everything would have been different. And then, shortly afterward, he reached a *literal* crossroad, where he had a choice between defending himself and letting himself be pushed aside. So how accurate is it to say that Oedipus was doomed no matter which path he took?

Now, you can say it wasn't a *real* choice, that it was illusory and, in reality, he didn't have the option of returning to Corinth. But why would that be the case? The most sensible response would be that it was all *preordained*. But that brings us to a third sense of "fate"—the one that I think is meant when *Oedipus Rex* is called a "tragedy of fate."

FIXED ON HIS NATAL DAY, OR "WHY ME?"

The reason the story of Oedipus feels so fate-laden to so many, and has become such a symbol of the idea of fate, is the existence and fulfillment of the prophecies. Because of the prophecies, it can be said that his fate was preset, predetermined, preordained—choose your preferred word. "Fate," in fact, comes from the Latin "fatum," which means "that which has been spoken."

This brings us to the second implication of Oedipus's discovery: that the prophecies had come true. At the moment of his terrible discovery, in addition to bemoaning the lives he cut down with his own hands, he cries: "Oh God! All has come true!" (lines 1306–07). He realizes that he hasn't, after all, escaped those dreadful prophecies he thought he had left far behind him. At the same time, he realizes that the awful words flung at him by Teiresias were also true.

I think, therefore, that if we're going to assert that *Oedipus Rex* is a play about the working out of fate, we should do so with this particular sense of "fate" in mind: a prophecy fulfilled (or, in this case, two prophecies). That sense of "fate" fits the story far better than the other two just discussed.

It also happens to be more consonant with the ancient way of thinking about fate. In Greek mythology, as in the mythologies of many other cultures, fate was personified by female figures—the

Moirai, to the Greeks—who determined in advance the course of everyone's life. (The Norns, in Norse mythology were very similar.) They literally wove the tapestry of our destinies, and even the gods themselves could not make changes to their plans. In this view of fate, everything is fixed *in advance.* As Homer has Hector say in the *Iliad*: "No one alive has ever escaped [fate], neither brave man nor coward, I tell you—it's born with us the day that we are born."[6] Seneca wrote in his version of the Oedipus story, "[O]n our natal day was fixed our day of death. Not God himself can change the current of our lives, which bears its own compelling force within itself."[7] Oedipus's fate was locked in at the outset. That, I believe, is why *Oedipus Rex* strikes people as a play about fate.

I think that much is clear. But there's something else about the role of fate here that's *not* so clear, and that is the question, Why Oedipus? Why did this calamity happen to Oedipus and not someone else? I think what's interesting about this question is that it's not discussed in the play. At the moment of discovery, Oedipus looks up and cries, "Oh God! All has come true!" But given the horror of the revelation, I think it's striking that there is no moment in which he looks skyward and, like Tevye in *Fiddler on the Roof*, asks, "Oh God! Why me? Why of all people was I the subject of such a fate?"

In fact, *no one* in the play asks this question—neither Oedipus nor the other characters nor even the chorus. The question simply is never raised. To see why this is significant, let's consider for a moment a work of literature in which the "Why me?" or "Why him?" question *does* get asked. For there are indeed such works of literature.

The classic example is the novel *The Bridge of San Luis Rey* by Thornton Wilder. Set in eighteenth-century colonial Peru, the novel opens with the deaths of five people when a heavily crossed rope bridge breaks and they fall into a steep canyon. A priest who witnesses the event wonders why this calamity happened to those five people and not anyone else. Trying to answer that question, he combs through the record of their lives, trying to learn everything he possibly can about them. His investigation of *why* is what the entire novel is about.

This simply doesn't happen in *Oedipus Rex*. There's no counterpart in the play to the priest in *The Bridge of San Luis Rey*—someone who looks into Oedipus's life to understand why he was singled out for this terrible punishment.

But what about us? Are we supposed to ask that question anyway? Is that what Sophocles expected us to do? Did he want us to play the role of the priest in *The Bridge of San Luis Rey* and scour the record of Oedipus's life?

Some scholars have done precisely that, examining whether his fate can be explained by his various flaws. And, as I mentioned in chapter 3, an untold number of scholars have found such flaws. Some, for example, think he was too reckless in killing an older man and marrying an older woman. Others are offended by his onstage conduct, finding him hubristic and temperamental. (For examples, see the appendix.) They argue, in effect, that Oedipus's character is his destiny.

This line of reasoning never made any sense to me, because no matter how obnoxious you may find Oedipus to be, to argue that his character flaws brought about his fate gets causation backward. How could his conduct be punished with a fate *that had already been determined before he was even born*? The prophecies didn't say, "You will suffer this terrible fate *if* you behave badly." Oedipus was given no out; the die was already cast, his fate already sealed.[8]

Instead, I think, the only good answer to the "Why him?" question is simply that it's not a fair world. We could go back, as some scholars do, and talk about the curse on Laius that I mentioned in chapter 3. But that gets us nowhere and yields no answer other than that it was bad luck for Oedipus to have been born the son of Laius.

(Such a focus on Laius also misses what was innovative about Sophocles's version of the story, which—in contrast with, say, the Aeschylean version—deliberately *suppressed* any reference to Laius's crimes, thereby putting the focus on Oedipus himself.)[9]

Ultimately, therefore, I think that the play is not a contemplation of the "Why me?" question. This is not a story in which someone gets lung cancer, and then we find out that he smoked all his life. Sometimes stuff just happens, and there's no satisfying answer to the question, "Why this person and not another?" Sometimes searching for an answer to that question in a person's life record gets you nowhere.

In fact, that's the ultimate conclusion reached by the priest in *The Bridge of San Luis Rey*. After many years of studying the lives of the five victims, he decides that there is nothing in their backgrounds explaining why they, and not others, were the ones who died when the bridge collapsed. He concludes, in other words, that slowly, over time, the ropes holding up the bridge weakened, and that therefore *somebody* had to be the last straw. Likewise, *somebody* had to have the misfortune of being Laius's son, and that lot fell to poor Oedipus.

So if the play is not a contemplation of the why, is there anything interesting about the role of fate in the play, beyond being a reminder that it's not a fair world and that bad stuff over which you have no control just happens? In other words, is there an interesting angle on fate in *Oedipus Rex* that has prompted so many to think of it as the preeminent tragedy of fate?

I think there is. It's not the question of why these events happened to Oedipus and not someone else but rather the question of *how*. In other words, what's truly interesting to me about the role of fate in *Oedipus Rex* is the mechanism by which his fate came about.

What's distinctive about Oedipus is not simply that his life's outcome was declared from the outset: It's that it was declared *to him*. The gods didn't utter the prophecies into the air on Mount Olympus. They *revealed* them, and not just to priests and seers but to the affected characters themselves—Oedipus and his parents, the very subjects of the prophecy. This makes them a special kind of prophecy which today we call *self-fulfilling*.

THE OEDIPUS EFFECT

Prophecies from Delphi could be maddeningly ambiguous and misleading. Mysterious statements are not said to be "Delphic" for nothing.

Consider the tale of the king of Lydia, Croesus, which I touched on briefly in chapter 2. In one of the most famous stories in his *Histories*, Herodotus (a friend of Sophocles) recounts how Croesus—he of "rich as Croesus" fame—was trying to decide whether to invade the Persian Empire, then controlled by Cyrus the Great. Croesus consulted the Delphic oracle, giving a lot of money, and received the following answer: "If you attack Persia, you will destroy a great empire." Based on that prophecy, Croesus proceeded to attack Persia—and lost. Cyrus conquered Lydia. The oracle was right: Croesus did destroy a great empire—his own![10]

According to Herodotus, after Croesus lost his empire, he asked the oracle why it had misled him. The oracle responded, essentially, "Why didn't you ask for clarification?!" The same question could have been put to Oedipus.

The term "self-fulfilling prophecy" was coined by the sociologist Robert Merton in 1948. It refers to predictions that, by becoming known, cause themselves to happen; they are beliefs about the future that become true by virtue of being believed and acted upon. The self-fulfilling prophecy is an important phenomenon, with applications throughout the social sciences—psychology, sociology, economics, education theory, and international relations. I've always found them fascinating.

They come in different varieties. In some cases, they are predictions about *good* things happening. There are different mechanisms whereby a prediction might itself lead to the predicted outcome. For example, the prediction might produce its predicted outcome based on the authority of the person making the prediction. Say the chairman of the Federal Reserve predicts that stocks will go up. As a result, investors—interpreting the chairman's prediction as a sign of confidence in the market—buy a bunch of stocks, thereby raising their values. Hence, the "prophecy" has been fulfilled.

Predictions like that can have a confidence-boosting effect. Or they can influence the outcome by planting in someone's mind a seed that might otherwise not have been there. *Macbeth* is a classic example of the latter. The witches predict Macbeth will be king, and he then proceeds to take steps to fulfill their prophecy. (This turned out not to be such a good thing for Macbeth, but that's another matter.) Or a prediction can work through what's called the "observer-expectancy effect." If a teacher gets into his head that a certain student has great potential, he will, by focusing his energy on that student, make that prediction come true.

Then there are predictions of bad happenings, the ones to be studiously avoided. Here, too, the different mechanisms are manifold. If a newspaper predicts a run on a bank, depositors (who are now spooked by the prediction) will bring about that run by demanding the return of their deposits. In this case, a bunch of selfish individual acts add up to a collective bad outcome that fulfills the prediction. Or take the opposite of the good-student scenario: If a teacher assesses a student as having low potential, by acting upon that belief and, say, *not* pushing the student to succeed, the teacher increases the odds that the prediction will come true. (This phenomenon is sometimes referred to as the "soft bigotry of low expectations.")

This discussion reminds me of a joke that made the rounds on the Internet a few years ago: A study showed that pessimists die younger than optimists—to which the pessimists responded, "See? We were right!" In other words, you can fulfill a sour prediction through a kind of confidence-*destroying* effect. Something bad is predicted, and through a kind of learned helplessness, you hasten its realization by resigning yourself to that undesired outcome.

The Croesus story illustrates yet another mechanism at play in some self-fulfilling prophecies. In effect, the oracle there was saying, "You will destroy your own empire," but Croesus misunderstood. He took its message as a prophecy of something good happening, so, ironically, he set about trying to fulfill it.

But the most ironic, and to me the most interesting, of all these scenarios is the one in which a prophecy that something terrible will happen is fulfilled by the very steps taken to keep it from happening. Now, usually, when you predict that something bad will happen, you do so to try to prevent it; the prediction is in the form of "If you don't do such and such or stop doing such and such, this or that will happen." Sometimes the prediction is taken to heart and disaster averted. As Yuval Noah Harari puts it in his book *Homo Deus*, "What's the point of making predictions if they cannot change anything?"[11] Sometimes the prediction is ignored and disaster ensues, as when a smoker ignores cancer warnings or the Trojans ignore Cassandra's predictions of doom. In the latter situation, the problem is a failure to take the gloomy warning seriously.

But sometimes the prophecy comes true precisely because it *was* taken seriously; paradoxically, the recipient would have been better off ignoring it altogether. That's the self-fulfilling prophecy, and *Oedipus Rex* provides us with not just one but two of the greatest examples of it. In fact, the examples are so vivid that the great twentieth-century philosopher of science Karl Popper (1902–1994) invoked Oedipus when he analyzed the phenomenon of the self-fulfilling prophecy, calling it the "Oedipus effect."[12]

After receiving the first prophecy, Laius and Jocasta cast out their infant son, producing the unintended result that he grows up without recognizing them and therefore, when the time comes, is able to kill Laius and marry Jocasta in complete obliviousness. They would have been better off raising him in Thebes. The lesson here? Sometimes it's better to keep someone close than send them off, because you never know what might happen once they're out of your jurisdiction. King Priam of Troy also learned this lesson. He received a prophecy that his son Paris would bring ruin to the city, so he sent him into exile on Mount Ida. But it was there that Paris was chosen to judge the beauty contest among the goddesses, which eventually led him to abduct Helen, which led to the ruinous war with the Greeks.

Trouble is also bound to happen when you try to keep someone in ignorance, which in effect was what happened to the child Oedipus. The events of his early life were never explained to him, so he had no frame of reference for his actions as an adult. Invariably, his ignorance was the cause of calamity.

This is a common theme. In "Sleeping Beauty," the evil witch places a curse on the princess that one day she will die by pricking her finger on a spindle. To protect her from this fate, her father, the king, orders all spindles and spinning wheels removed from the kingdom. The princess grows up never having seen a spinning wheel, but one day she finally encounters one that was secretly preserved. Being unfamiliar with this strange device, she pricks her finger, and the curse comes true (or, more accurately, a modified version of the curse, as after the curse was placed on her, a good witch was able to reduce the curse to a hundred-year slumber).

The second self-fulfilling prophecy in *Oedipus Rex* was the one received by Oedipus himself. After being warned that he will kill his father and marry his mother, Oedipus seeks safety by fleeing Corinth, which leads him right into the jaws of his awful destiny. Again, you've very likely seen this plot point in other stories. In the movie *Alien*, the protagonist, Ripley, blows up her entire ship to kill the alien, only to find it hiding in the small escape capsule with her.

There's a traditional Arabic story sometimes called "The Appointment in Samarra" that I've always loved. A servant at a bazaar in Baghdad encounters Death. He is terrified because he is sure that the look on Death's face signifies that Death was there at the bazaar to take him away. He runs home to ask his master for a swift horse to take him to Samarra, to escape Death. Later that day, the master bumps into Death and asks him why he scared his servant with a terrifying look. Death says, "I didn't mean to scare him. The look on my face was surprise, for I have an appointment to meet him in Samarra tonight."

In these stories we see the protagonist struggling in front of our eyes to avoid his fate. In *Oedipus Rex*, the struggle to escape took place in the backstory. What we are seeing onstage is the realization phase, during which Oedipus discovers, to his horror—and after the fact—that he has failed to win his struggle against fate. The horror is intensified by the fact that he thought he had won the struggle, and now he realizes that not only did he lose the fight against fate, it was his very efforts in attempting to thwart it that eventually brought it about. He realizes, in other words, that he has been cruelly tricked.

"FOUL DEEDS WILL RISE"

Several of the world's leading classicists have argued vehemently against the notion that *Oedipus Rex* is a tragedy of fate. Bernard Knox devotes the first chapter of *Oedipus at Thebes*, which I discussed in chapter 3, to arguing against the tragedy-of-fate interpretation, and a similar argument takes up a major part of E. R. Dodds's classic essay "On Misunderstanding the *Oedipus Rex*." I understand why they make this argument and am sympathetic to it. It's important to them that Oedipus be portrayed as a great man, a hero of truth. They hate the image of Oedipus as a worm on a hook, a fly in a spider's web. For them, the problem with calling *Oedipus Rex* a tragedy of fate is that it means undermining the heroic image of Oedipus.

In support of their arguments against the tragedy-of-fate thesis, they make the observation that while the prophecies in the story foretell that Oedipus will kill his father and marry his mother, they say nothing about the truth being made known, let alone that Jocasta will kill herself and Oedipus blind himself.[13] And therefore, they argue, it cannot be said that what happens in the play is a tragedy of fate—a subtle distinction. Maybe Oedipus's overall life is a tragedy of fate, but what we're seeing in the play itself is not.

When I first encountered this argument, I thought it was kind of hyper-technical. It sounded to me like one of those disingenuous legal arguments that fault the other side in a negotiation for failing to specify something that everyone assumes is implicit. ("Oh, you wanted the tires, too? You didn't say that—you only paid for the car.") It struck me as a little like complaining that the prophecy forgot to say, "Simon says." Wasn't it implicit in the prophecies that the truth would eventually be made known?

But over time, I decided that the problem with the argument wasn't so much that it's too technical as that it misses an important issue with the play. The argument by the anti-fatalists (Knox, Dodds, et al) jumps from the fact that the prophecies are silent about the revelation to the argument that the revelation occurred only because of Oedipus's efforts. This sets up a false choice: Either the revelation (and resulting suicide and self-blinding) was part of the prophecy (in which case it would be considered "fated"), or it's the product of Oedipus's unrelenting search for the truth. But this misses an important in-between possibility: that the truth was bound to come out because of its very nature, regardless of what Oedipus did on stage.

In skipping over this possibility, the anti-fatalists miss an interesting area of inquiry about the play, which includes questions like: Why *did* the truth come out? Were there forces working toward exposure of the ugly reality behind the illusion? And if so, how strong were those forces?

These, of course, are questions that can be asked about an infinite number of things, not just *Oedipus Rex*. They are important inquiries about the nature of truth. To what extent does the truth contain the seeds of its own unfolding? What are the forces that push the truth to the surface, ensuring its exposure and, at the same time, defeating falsehood and illusion?

The answers are different in each sphere of life. The laws of nature and mathematics seem bound to come out at some point. If Isaac Newton hadn't figured out the laws of motion, eventually someone else would have. The brute facts of the natural world don't stay hidden forever. The New World and the moons of Jupiter were destined to be "discovered" at some point.

But I don't think we're quite as bullish about the truth surfacing in the human world. Some political scandals eventually get unearthed, but surely not all. While we're reasonably sure some genius other than Johannes Kepler would eventually have discovered the laws of planetary motion, how confident are we that Watergate would have surfaced without Bob Woodward and Carl Bernstein? We'll never know the number of undiscovered Watergates.

Sometimes, cold-case murders resurface after many years and are solved. Creon had long ago closed the file on the murder of Laius Rex; it became a very cold case indeed, but the plague brought it back out from the storage files, and with renewed scrutiny, it got solved.

On the other hand, I read once that around a third of murders in the United States remain unsolved—they are cold cases that stay forever cold. Each one of those is a truth failing to surface. In many cases we don't even find the body, let alone the murderer. Sometimes the murdered victim, buried in a shallow grave, is uncovered by a passing dog or washes up on shore; Hamlet famously said, "Foul deeds will rise, though all the earth o'erwhelm them."[14] But we know that's not always true—some things stay buried, regardless of how much or little earth o'erwhelms them. Jimmy Hoffa's body hasn't surfaced yet; it's a pretty good bet by now that it never will.

And those are just the known unknowns—we know there was a murder; we simply have to find who did it. But then there are all the unknown unknowns, situations in which we don't even realize that there's a question, a crime that was committed, a mystery to be solved.

Arthur Miller's phrase "return of the repressed" doesn't imply that the truth *always* emerges (and if it did, it would be wrong). Sometimes the repressed stays repressed.

SOMETHING IS ROTTEN IN THE STATE OF THEBES

So what about the repressed facts in *Oedipus Rex*? Was the truth about the past in the play a poorly buried body that eventually would be sniffed out? Or was it lying at the bottom of the sea, already eaten by sea creatures?

Knox and the other anti-fatalists simply assume that it took Oedipus himself to bring out the truth. For them, Oedipus was Woodward and Bernstein, without whose diligence and drive the truth might never have emerged, not a Columbus who "discovered" something that would inevitably have been discovered anyway. After all, the whole investigation begins when Oedipus takes the initiative in sending Creon to the oracle.[15] And when he learns the oracle's response, he immediately snaps into action. Throughout the play, he's encouraged to quit, first by Teiresias, next by Jocasta, and finally by the Theban. But he doesn't. He persists until everything is out—*everything*.

The Oedipus we see on stage, the anti-fatalists argue, is a man driving his own destiny. This is the Oedipus of the Sphinx episode, courageous beyond normal human capacity, throwing all caution to the wind. "Let it burst!" he cries. "Whatever will, whatever must! I must know my birth" (line 1184). It is Oedipus's character, his greatness of spirit, that leads to the revelation about his identity, which might never have been revealed otherwise.[16]

But can't an equally strong case be made that the revelation was *not* contingent on Oedipus's efforts, and that the truth might well have surfaced even if Oedipus were a different sort of person, one who was willing to let sleeping cold cases lie? Yes, Oedipus sent Creon to the oracle and pushed hard to find the truth. But, as we discussed in chapter 4, with the arrival of the Corinthian and his news about the death of Polybus, a whole new play begins. It was inevitable that the Corinthian would have come with his news, because it was inevitable that Polybus, Oedipus's adoptive father, was going to die. And once he died, of course someone would come to tell Oedipus, the heir to the throne of Corinth.

Recall that it's the Corinthian's news, and not the murder investigation, that results in the truth coming out. In the scene with the Corinthian messenger, the truth that Oedipus was a foundling emerges not from his brave examination of the messenger but from the messenger's examination of *him*:

Messenger: Wait, who is this woman, makes you so afraid?

Oedipus: Merope, old man. The wife of Polybus.

Messenger: The queen? What's there to fear in her?

Oedipus: A dreadful prophecy, stranger, sent by the gods.

Messenger: Tell me, could you? Unless it's forbidden other ears to hear.

Oedipus: [*Recites the prophecy.*]

Messenger: You're afraid of that? That kept you out of Corinth? (lines 1084–97)

At this point, Oedipus is a passive recipient of fate, tossed about like a boat in a storm, not a bulldog seeking the truth. He becomes a bulldog later, in his questioning of the Theban shepherd over the impassioned objections of Jocasta. But, as one commentator put it, how many people would lose interest in their origins once they learned they were adopted, especially when the source of that information was already on his way and available for examination?[17] Probably not many.

Furthermore, once Jocasta becomes aware of the awful truth, at the end of the dialogue with the Corinthian, she chooses suicide. Thus, even if the Theban shepherd were to hold his tongue—even to the point of death—she would still be dead by her own hand. And at that point, how could Oedipus—or anyone, for that matter—fail to understand the enormous implication? Therefore, we can say with certainty that the truth was almost certain to come out even without the benefit of the Theban shepherd's testimony, which located the infant Oedipus all the way back to Jocasta's womb. Indeed, it can be, and has been, argued that the truth would have surfaced even if there were no Corinthian messenger with news of Polybus's death, because eventually, somehow or other, the truth would have caught up to Oedipus and Jocasta.[18]

And let's not forget perhaps the strongest force pushing the truth to the surface: the plague. For a long time, I didn't particularly focus on its role in the play. It had nothing much to do with the Circular Detective theme or the mysteries of the past, the main ideas that had preoccupied me. But eventually I understood its significance: It's the herald of the rising foul deeds. Like the ghost of Hamlet's father, it tells us that something is rotten in the state of Thebes. It's the gods' way of saying that they will not leave Thebes alone until the truth about Oedipus is brought out into the light—the epidemiological equivalent of a shallow grave disgorging a dead body.

The plague was not part of the myth that Sophocles inherited; as far as we know, he invented it.[19] But by introducing the plague into the story—a stroke of literary genius—wasn't Sophocles in effect saying, two thousand years before Shakespeare, that foul deeds *will* rise?

These are some of the points that could be used to counter the Knox/Dodds position that without Oedipus's courage and persistence, the truth wouldn't have surfaced.

Of course, the anti-fatalists might respond with counter-counterpoints. For example, they might ask: Why assume that Jocasta's suicide was inevitable? Living with a buried past doesn't seem out of character for her. After all, she was perfectly content to leave unexplored the coincidence that Laius was killed and Oedipus did his killing at the same crossroad. In support, they could point to the fact that in some versions of the Oedipus story, such as the once-famous epic *The Thebaid* by the first-century-AD Latin poet Statius, Jocasta does *not* kill herself but lives on for many years.

One could go on like this indefinitely, with points and counterpoints, evidence and counterevidence, arguing about what would or would not have happened but for such and such. We do this all the time in real life, in which it's generally impossible to say with certainty what would have happened in an alternative world. Outside the laboratory, you can't rerun the tape of life to see how things would have come out on a second or third showing—you don't know if there would have been a World War II if Hitler had never been born, and so on. How can we say for certain what would have happened in the absence of Oedipus's heroism and persistence?

One can, in fact, imagine a version of *Oedipus Rex* in which the truth never emerges. Indeed, some of my favorite works of literature and movies turn precisely on a scenario in which the truth comes tantalizingly close to surfacing but remains hidden except to the reader or audience. In Tom Stoppard's *Arcadia*, the modern-day scholars researching the happenings among a group of people in the early nineteenth century never discover the truth about them. We in the audience do, however, and the contrast between what the present-day scholars believe and what actually happened is the central irony (and tension) of the play. A. S. Byatt's novel *Possession* is similar.

One of the most spine-tingling film endings of all time turns on this idea. At the very end of *Citizen Kane*, we learn what "Rosebud" refers to, while the reporters who spend the whole movie in search of its meaning are left to speculate. Anyone who's ever seen the film will never forget the image of the sleigh beginning to burn up in the fire, signaling that the mystery will always remain unsolved.

The larger point I'm making is that *Oedipus Rex* lends itself to this debate about the nature of truth, just as it lends itself to the debate about the nature of fate we discussed earlier in this chapter. This is just one more thing about it that makes it the timeless masterpiece that it is.

Oedipus's first discovery, that he had committed patricide and incest, helped me think long and hard about the obligations each person owes to everyone else in the world. His second discovery, that the prophecies were right, led me to the different meanings of fate, self-fulfilling prophecies, and questions about the nature of truth.

And then there's Oedipus's third discovery: All this time, he was actually home.

Chapter Seven

The Man Who Didn't Know He Was Home

If you were to look at multiple translations of *Oedipus Rex*, you might be puzzled by a curious thing about them: In some translations, the play is called *Oedipus Rex*; in others it's called *Oedipus Tyrannus*. Why the different names? What's the difference?

I, too, was puzzled at first. When I looked into it, I learned that, actually, there was an important distinction in ancient Greece between a ruler who was a "tyrannus" ("tyrant") and one who was a "rex." "Tyrannus" means "tyrant," though not in the modern sense of a bad, autocratic ruler; it simply refers to a ruler who acquired power through his own actions, possibly but not necessarily through the use of violence. A "rex," a king, on the other hand, is a hereditary ruler.[1] Thus, Dionysius I was the tyrannus of Syracuse, but it doesn't mean he was an evil despot; it means that he didn't inherit his crown. Leonidas I of Sparta, on the other hand, was a king because he inherited the crown from his father.

That its various translators haven't been able to land on one or the other for the play reflects another giant irony: Oedipus was both. (Bernard Knox cleverly skirts this problem by calling his book *Oedipus at Thebes*, a nice contrast with *Oedipus at Colonus*.) For all the years he ruled Thebes, he was believed to be a tyrannus because he was from elsewhere, a prince of Corinth. He achieved power through heroism, not birth. But unbeknownst to anyone, all along, he was actually the hereditary king. He was rex. And even more ironically, the minute he learned that he was Laius's son, he stopped being either tyrannus *or* rex! In a sense, he learned he was legitimate and illegitimate at the same time.[2]

This all relates to the third implication of Oedipus's discovery: Throughout his sojourn in Thebes, he was home.

THE "ALL-ALONG FEELING"

The shock of self-recognition we talked about in chapter 2 is a spine-tingling moment—one of the most powerful in literature, and in life, too. This is actually a subset of a broader feeling that, for lack of a better term, I call the "all-along feeling." It refers to that precise moment when a character discovers, with enormous surprise, that *all along* the world has been a different place than he thought. *He* is different. The whole situation is different.

To be clear, not every surprise is accompanied by the all-along feeling; it's a very special kind of surprise. The Marion Crane character in *Psycho* is surprised when the psycho stabs her in the shower, but there's no all-along feeling. It's just a surprise.

In *The Wizard of Oz*, though, Dorothy learns that *all along* she had the means to return home. Here are a few other well-known examples that illustrate what I have in mind:

- *The Shining*. In one of the most chilling moments in this Stanley Kubrick masterpiece, the wife (played by Shelley Duvall) comes across the manuscript that her husband, an increasingly deranged writer (played by Jack Nicholson), has been writing all winter long. The manuscript is hundreds of pages long but consists of nothing but the line "All work and no play makes Jack a dull boy," typed over and over again. That is the book he claims to have been working on *all along*.

- *Cyrano de Bergerac*. At the end of the play, Roxane finds out that *all along* it was Cyrano she was in love with, not Christian.
- *Othello*. Othello realizes at the end that *all along* Desdemona was faithful and that he, not Desdemona, has destroyed their love.

At its most powerful, the all-along feeling can send shivers up and down your spine. An example from recent years that I find particularly spine-tingling is the movie *The Sixth Sense*, directed by M. Night Shyamalan. Bruce Willis plays a child psychologist who, in the movie's first scene, is shot in the abdomen by a deranged patient. In the next scene, set several months later, we see Willis, presumably recovered from his gunshot wound, standing outside the home of a young boy. Willis's character appears to have taken the boy on as a special patient, as he visits him at his home regularly.

Over the course of the movie, we learn that what's troubling the boy is that he sees dead people walking around as if they were still alive; in fact, dead people seem to seek him out because of his gift. We, the moviegoers, can see the dead people the boy sees; Willis can't. But Willis does make headway in helping the boy come to terms with his special gift. The boy learns to listen to the dead people and help them solve whatever problem has caused them to become ghosts and kept them from passing into peaceful eternity.

Meanwhile, Willis has been becoming increasingly estranged from his wife (whom we saw hovering over him when he had the gunshot wound at the beginning). They can't seem to connect. She ignores him when he speaks, and she even seems to be going on dates with other guys. The movie's climax arrives when Willis sees her crying, tries to talk to her, and then notices that she has dropped his wedding ring. This finally forces him to realize that he didn't survive the shooting after all, and that all along he has been dead.

In a flood of flashbacks, we see some of the key scenes in the movie and realize how everything fits with the new information that he is dead, including the complete absence of contact between him and his wife and between him and the boy's mother. Re-watching the movie adds to your admiration for Shyamalan and the brilliant way he achieved this effect. I've watched *The Sixth Sense* multiple times because I find it so masterful—seeing Willis realize that all along he has been dead raises those proverbial hairs on the back of my neck every time I watch it.

It may seem strange to find, in a book about *Oedipus Rex*, a lengthy description of a thriller about a boy who sees dead people and a psychiatrist who doesn't realize that he himself is dead. But they actually have more in common than first meets the eye: They are both about men who are trying to help and protect others—men who do not realize that they themselves constitute the very thing they are combatting. The people of Thebes are suffering from a plague; the boy in the movie is plagued by dead people. Oedipus thinks he will save his people from the plague; Willis thinks he is helping to shelter the boy from dead people. Then they both learn that they themselves are the problem (or, for the Willis character, part of the problem). In addition, in both stories, the question of whether someone is alive or dead plays a huge role: In *The Sixth Sense*, his wife knows the Bruce Willis character is dead while he thinks he's still alive; in *Oedipus Rex*, the wife (and mother) thinks that her infant, who grew up to be Oedipus, is dead, while Oedipus of course knows that he's alive (though he doesn't yet know he wasn't supposed to be).

Also, in both stories, there's a moment long before the revelation when the protagonists are told the truth point-blank but don't realize it because they are (metaphorically) blind. Early in *Oedipus Rex*, Teiresias, goaded by Oedipus's anger, blurts out the whole truth. In the scene in *The Sixth Sense* in which the boy confesses his affliction to Willis (delivering the movie's signature line, "I see dead people"), he tells Willis that some dead people walk around without realizing they're dead. He is looking Willis right in the eye when he speaks, and Willis fails to pick up the clue.

But the main reason *The Sixth Sense* reminds me so much of *Oedipus Rex* is the intensity of the all-along feeling in the two stories. *The Sixth Sense* is my favorite recent example of this sensation, but just as I think of *Oedipus Rex* as the mother of all backstories, so I think of it as the matriarch of the all-along feeling in literature. Here's a character who discovers that *all along* he is, in the most literal sense, a different person than he thought he was.

Thanks to film technology, we get to see Willis's flashbacks. Not so in *Oedipus Rex*. But we see Oedipus's flashbacks all the same—he turned the wrong way after leaving Delphi, the man at the crossroad was his father, and so on. Is there a character in literature who experiences a more intense all-along feeling than Oedipus?

And I think the most striking implication of Oedipus's discovery—the aspect of it that produces the greatest all-along feeling—is that *all along* he has been home. Without realizing it, he is back where he started his life's journey; his life has come full circle.

CIRCLES, CYCLES, AND CIRCUITS

The circularity of Oedipus's journey strikes a strong chord. But why? What is it about circles that we find so appealing?

A love of circles seems to be ingrained in us; call it "circulaphilia." The Greeks were fascinated by them. They thought the circle was the most perfect thing possible and the pattern by which all things progress, especially the stars and other heavenly orbs.

Cycles and circuits are all around us, everywhere we look. They are an elemental part of the natural world and the course of our own lives: the cycle of the seasons, the journey of water from rain to river to ocean to cloud and back to rain. "All the rivers run into the sea; yet the sea is not full; unto the place from whence the rivers come, thither they return again," as it is written in the book of Ecclesiastes.[3] There's the cycle of each day, from morning to night and back to morning. Ecclesiastes again: "The sun also ariseth, and the sun goeth down, and hasteth to his place where he arose."[4]

Circles are everywhere in our quotidian routines—our daily journeys that take us away from home and then back again. And they mark our overarching journey through life: we begin and end as helpless creatures, as in the Sphinx's riddle. Again, biblical wisdom is apt here. "Naked came I out of my mother's womb, and naked shall I return thither," says Job.[5] "In the sweat of thy face shalt thou eat bread, till thou return unto the ground; for out of it wast thou taken: for dust thou art, and unto dust shalt thou return," as it is declared in the book of Genesis.[6]

We are primed by nature and by our own lives to seek, if not demand, cycles. Think about music: We find it satisfying when a song ends on the same note it began with.[7] We also like to see circularity in stories. We like it when physical objects are restored to their rightful place. Wagner's Ring Cycle, an opera tetralogy, begins with Alberich the dwarf stealing the gold of the Rhine River (the Rhine gold) from the Rhine maidens. Over the course of the four operas—*Das Rheingold*, *Die Walküre*, *Siegfried*, and *Die Götterdämmerung*—the ring bounces around from one person to another, and at the very end, the ring is washed back into the Rhine River, returned to its original owners (just as the ring in J. R. R. Tolkien's epic *The Lord of the Rings* eventually goes back to where *it* came from).

Earlier in the book, I talked about Willkie Collins's novel *The Moonstone*, in which the protagonist discovers that he himself has stolen a priceless diamond. After it's recovered, the diamond is returned to the forehead of the statue of the Hindu goddess from whom it had been stolen many years earlier—a satisfying resolution.

We like it when people return to their original station. There's a wonderful children's story about a Chinese stonecutter who sees the emperor passing by, carried on his throne. He wishes he were the emperor. Magically, his wish is granted, and he suddenly finds himself carried by servants on the royal throne. The sun, however, is beating down on him, making him miserable. He now wants to be the sun, and the sun he then becomes. But a storm cloud drifts by and blocks him out, so he becomes a storm cloud, reveling in his ability to rain. But then he sees that the water he has produced is being channeled by a mighty river. So that's what he becomes next. But then he is dismayed to find a mountain obstructing his path, causing him to divide him in two. He becomes the mountain and is happy for a while, until one day a stonecutter climbs him and begins chipping away at his rocks. In the end, he decides to return to his original condition.

The stonecutter returned to his origins voluntarily. Not so with the protagonists in the Grimm Brothers story "The Fisherman and His Wife." In the tale, a fisherman catches an enchanted flounder that, in return for being released and thrown back in the water, promises to grant the fisherman whatever he wishes. At first, he wishes for a pretty cottage so he and his wife no longer have to live in their filthy hovel. But the fisherman's wife, sensing a good thing, makes increasingly grandiose requests, including being turned into a king, then emperor, then pope, until ultimately, she asks to be made into God. This is too much for the flounder, which sends them reeling back to their filthy cottage. (There's a bawdier version of this story in *The Thousand and One Nights*, about a man who, being given three wishes by a jinni, at his wife's prompting asks for a bigger "zabb" [penis]. When he gets one that is much too large, he asks for it to be reduced and, of course, is given one that has shrunk to almost nothing. He then has to use his last remaining wish to restore it to its original size.)

And finally, we like it when *people* return home, when they complete a circuit in a literal, geographic sense. In most cases, the return home is deliberate: Our hero leaves home on a journey and returns in the end, as salmon return home to spawn and end their lives. (I was delighted to learn that there's a word for this phenomenon in nature; such creatures are said to be "anadromous."). Bilbo Baggins, in *The Hobbit*, travels "There and Back Again," the title of his memoirs. Phileas Fogg journeys "around the world in eighty days" in the Jules Verne novel, arriving home at precisely the moment necessary to win a bet. Joseph Campbell's "hero with a thousand faces" finds himself home at the end of his heroic journey. It's a happy homecoming.

THE ARC OF ONE'S LIFE

Even more interesting in a narrative is when the hero has *unknowingly* returned home. This is what happens in another unforgettable movie ending that includes one of the greatest apocalyptic images in film: the end of the original 1968 version of *Planet of the Apes*. Astronaut George Taylor, played by Charlton Heston, has traveled to what he believes to be a distant planet. It's very similar to Earth, except it's ruled by apes. At the end, when he sees the crowned head of the Statue of Liberty washed up on the beach, he discovers that he has been back on Earth *all along*: "Oh my God . . . I'm back. I'm home. All the time . . ."[8] (Like Oedipus, Taylor is warned not to look for the answer. The orangutan Dr. Zaius—rhymes with Laius!—cautions Taylor that he may not like what he finds.)

Like Taylor, Oedipus is the Man Who Didn't Know He Was Home. He, too, thought he was leaving home when he journeyed out from Corinth on his adventures, and when he arrived in Thebes, he thought he was far away from his life's starting point. But in the end, he discovers that he wasn't just a ruler *of* Thebes; he was a ruler *from* Thebes. He wasn't tyrannus; he was rex. And he also came to understand what Teiresias meant when he said that soon a stranger "will be revealed a native Theban but he will take no joy in the revelation" (lines 515–16).

This line of thought led me to another epiphany about the Sphinx's riddle. The first, as discussed in chapter 2, was that the riddle was in the form of a Circular Detective story: Someone is asked to identify a culprit, and it turns out the culprit is that person himself.

But here's an interesting question about this famous riddle: Why is it even a riddle? What makes it tricky? It's tricky because it takes something familiar and turns it into something unfamiliar. The riddle *seems* to be describing a strange, unfamiliar creature with a jumble of morphing body parts. But, in fact, it's describing something very familiar indeed—man himself. Oedipus's exchange with the Sphinx is a metaphor for his life.

The people he encounters are familiar in the most literal sense—they are *family*. A man on the crossroad, a woman given to him as queen: They are family—his mother and father. But he doesn't recognize them as such, even though he is able to recognize the familiar in the riddle. And then he arrives at the city where he was born, and he doesn't recognize it, either.

With his discoveries, Oedipus now sees the whole trajectory of his life and what it all means. He realizes that the arc of his life is a great big circle.

Earlier, I pointed out that Oedipus's discovery of his true identity had three critical implications. But there are actually two more.

One of those additional implications is that he now knows how and why he got his name and the scars on his feet. As I mentioned in the introduction, "Oedipus" means swollen foot. For as long as Oedipus remembers, from his earliest childhood, he has had scars on his feet. He must have wondered where those scars came from, and why he was given that odd name. This isn't resolved in any of the extant writings about the Oedipus myth, but we can fill in the gaps by assuming that his Corinthian parents, Polybus and Merope, made up a story about an accident that happened when he was an infant, leading to both the scars and the name. Presumably it's the same story he would have told Jocasta if she ever asked. Now he learns the real meaning of his name. He now understands not just that it means "swollen feet" but exactly how and why they were swollen—another irony, for the man who was clever about feet in answering the Sphinx's riddle was ignorant about his own.[9]

The other, and related, implication is that his parents had tried to kill him.

This adds a whole other layer of complexity and another huge irony, for Oedipus didn't just learn that the man he killed was his father; he learned that that very man had tried to kill him as an infant. There would be a kind of rough justice, then, in killing Laius. Oedipus himself makes that observation in *Oedipus at Colonus*.

That doesn't mean that an ancient Athenian audience would have viewed Laius's actions with disgust. We in the modern world are revolted by it: In German poet and dramatist Hugo von Hofmannsthal's version of the Oedipus story, *Oedipus and the Sphinx*, Jocasta feels such intense revulsion at Laius's act of infanticide that she convinces herself that the son she believes is dead has sent the Sphinx as punishment and that the "robbers" who killed Laius were merely acting as instruments of the wrongly killed baby. But, of course, that's an early-twentieth-century sensibility at work. Views were very different back in ancient Greece; infanticide was more acceptable in those days, even in supposedly enlightened fifth-century Athens.[10] It's a bit unclear just how it would have been viewed by the Athenians watching the play; scholars disagree on the subject. (See the appendix.)

The record in the play itself is mixed. On the one hand, when Jocasta tells the story to Oedipus about her child, she exhibits no shame or remorse. And Oedipus himself has no reaction to the information, which might lead us to infer that he's not bothered by it. On the other hand, Jocasta, in her description of the infanticide, says that it was Laius, not she, who ordered the infant to be killed, as if distancing herself from the act. (Interestingly, the shepherd attributes the order to Jocasta, not Laius.). As to Oedipus's non-reaction upon hearing Jocasta mention the fate of her newborn, it's possible that this isn't nonchalance but failure to hear the reference to infanticide because it comes right after he is stunned to hear the description of the site of Laius's killing.[11] So we really don't know from that scene how he feels about his parents' actions.

Moreover, there is a tellingly ambiguous moment in the dialogue with the Theban. When the Theban says that Jocasta gave him the infant to be killed, Oedipus responds: "Her own child. How could she?" It's possible that he merely meant to ask *why* she would do such a thing (the Theban responds that she was afraid of frightening prophecies), but it's also possible that Oedipus was genuinely horrified at the thought of his wife doing such a thing to her own child. Several translations of *Oedipus Rex* use the same judgmental tone: Luci Berkowitz and Theodore F. Brunner ("Her own child!); Dudley Fitts and Robert Fitzgerald ("An unspeakable mother!"); R. C. Jebb ("Her own child, the wretch?"). But others are not so clear: Ruby Blondell ("Her own child, wretch?"); Albert Cook ("When she bore him, the wretch"). In these last two, it's unclear to me if "wretch" refers to Jocasta, Oedipus, or even the Theban to whom Oedipus is speaking.

The moral question is probably irresolvable. But without forgetting the difficulty of reconciling twenty-first-century morals with ancient drama, we shouldn't lose sight of the fact that even if Oedipus doesn't consider infanticide a moral outrage, he is still learning something horrifying about his own past. He isn't just learning about Jocasta's attempt to commit infanticide against some unknown infant—*the infant was him.* He is learning that he was unwanted from the beginning and meant to be killed. That must add to his sense of heartbreak, and it adds to our sense of tragedy.

"Tragedy"—what does that word mean, anyway?

Chapter Eight

"Is There a Man More Agonized?"

About ten years ago I was working as a lawyer at a government agency in Washington, DC, where I live. On Valentine's Day, a coworker I was in regular contact with was heading home, crossing the street from our building to the Metro. It was a winter evening, so it was fairly dark. As she was walking, a city bus was making a left turn from a blind spot behind her right shoulder, so she didn't see it coming. The bus was going unusually fast and hit her. She died instantly.

The whole agency was in a state of shock the next day after learning about the accident. She was well known and liked throughout the agency. She was in her forties, and after she died, I learned that she had recently married. It was the first marriage for both her and her husband; after many years alone, they had finally found happiness with each other. As the accident was happening, her husband was preparing a nice dinner to celebrate what would have been their first Valentine's Day together.

We hear or read or learn about other people's deaths all the time. Sometimes it's people we know well—family and friends; sometimes it's people we know but not well, like my colleague from the agency; and most of the time it's people we don't know at all. When someone dies, it's always sad, but deaths are sad to different degrees and in different ways. Her death struck me—and still does—as sad in a particular way, a way that I associate with a particular word. That word is *tragic*.

I've spent many pages so far talking about *Oedipus Rex*, but I haven't really said much yet about the fact that it's a tragedy. I talked about the "tragedy of fate" concept, but that discussion was really focused more on fate than tragedy. The truth is that for many years, I didn't really think of the play as a tragedy. This may sound strange, given that it's not only a tragedy but one of the genre's towering examples. But I didn't really approach it in those terms. I guess to me, the play was more like a great work of literature that happens to be a tragedy.

But you can't spend years contemplating *Oedipus Rex* without eventually asking about its relationship to the concepts of tragedy and the tragic, and so I did.

We use the terms "tragedy" and "tragic" all the time to refer to events in the real world that strike us as particularly sad, or sad in a certain way. But the first thing to understand about these terms is that a "tragedy" like *Oedipus Rex* or *Hamlet* or *Antigone* isn't called a tragedy because it's so "tragic."[1] It's actually the other way around: "Tragic" in the real-world sense comes from the ancient Greek "tragedy," which was coined in the sixth century BC in Greece to describe a drama that was performed in a certain way in a certain setting. The word came from the Greek words "tragos," meaning "goat," and "oide," meaning "song" (think of "ode"). There are various theories as to how the goat got in there; one is that the prize for the best drama was a goat (a kind of reverse *Let's Make a Deal*).[2] Whatever its origins, the word stuck, and it was used throughout the fifth century BC to refer to all those great plays by Aeschylus, Sophocles, and Euripides, and then eventually those of Shakespeare, the great French tragedians like Racine and Corneille, and on into the modern age.

So, the word refers to both a type of theatrical drama *and* a type of event in the real world (and our emotional reaction to it).

The first question I ask in this chapter is whether the various definitions and theories relating to tragedy in the theatrical context tell us anything helpful about *Oedipus Rex*. The conclusion I reach is no: There have been vicious academic debates about the meaning of a theatrical tragedy, but they don't shed much light on why *Oedipus Rex* is so special. Then I turn to the way we use the terms "tragedy" and "tragic" in an everyday sense. I believe that we do have an intuitive sense of the tragic in relation to real life, and that that intuitive sense of the tragic does help explain exactly why and how the play tugs at our heartstrings in the way it does.

SOMETHING TO DO WITH A GOAT

By the time of Sophocles, the word tragedy had long since shed its association with goats and meant pretty much what we mean by it today when we refer to a drama as a "tragedy." But what exactly *do* we mean by it today?

Let's start with Aristotle, whose description is still influential. In *Poetics*, he offers the following definition:

> Tragedy is an imitation of an action that is admirable, complete and possesses magnitude; in language made pleasurable, each of its species separated in different parts; performed by actors not through narration; *effecting through pity (eleos) and fear (phobos) a catharsis.*[3]

The last clause is the important part—the rest of the paragraph seems to be just describing theater—and has been subject to scholarly torture for centuries. As we discussed in chapter 3, Aristotle borrowed the concept of catharsis from medicine; it refers to some kind of emotional release or cleansing—a purgation—experienced by the audience.[4] Modern scholars have debated ad nauseam what exactly Aristotle meant by it. There has been some further scholarly dispute about what Aristotle meant by "eleos" and "phobos"—one scholar, for example, prefers "terror" to "fear"—but the differences are fairly subtle.[5]

In any event, modern definitions of the term have mostly dropped the "fear" and "catharsis" requirements and are thus a little more expansive. Definitions vary depending on whom you ask, but if you smush together several common ones you get something like "a drama that involves suffering, pitiable and unfortunate events, and a bad ending, especially the downfall of the main character."

For some purposes, that definition is fine—a useful label for placing fiction in different boxes, like "rom-com" or "action flick," so you know what you're in for that evening (or what to avoid if you're in the mood for something else). But a simple, generic definition masks the huge amount of debate and controversy about the art form—one that many thinkers, over the years, have considered an enormously important vehicle for conveying profound messages about the human condition. And when you drill down on the standard definition, you find all kinds of problems. It turns out that it's next to impossible to find a least common denominator, some feature that all works described as "tragedies" have in common and that sets them apart from everything else.

Take suffering. Even many comedies contain some degree of suffering. I suppose, then, you could argue that tragedies have "lots and lots of suffering." But then how does that distinguish tragedy from a disgusting torture movie? Tragedy can't just mean physical pain or blood and gore; *Oedipus Rex* would qualify here ("black hail of blood pulsing, gushing down" [line 1414]), but so would *The Texas Chain Saw Massacre*.

Or consider a "bad ending." When we think of Greek tragedy, for example, we think of characters on stage gnashing their teeth and rending their garments when the curtain comes down—a bad ending, just as sure as a happy ending defines comedy. But not every tragedy has a bad ending; there are so-called "happy tragedies."[6] Many horrible things happen in *The Oresteia*, including the murder of a father and then the murder of a mother. But it ends happily. So, for that matter, does *Oedipus at Colonus*; in the end, Oedipus is given permission to come to his final rest in Athens. In *Iphigenia in Tauris*, by Euripides, Agamemnon's daughter is rescued at the last minute as she is about to be sacrificed. Conversely, not everything that has a bad ending is a tragedy. *Dr. Strangelove* ends with the entire world blowing up, but no one calls it a tragedy.

For some people, to truly be tragic, a drama must include a profound exploration of big issues like fate and free will, the nature of good and evil, and so on. One scholar defines tragedy as a "story with an unhappy ending that is memorably and upliftingly moving rather than simply sad."[7] But the meaning of those terms isn't self-evident. Similarly, some talk about suffering that "ennobles" the viewer. Samuel Johnson defined tragedy as "a dramatic representation of serious actions."[8] But, as with "sadness," what is "moving," "ennobling," or "serious" is in the eye of the beholder.

These problems of definition have led one commentator to say, "The truth is no definition of tragedy more elaborate than 'very sad' has ever worked out." (Schopenhauer, trying to keep it simple, defined tragedy that way.)[9] We could cut through all this by just saying, "I know tragedy when I see it," or by defining it by agreed-upon examples, as in, "'Tragedy' is a drama like *Oedipus Rex* or *Hamlet*," without specifying what that means, as some have done.[10] And in fact, that may be the best we can do. But then we would have no reliable standard for deciding what else is in and what's out.

Maybe none of this is terribly important. After all, nothing much turns on who calls what what. This is true in most disputes about definitions, at least among those outside of the law, where definitions have legal significance. But sometimes, fights over definitions are really about something else, and I think that's the case with tragedy. Much of the fight about the definition of tragedy is really about quality—not whether this work or the other is a tragedy but whether it's a *great* tragedy.

As we discussed in chapter 3, Aristotle opined that the best tragedies are those that combine what he called "reversal" (unintended, ironic effects) and "recognition" ("a change from ignorance to knowledge"). Note that this criterion excludes many great tragedies (including the other two plays in Sophocles's Theban cycle), and it includes lots of non-tragedies. In fact, I would wager that the Oedipus-type revelation shows up more in comedy than in tragedy, such as in *H. M. S. Pinafore* and Oscar Wilde's *The Importance of Being Earnest*. It's what underlies much of the "comedy of errors" genre, which is why it wouldn't be that hard to turn Oedipus into a comedy—in fact, it's been done on several occasions, such as, for example, in the mock oratorio *Oedipus Tex* by Peter Schickele (aka P. D. Q. Bach).

According to one scholar, "Most of the questions about tragedy which continue to vex us today were first formulated by Aristotle."[11] After Aristotle, the most influential thinker on tragedy was probably Hegel. I've always found Hegel almost impossible to understand, but his theory of tragedy is actually comprehensible, and it isn't bad. His big idea about tragedy is that it's about conflict, not between right and wrong but between right and right. The best and highest form of tragedy, for Hegel, is one in which the protagonists are in conflict but each one is right in his own way, or at least there's no clear right or wrong.

Hegel loved Sophocles and *Oedipus Rex*, but unlike his fellow German Schiller (and unlike Aristotle), his favorite tragedy is *Antigone*. In his view, it embodied his conception of tragedy as a conflict between two irresolvables. When Antigone's brother Polyneices falls in battle trying to retake Thebes, her uncle, Creon, who at this point in the saga is ruler of Thebes, orders that the body of Polyneices be left unburied. Antigone secretly buries her brother, but when Creon finds out, he orders her to be buried alive, creating a chain of events that ultimately ends with the deaths of Antigone, her lover, Haemon—Creon's son—and, due to anguish over her son's death, Creon's wife, Eurydice.

Tragedy results in *Antigone*, said Hegel, from the clash of two justified but irreconcilable claims: a ruler's interest in restoring civic order by shaming and punishing those wishing to overthrow it, and a sister's moral obligation to give her brother a proper burial. They're both right, says Hegel, and they're both wrong—and they both suffer. Damned if they do, damned if they don't.

Nietzsche, whose views on *Oedipus Rex* we discussed in chapter 3, has also played a big role in the debate about the meaning of tragedy (his first major publication was a work titled *The Birth of Tragedy*). Like Hegel, he thought conflict is at the heart of tragedy, but for Nietzsche the conflict was between two forces: the wild, untamed force of nature (which he called "Dionysian," after the god of pleasure and drunken merriment) and the force of careful thought and reason (called "Apollonian," after the god of reason and light). In Nietzsche's view, Greek life and Greek drama were far more Dionysian—in a word, wild—than was acknowledged by his contemporaries, who held that ancient Greece was all "sweetness and light."

According to Nietzsche, Greek tragedy represents the thrilling clash and combination of these two forces, the Dionysian in the form of the chorus and the Apollonian in the form of dialogue among the characters. Aeschylus and Sophocles struck exactly the right balance between the two forces, he felt. But, like Don McLean in "American Pie" claiming that rock 'n' roll died with Buddy Holly, Nietzsche thought the art form went downhill after those two playwrights. (It started with Euripides, whose dramas Nietzsche found too "rational.")

The last century has seen an enormous amount of writing and discussion about tragedy—so much so that a new field of inquiry seems to have sprouted up called "tragedy theory." (The large range of views and preoccupations within this genre can be detected in the following book titles: *Christianity and Tragedy*; *Philosophy and Tragedy*; *Tragedy and Philosophy* [there are two books with this title]; *Greek Tragedy and the Modern World*; *Modern Tragedy*; *Tragic Drama and Modern Society*; *Tragedy and the Theory of Drama*; *Tragedy and Theory*; *A Definition of Tragedy*; *Elements of Tragedy*; *Principles of Tragedy*; *Ideas and Forms of Tragedy*; *The Idea of the Tragic*; *Tragedy and Comedy*; *Tragedy and Truth*; *Tragedy and Social Evolution*; *Tragedy and Civilization*; *Tragedy: Contradiction and Repression*; *The Harvest of Tragedy*; *The Paradox of Tragedy*; *The Psychology of Tragedy*; *The Psychology of Tragic Drama*; *The Pleasures of Tragedy*; and *Why Does Tragedy Give Pleasure?*)

One of the more interesting debates today is whether, in the modern world, we've lost the ability to produce tragedies because we no longer have a "tragic vision" of the world.

George Steiner, in his aptly titled book *The Death of Tragedy*, argues that "true" tragedy reflects what he calls the "tragic vision," which is something the Greeks and Elizabethans had but we moderns don't. According to Steiner, they viewed their lives as being ruled by large, impersonal forces over which man has no control, while we tend to think that we can improve our lives through changes in technology, laws, and society. In the plays of Henrik Ibsen, for example, problems and conflicts are all believed to be solvable through social and legal means. Needless to say, many people have rejected Steiner's arguments.

A parallel debate is whether a "true" tragedy must involve a great man or woman—that is, someone who can fall from a great height only because he or she is already up high, like a king or a hero. This is the traditional definition. As with Steiner's theory, it's based on a fundamental claim about the difference between the modern and premodern worlds. In the modern world, it's argued, we no longer have heroes; we're all consumed by petty things. Hence *real* tragedy is impossible today.[12]

But most scholars take the democratic, anti-elitist side: Dramas about the common man can be just as dramatic as the great Greek and Elizabethan tragedies, if not more so. The quiet desperation of the common man living out his daily life can be truly tragic. That's the whole point of a work like *Death of a Salesman*. As is stated in that great play, "attention must be paid" to such a person. And as Arthur Miller himself put it in a manifesto: "I believe that the common man is as apt a subject for tragedy in its highest sense as kings were."[13]

Indeed, some have gone even further and have argued that *only* a story about a common man can be a great tragedy, a perspective that has the strange result of excluding all the famous Greek tragedies. Under this view, tragedy is not necessarily about the big, cataclysmic, disastrous events—patricide, self-blinding, the sudden fall of great princes. It can be about the quotidian, the grayness of daily life, never-changing, nothing ever happening.

Some existential critics go even further. For them, life itself is tragic, not just events or even nonevents. And, according to them, tragedy doesn't just happen to certain people who are fit for it. Life is tragic for everyone, because of the essential meaninglessness of our lives, especially in light of the knowledge that we are going to die, the inherent meaninglessness of the cosmos, our radical isolation from each other, and all the other stuff that existentialists talk about, all of which added up makes life a vale of tears. Life sucks, and then you die. For those with this existentialist bent, such as the late Norwegian philosopher Peter Wessel Zapffe, a "true" tragedy has to bring out that basic fact about the human condition.

THE MODEL TRAGEDY?

No one has ever argued that *Oedipus Rex* doesn't qualify as a tragedy. In the play, there's a fall from a great height, a bad ending, sadness, profundity, and so on. It satisfies all the traditionalists by reflecting the ancients' "tragic vision" of the world; if Oedipus isn't wrestling with fate and the gods, no one is. It would be indeed a peculiar definition of tragedy that excluded *Oedipus Rex*, especially given that some of the definitions and criteria applied to the form were *inspired* by the play.

But the question isn't whether *Oedipus Rex* meets the minimal test for tragedy. That's a no-brainer. The question is, do any of the theories of tragedy shed any light on why it's so great?

Some of the theories of tragedy we discussed fit the play like a glove. As one modern scholar put it:

> We are a little unwilling to believe that [*Oedipus Rex*] could fall short, if rightly examined, of any of those attributes that a great tragedy might be expected to possess. Tradition has built up a list of such attributes, and criticism of the *Oedipus Tyrannus* consists largely in the effort to demonstrate that the play, if only we adopt the right point of view, really does square with every conceivable demand that could be made of it.[14]

Oedipus Rex "contains the shape of tragedy as no other does," says another scholar, echoing the sentiment.[15]

But there are other theories of tragedy that don't particularly fit *Oedipus Rex* and therefore don't tell us much about what makes it tick. It's not *everyone's* model tragedy. For Hegel, *Antigone* was the model, not *Oedipus Rex.*

If your preferred tragedy is one that deals with the common man struggling with daily life, then *Oedipus Rex* obviously isn't in your bull's-eye. First, of course, he's a king, not a common man. But more importantly, his tragedy isn't of the "quiet desperation" type. It's about sudden, earth-shattering calamity, not about tedium and soul-destroying drudgery. He's neither a salesman nor a man in a gray flannel suit.

But it would be silly to argue that *Oedipus Rex* isn't a true tragedy on the grounds that it doesn't fit the modern mold, just as it would be silly to argue (as some have) that *Death of a Salesman* isn't a true tragedy just because Willy Loman is a salesman. They're just different flavors of tragedy. Who says we have to choose? I love them all. And so did the man most associated with the tragedy of the common man, Arthur Miller, who, as we discussed in chapter 5, wrote that he was inspired by *Oedipus Rex* in writing *All My Sons*.

How about the existential theory that tragedy should reflect the tragic nature of the human condition in general? Some scholars have, in fact, viewed *Oedipus Rex* as doing exactly that: reflecting the tragedy—indeed, the horror—of the human condition. Harvard's Charles Segal, for example, wrote that "*Oedipus* [*Rex*] touches another area of anxiety, existential rather than sexual or psychological: the fear of meaninglessness."[16] In fact, Segal said that *Oedipus Rex* calls to mind the famous words of the satyr Silenus: "For mortals, best of all is not to be born"—a view of life reflected in today's so-called "anti-natalist" position, which holds that because life is inherently painful, it's immoral to bring children into the world. Philip Vellacott wrote of *Oedipus Rex*, "The only lesson to be drawn is one of *total pessimism*, and the only attitude encouraged is that of *uncomprehending resignation*."[17]

I understand why they say this. Sometimes life does seem absurd and pointless, and no character has a greater right to feel that way than Oedipus. A story about terrible things happening at random, out of the blue, for no apparent rhyme or reason—those are the stories that fill me with existential dread. A story, real or fictional, about little children being killed in a school shooting, or about a virtuous person being blown up by a terrorist's bomb, can evoke intense feelings of despair.

But that's not *Oedipus Rex*. It has never given me the feeling that life is meaningless; quite the contrary. As many before me have said, a great tragic work of art gives meaning to life, and none more so, I think, than *Oedipus Rex*. When the truth is revealed, Oedipus's discovery is not that life and the universe are meaningless. He learns the exact opposite: His life had a meaning—a horrible one, but a meaning nonetheless.

It's true that Jocasta says, "It's all chance, chance rules our lives. Not a man on earth can see a day ahead, groping through the dark. Better to live at random, best we can" (line 1072). That's as strong a statement of existential resignation as anything spoken by any character in literature. But she says the line *before* the truth hits her. Like Oedipus a little later in the play, she discovers *exactly* what her life has meant, and she returns to the dominant world view of her time—that everything happens according to a giant cosmic plan.[18]

So the "existential dread" theory doesn't work for me. What about the other feelings that great tragedy is supposed to provoke? According to Aristotle, I should experience pity, fear, and catharsis when I witness a tragedy. How useful is that formula in accounting for my reaction to *Oedipus Rex*?

Let's start with catharsis. As I mentioned earlier, scholars have been arguing over what Aristotle meant by this term for centuries; indeed, there's almost as much debate about the meaning of the term as there is about the meaning of "tragedy." I'm not equipped to take a side in this debate. But I can say that whichever emotion Aristotle believed would be evoked by catharsis, *Oedipus Rex* has never caused me to experience it. I've never cried over Oedipus; I've never felt cleansed and purified, emotionally or intellectually. Thomas Cahill describes catharsis in the following terms:

> We leave the theater warned by what we have witnessed but purged of negative emotions. We are pleasantly exhausted now, as if we had recently expelled a poison from our body. We are at

> peace . . . restored by this vicarious brush with destruction and death. [I think] I didn't die. I am still alive—and can face tomorrow with a certain placid wisdom.[19]

Personally, I've never felt that way after reading or watching a performance of *Oedipus Rex*, or any tragedy for that matter. I don't know what negative emotions Cahill had in mind, but I don't think I've ever been "purged" of them, nor I have felt "pleasantly exhausted" or "at peace." It's not because I'm coldhearted or bottled up. I cry all the time during all kinds of schlocky, sentimental movies. I've cried at mediocre movies, even as I resented the way the moviemaker had manipulated my feelings. I feel passionately about *Oedipus Rex*, obviously, or I wouldn't have written a whole book about it. But I experience no catharsis from it. (While we're on that subject, it's worth pointing out that according to recent psychological research, the benefits of catharsis are overstated, like the alleged benefits of "primal scream" therapy.)[20]

What about pity and fear? I don't feel fear when I think about *Oedipus Rex*, and I doubt anyone else does. I feel fear when I see a movie about a man in his prime getting brain cancer or about shark attacks in shallow water—events that seem closer to home. I feel more fear watching *Jaws* than reading *Oedipus Rex*, despite the fact that *Oedipus Rex* is a greater work of art. (Not that I mean to slight *Jaws*, which is a terrific movie.)

Pity is much closer to the mark. I certainly pity Oedipus, one of the great exemplars of human suffering. Scholars have frequently compared Oedipus to the other great sufferers in literature. "The play stands with the Book of Job, *Hamlet*, and *King Lear* as one of Western literature's most searching examinations of the problem of suffering," says Charles Segal.[21] The great German classicist Werner Jaeger (1888–1961) compared Oedipus to Jesus, arguing he is "suffering humanity personified."[22] Notice that both men had their feet pierced—Oedipus at the beginning of his life, Jesus at the very end.[23] And when Oedipus says, "I alone of all mankind can carry these afflictions," it's impossible not to think of Christ on the cross.[24]

Still, the quantum of pity isn't a reliable indicator of artistic greatness. In the first place, who's to say that what happened to Oedipus was the very worst thing that could happen to a man? I can think of worse things, both in real life and in literature. I can't imagine the horror I'd feel if I learned, like César in *Jean de Florette*, that I had killed my own child. Or think about a modern tragedy like *Sophie's Choice*, in which a mother is forced by the Nazis to choose which of her two children will live and which will die. As a parent, I find it hard to imagine anything worse than that.

Or consider Euripides's play *The Trojan Women*. After losing their city and seeing all their men killed, the women in the play are taken into captivity by the Greeks, who, the women know, will treat them as sex slaves. On top of all these horrors, they are then forced to witness their children being thrown from the towers of Troy. I can't say that what happened to Oedipus is any worse than that. Yet *The Trojan Women* has not captured my imagination over the years.

My point here is that *Oedipus Rex* isn't a great tragedy because Oedipus is an icon of suffering. Rather, Oedipus is an icon of suffering because *Oedipus Rex* is such a great tragedy. So, at the end of the day, academic theorizing about theatrical tragedy fails to deliver the goods on *Oedipus Rex*.

THE SENSE OF THE TRAGIC

But what about the other use of the terms "tragedy" and "tragic"—those descriptions of unfortunate real-world events? In addition to studying the academic literature on tragedy in the theatrical context, I've also explored what makes a real-world event feel tragic. For this study, I relied more on my intuition than scholarly research, and—perhaps because of this—the exploration turned out to be more fruitful.

If you Google the word "tragedy," you'll get a return of the multiple news headlines that have used it within just the last couple of hours of your search. If you Google "tragedy of," you'll get suggested completions of the phrase covering everything from "the tragedy of the commons" to "the tragedy of Sarah Palin" to "the tragedy of the euro."

This drives language mavens crazy, because they feel that the word should be limited to only the most catastrophic events—ones involving lots of people or ones that are really, really sad. They hate to see words devalued, as when we say we're starving when we're just a little hungry or freezing when we're just a little chilly. Some of the "tragedy theorists" we were discussing earlier in this chapter would prohibit the use of the word for anything other than literary tragedies, on the principle that only in art can something as elevated and profound as tragedy take place. At the other extreme, as I mentioned above, some scholars (and some regular people) see life itself as being tragic.

Personally, I'm more inclined to view life as a comedy than as a tragedy. And I'm not a language maven, so I don't freak out every time the word is used loosely ("It's a tragedy that my child didn't get into that preschool program"). My goal is not to police the perfect dictionary definition of the word. What interests me is how I react to specific events in life. I'm testing my intuition: Which real-world events fill me with what might be called a "sense of the tragic" (not to be confused with the "tragic sense of life," a concept developed by the Spanish philosopher Miguel de Unamuno that stresses spiritual anxiety as the source of man's continual quest for improvement)? It's analogous to asking, for example, which things in the world produce a sense of awe in us, or a sense of the sublime, or a sense of the beautiful—something Edmund Burke did in his *A Philosophical Enquiry into the Origin of Our Ideas of the Sublime and Beautiful*. I want to explore the events in real life that produce in me a sense of the tragic. Once I have figured that out, then I can apply what I've learned to *Oedipus Rex*.

So, the question is, why did my work colleague's death feel so tragic to me, but not my father's when he died from cancer at the age of seventy-eight? His death made me extremely sad and left a big hole in my life, but it never felt or seemed tragic to me. Obviously, age has something to do with it—he died after a full and good life. But it's not just age. The difference, I think, has something to do with the timing, the fact that my work colleague had just found happiness.

My wife and I had a friend who, like my agency colleague, also found love later in life and died very shortly thereafter—of cancer, in her case. Her death gave me that same tragic feeling. It wasn't their ages that affected me similarly; our friend was about ten years older at the time of her death than my colleague at the time of hers. The deaths were different—one died instantly, the other slowly. I knew our friend better than I knew my colleague. But in both cases, the death had a cruel irony—people being stripped of life just at the moment when their lives had turned a corner, when they had finally found a degree of happiness that had previously been missing in their lives, when they felt most alive.

I would probably also feel the same way if I heard about a man who had been in prison for many years for a crime he committed as a youth and then died or was killed right when he was about to be released, or shortly thereafter. Or one of those stories you've heard about a military pilot or soldier who dies on his very last mission, right before being sent home. Or a story about someone who died right before something he had done was celebrated as a great success. Georges Bizet died after completing *Carmen* but before he knew it was considered a masterpiece. Jonathan Larson, the creator of the acclaimed rock opera *Rent*, collapsed and died within just a few days of its premiere. He had been working on the musical for seven years.

The women in my two stories—my agency colleague and our personal friend—were both lovely people. The convict who dies before he's about to be released might not be as nice; he might be tough and hardened. But if he'd been rehabilitated and about to start a new life, I would feel the same distinct sense of tragedy at his death.

I think what these examples have in common with one another is that they all involve a cruel illusion. You are given reason to hold a certain set of optimistic expectations, and then you realize you were being toyed with by fate, or the gods, or the powers that be.

Notice that the sense of the tragic is not just about sadness and loss. Tragic events are extremely sad, but not all sad events are tragic. The death of every person is sad to someone. Some deaths are sadder than others, depending on circumstances, including age. But not all deaths strike me as tragic.

Nor is it a matter of suffering—there can be great suffering without any tragedy. Just because someone dies in great pain does not necessarily make his death tragic. It may have been pitiable or gut-wrenching, yet not tragic in the sense I am talking about. And, conversely, there can be tragedy without any suffering. My work colleague didn't suffer at all, physically or mentally. She died instantly. Her death was, nonetheless, a tragedy.

"Tragic" is also not the same as "pitiable" or "pathetic" or "heartrending." An eighty-year-old woman mourning the death of her husband can be all of those. She might be inconsolable. It hurts to see such emotional pain and suffering. But unless there's something special about the circumstances of his death, I don't get that deep sense that it's a tragedy.

Of course, it's all a question of degree. If a death is *really* premature, as in the case of a child, then yes—I do have a sense of the tragic every time I hear of a small child dying. The funeral for the five-year-old son of friends of ours was unlike any I'd ever attended. It was the most intense and silent funeral I've ever experienced, with little talking by anyone, and none of the nervous laughter that occurs at other funerals. Tragedy may not be a strong enough word for that situation. I felt more horrified than anything else.

Now, what does all this tell us about *Oedipus Rex*?

WHAT'S SO "TRAGIC" ABOUT *OEDIPUS REX*?

Oedipus Rex is overflowing with the horrible, the sad, the heart-rending, and the cataclysmic. So, what exactly about *Oedipus Rex* is tragic in the sense I just discussed? Stated differently, if the play were a reconstruction of actual events, like the death of my work colleague, what about it would fill me with that sense of the tragic?

In a sense, everything would, because Oedipus's whole life was one bitter irony. No literary character has been more cruelly tricked by the gods or fate (or some other agent of destruction) than Oedipus.

Let me break this observation down: As a young man, Oedipus found himself forced to leave the parents he loved. As Oedipus said to the Corinthian, "To see one's parents and look into their eyes is the greatest joy I know" (line 1095–96). He was deprived of that joy. That was cruel, and it was ironic because it turned out to be unnecessary; if he had stayed in Corinth, he would have been safe. Because of the prophecy, he was driven away from home. In fact, Oedipus is a man who was driven away from his home three times in his life: first, as an infant, from Thebes; second, as a young man, leaving Corinth; and third, as a helpless, blind beggar, leaving Thebes again.

We also need to consider the mental agony Oedipus had been living with since receiving the prophecy about incest and patricide. Imagine being told you are going to commit some unspeakable acts and there is nothing you can do to prevent it. What agony you would be under, your whole life, a torment as painful as if you were told when and how you were going to die! This tragic aspect of the story is brilliantly captured by Hugo von Hofmannsthal in his play *Oedipus and the Sphinx* (essentially a prequel to *Oedipus Rex*), which portrays Oedipus as virtually suicidal after receiving the horrible message from the oracle about his destiny.

He's also a man who thinks that he's the savior of his people but learns, to his horror, that not only is he *not* their savior, he is the very cause of their misfortunes. This is yet another cruel joke played on him by the powers that be. On top of this, his ruin comes about through his own efforts. His sincere search for the truth ends with a truly shocking reward. His is the tragedy of the good man trying to do the right thing and finding that no matter what he does, he brings pain to all around him. In the words of one scholar, "[I]t is the very core of his tragedy that, by using his high intellect honestly and uncompromisingly, he brings doom upon himself."[25]

And there's another cruel irony: Oedipus is a man who loses his mother just as he discovers who she is. The horror of this was brought home to me by another powerful story—Victor Hugo's *The Hunchback of Notre-Dame*. This aspect of the novel is not well known because it has been left out of the movie versions I have seen and it is separate from the Quasimodo story, but in the novel itself, there's an old, reclusive woman who lives in a dank little cell of a building near Notre Dame. Because her infant daughter was stolen from her by gypsies, the recluse has formed an intense hatred of Esmeralda, the novel's primary female protagonist, who the recluse believes is a gypsy. Meanwhile, the evil Frollo, the archdeacon of the Notre Dame cathedral, decides to have Esmeralda executed because she rebuffed his sexual overtures.

In the book's climax, Frollo tracks Esmeralda down to the square where the recluse lives and, knowing that the recluse hates Esmeralda, asks her to keep Esmeralda confined while he retrieves soldiers. Her hatred of Esmeralda makes her only too willing to oblige. During those few minutes they are together, however, they make the novel's most remarkable discovery. What they learn is that Esmeralda is not a gypsy herself but was raised by gypsies. She is, in fact, the very infant daughter who was stolen from the recluse. As in so many other recognition stories, they discover this through a sign. Throughout the novel, Hugo refers to the little pouch worn by Esmeralda around her neck; in the recognition scene we finally learn its contents—a little shoe. It is one in a matched pair of shoes worn by Esmeralda as an infant; the recluse has the other one.

But they make the discovery too late; the soldiers arrive to take Esmeralda away, and she is promptly executed. By confining Esmeralda at Frollo's request, therefore, the old woman has killed her own daughter (another example of unknowingly harming a close relative). Mother and daughter are separated forever right at the moment in their lives when they have finally been reunited. Likewise, when Oedipus bursts into Jocasta's room, he is seeing his mother for the first time. He has known her as his wife, but now he knows that she is his real mother and she is dead. It's hard to think of a crueler irony than that.

> And there we saw the woman hanging by the neck, cradled high in a woven noose, spinning, swinging back and forth. And when he saw her, giving a low, wrenching sob that broke our hearts, slipping the halter from her throat, he eased her down, in a slow embrace he laid her down, poor thing. (lines 1395–1400)

This is all looking at it from Oedipus's point of view, which brings up an interesting point about the play: Our gaze is so focused on Oedipus and his suffering that it's easy to forget the agony of the other characters—first and most importantly Jocasta. I think of her as generally less sympathetic in the play than Oedipus. For one thing, she is not the great champion of truth that Oedipus is; to the contrary, she is a force *against* the truth, doing her best to keep the sleeping dogs asleep. Her motives are understandable, but I generally side with the Oedipuses of the world who want to bring the truth out, not keep it buried (though if there was ever a time to keep a truth under wraps, it was this one). And then there's the matter of the infanticide, which I discussed at the end of the last chapter. In her speech to Oedipus, she puts the blame on Laius, but the shepherd gives us reason to doubt her account, and he's a more credible witness. But she is still a tragic figure, like Lady Macbeth and like Joe Keller from *All My Sons*, who too committed unspeakable crimes.

Jocasta's story is particularly parallel to Keller's. They both did a horrible thing years before we meet them, apparently without feeling much remorse. But they don't know the full significance of what they did: Jocasta didn't know her infant child survived, and Keller didn't know that he had driven his son Larry to suicide. They both suffer under the cruel irony of believing they are safe and secure while in actuality they are in terrible danger. And then, when each of them learns the truth, they kill themselves.

Because Oedipus is such a towering tragic figure, it's easy to overlook the fact that Jocasta is one of literature's greatest tragic characters in her own right. In Jocasta's final scene, she implores Oedipus to drop his inquiry. She begs him: "Stop—in the name of god, if you love your own life, call off this search! My suffering is enough" (lines 1162–65). There aren't too many moments in literature more horrible and heartrending than the one in which she exits the scene, knowing what is coming but having failed to dissuade her son from rushing headlong into horror.[26] "You're doomed—may you never fathom who you are! . . . man of agony—that is the only name I have for you, that, no other—ever, ever, ever!" (lines 1173, 1176–77).

Some scholars have also detected tragedy in the story of the two old men, the Corinthian and the Theban.[27] And I think these scholars have a point, for life played a cruel trick on them, too. All those years ago, they took pity on a helpless infant, believing they were rescuing him. Now they realize that what they thought was a kind and charitable act resulted in horror. This is why the Theban tries so desperately hard to avoid answering Oedipus's questions.

Finally, we shouldn't ignore the tragedy suffered by the people of Thebes, and I don't mean from the plague. Like the other characters in the play, they too have suffered a cruel irony: They had a great leader. He saved them once, from the Sphinx. They look to him to save them again, and not only does he fail to save them, he turns out to be the source of their woes. And then they lose him forever.

Are these the greatest sufferers in the history of literature—Oedipus, Jocasta, the two old men, the people of Thebes? Of course not. As I mentioned earlier in this chapter, how can one say that they'd be the winners in a suffering contest, given how much suffering there is in this world? And yet somehow, *Oedipus Rex* fills me with a sense of the tragic in a way that few if any other works of literature do, even ones that involve great suffering. Why? Because the cruelty he suffers couldn't be more ironic, and the irony couldn't be crueler.

Based on the reflections I've described in this chapter, I think I have a good sense of what makes *Oedipus Rex* so tragic in the real-world sense. The feeling I get from the play is comparable to the feeling I get when I think about the death of my work colleague right after she found marital happiness, or the friend who died of cancer likewise shortly after finding personal joy. There's no doubt that the sense of the tragic I feel about Oedipus and his fellow Theban sufferers is a critical part of its enormous power.

But as the years roll on, I've realized something else about my feelings when it comes to *Oedipus Rex*: I find *Oedipus Rex* to be the most moving work of literature I know and Oedipus a hero for all time, not because of how Oedipus suffers but because of how he behaves in the face of his suffering. While I have a strong sense of the tragic when I think about Oedipus, over time a much more potent feeling about him began to overtake me: a sense of admiration.

Chapter Nine

The Meaning of Heroism

When I was young, I thought that the most important personal trait—the trait most relevant to my success in the world—was cleverness. The highest compliment that someone could pay to me was to laugh at something I said, confirming that I was funny, or to praise my wittiness. The people I tried most to emulate were the great wits. I had a few friends who fell into that category, and I was jealous of how naturally they were able to say funny and clever things. I was always working on improving my "personality," which I took to mean how I came across to others—an entirely external thing. I was most proud of those times when I was able to keep a group of people laughing.

I remember a time, when I was in high school, when my father picked me up from a friend's house. On the way home, I referred to my friend's father as a drip, because I thought he was boring. I'll never forget my father's reaction. It wasn't exactly anger—more like disappointment in me for using that term to describe my friend's father. "He's not a drip," my father said. "He's a good man. He's a good father and a good husband and a good member of the community—a solid person." At the time, I didn't appreciate my father's point. I didn't really know what character meant.

As I started approaching college age, I began to appreciate intellect. I had always done well in school but generally took that for granted. As I got to college, and then law school, I leaned more heavily on my intellectual strengths and realized the singular importance of brainpower. I came to count on my intellectual capabilities to sustain me and bring me success. My brainpower, such as it is, got me into a good college, where I did well enough to get into a good law school, where I did well enough to get good legal jobs and have a relatively successful legal career. The things that made me the proudest, at least in the work world, were intellectual—the strategies that I came up with for winning cases, the articles I wrote.

As the years went on, however, I started becoming more aware of the importance of inner strength. Because of my academic success, I didn't have too many failures during my childhood, but as I moved along in life, failures came my way, and at times I was forced to confront the need to be strong on the inside, not just clever on the outside. In my late thirties, for example, I read a book about "emotional intelligence," which I consider basically another name for resilience. A career failure—of which I've had my share—demanded that I develop this different sort of intelligence.

Integrity also became more important to me over time. This hit me the most during those times when I failed to muster as much of it as I should have. Sometimes I learned from my mistakes; sometimes I didn't. Sometimes I did the right thing, sometimes I didn't. But one thing was for sure—the days when being clever and having a great "personality" meant everything were far behind me. As I reached middle age, the people I most emulated were no longer the witty ones or the brilliant ones but the *good* ones.

Here's an example: About seven years ago, an older colleague of mine died suddenly from a heart attack. He was sixty. I had only worked with him for about ten months when he died, but in that short time, I had become extremely fond of him and grown to admire him. At his funeral, several of the speakers referred to him as a "mensch," a Yiddish word usually translated as "an upstanding man"; I think it can also be translated as "someone with real character." This, of course, wasn't the first time I'd heard someone referred to as a mensch, but because it was used to describe someone who had just died, I thought about how I would be described after I died and what I would most want people to say about me.

I still admire great wits and towering minds. But for me, now, character is king. That's not a claim about how much of it I have; I know that I still have a long way to go. Rather, it's a statement of how important it is to me. I have come to believe that being a successful human being—successful in the most important ways—is a matter of character.

This change in my values is reflected in how I view *Oedipus Rex*. Today, I think of Oedipus as the greatest hero in literature, but not just because he is the protagonist of what I consider the greatest drama of all time. For me, he is the greatest hero because of his character—that quality that, for so long, I undervalued. More than any other character in literature, Oedipus has taught me the meaning of heroism—*true* heroism. That's the subject of this chapter: What makes a great hero, not in mythology but in life?

MARTYR TO TRUTH

As you may recall, in chapter 3 I discussed how twentieth-century mythologists like Lord Raglan and Otto Rank placed Oedipus in the context of mythology, putting him at the very top of their list of mythological heroes. Naturally, given my love of the Oedipus story, I was pleased to see him rank so high. His stellar standing in the pantheon of the great heroes seemed to confirm his importance and centrality in the history of mythology. I feel silly about it now, but when I learned about his accomplishment, I actually felt proud, as if someone had complimented one of my own children. "Attaboy,

Oedipus," I thought to myself. According to esteemed intellects, he ranks higher on the hero scale than Heracles, Jason, King Arthur, or any other mythological hero.

Rank's and Raglan's mythological perspectives are useful and interesting; they help place the Oedipus myth in a broader context. But their focus is different from mine. They emphasize what Oedipus has *in common* with other heroes. I'm interested in how he *differs*.

This means that there are elements of the Oedipus story that are important to me but not to them. For example, hardly any of the other hero stories they consider (e.g., Moses, Jesus, Heracles, Arthur, et al) involve unintentional patricide and incest, even the ones in which the hero is sent away as an infant and grows up ignorant of his true identity. The self-fulfilling prophecy plays no role in their mythological treatments, either. And the conquest of the Sphinx is treated as if it were just like any dragon slayer's act of courage and feat of strength. By the mythologists' telling, Oedipus might as well have killed the Sphinx with a sword (which, by the way, is how it's done in Hesiod's version of the Sphinx story, *Theogony*—but it's Heracles, not Oedipus, who slays the monster).

This is not to denigrate Oedipus's physical strength. After all, he must have been powerful to have single-handedly killed Laius and his retinue. (Whenever I think about the crossroad incident, I get into my head the analogous image of Samson slaying the Philistine army with the jawbone of an ass. After all, Oedipus did the job with nothing more than a shaft.) And just try to imagine the superhuman pain of gouging out your own eyes. But those physical feats merely make Oedipus another he-man, like Hercules and Samson and Jason. That's the least interesting aspect of the Oedipus story to me.

But most importantly, the mythological approach is silent on the topic of what makes *Oedipus Rex* the masterpiece that it is: the Circular Detective story at the beginning, the irony of the self-cursing, the subsequent exploration of Oedipus's past, the process by which he learns the truth, and the horrible acts that flow from those discoveries. This is not a flaw in Rank's and Raglan's analysis. They're not trying to solve the Riddle of Oedipus; they're trying to place Oedipus in line with his brother heroes.

At the heart of *Oedipus Rex* is a different kind of hero, a man apart from the other great men of mythology. This is in large part because he is not searching for a physical object, like the Holy Grail or the Golden Fleece, or a way to kill a woman with snakes coming out of her head or to clean out a king's filthy horse stables. He's up to something entirely different. He's seeking the truth.

Let's face it: Oedipus isn't the smartest hero ever. He's smart, but I can think of cleverer heroes, starting with one of the first great heroes in literature, Odysseus. Odysseus came up with the Trojan Horse. He thought up the idea of binding himself to the mast of his ship and putting wax in his men's ears so that he could listen to the Sirens without endangering himself and his crew by ordering them to approach the rocks. He told the Cyclops that his name was "Nobody," so that when the Cyclops sought help from his fellow Cyclopses after being blinded, his shouts that "Nobody blinded me!" kept them from coming to his aid.

Nor is Oedipus obviously the greatest ruler of legend. When the play begins, he is depicted as a great ruler who is loved by his people. He has taken initiative to combat the plague even before the town leaders implore him for help, sending Creon to the oracle. And as soon as he receives the oracle's answer, he begins his search. But there are other great rulers of legend: Moses, King Arthur, Henry V (of Shakespeare, not history), and many more. Some scholars have argued that, in fact, Oedipus is *not* a great ruler. As I mentioned in chapter 3, some believe that he exhibits hubris in the play, pointing especially to his bragging about having previously vanquished the Sphinx. And, to be sure, he is a touch cocky in that opening scene. Other scholars have argued that he is too quick to anger. Some scholars find him a raw despot; one characterized him as "a primitive, pre-Hellenic chieftain."[1]

Some have even gone so far as to say that it was because of these character flaws that the gods punished Oedipus. They treat *Oedipus Rex* as if it were a cautionary tale about egotism, with a clear moral ("Don't be egotistical").

I think it's ridiculous to treat the play as if it were "The Boy Who Cried Wolf" or some other Aesop-like fable with a simple moral. In the first place, as discussed in chapter 6, by the time the play commences, the die of Oedipus's fate has already been cast—the punishment would precede the crime. And what possible crime does he commit that would warrant such an extreme punishment—a little bragging? In any event, I don't think there is meaningful evidence of misconduct on stage, certainly not anything severe enough to detract from Oedipus's greatness as a man and as a ruler. He gets angry with Teiresias, but that's because—from Oedipus's point of view—Teiresias is stubbornly withholding valuable information.

Also, as the classicist Bernard Knox has pointed out, Oedipus exhibits an admirable democratic temper during the play. He is not the kind of leader who shelters himself from his people, speaking to them through messengers. To the contrary, he circulates among them, and when Creon—no democrat—suggests that they move indoors, away from the people, to discuss his news, Oedipus rejects the suggestion, saying, "Address yourself to all."[2]

Oedipus has flaws, but who doesn't? As classical scholar E. R. Dodds noted, scholars have "gone over the play with a microscope looking for moral faults in Oedipus, and have duly found them—for neither here nor anywhere else did Sophocles portray that insipid and unlikely character, the man of perfect virtue."[3]

So if he's not the smartest and not necessarily the greatest ruler, then what is it about Oedipus that sets him apart and makes him, for me, the greatest fictional hero ever? The answer is twofold.

First, it's his bravery in pursuit of the truth. That alone makes him one of the greatest heroes of the truth in all of literature and, for me, a man of stunning character. Much of the "action" in the play actually revolves around efforts to stop his inquiry. Early in the play, Teiresias warns him against continuing his search. Jocasta does the same after she figures out the truth, and the Theban gives him a final caution.

Dodds is correct that "Oedipus is a kind of symbol of the human intelligence which cannot rest until it has solved all the riddles."[4] And Knox applauds the way Oedipus "admits no mysteries, no half-truths, no half-measures," and the way he refuses to accede to "both Teiresias' and Jocasta's attempts to stop him from pressing on to the end." He illustrates this point with Oedipus's examination of the Theban, arguing that

> He already knows the truth—that Jocasta was his mother and Laius his father—yet there is one detail he does not understand. It is not a detail that offers any hope that the whole story may be false, it is merely a question of the shepherd's motive. "Why did you give the child to this man?" Even at the most terrible moment of his existence, he must have the full story, with no trace of obscurity in it anywhere. He must complete the process of inquiry, remove the last ambiguity.[5]

Schopennauer expressed his admiration for Oedipus in a letter to Goethe in which he spoke of Oedipus as the model of the philosopher who has "the courage to search problems through to the end." In Schopenhauer's view, Oedipus "pursues his quest untiringly, even when he realizes that the answer holds only horror and terror for him."[6]

Not everyone agrees with this perspective; some scholars deny that Oedipus deserves all the praise heaped on him by scholars like Knox. But I side with Knox that "Oedipus represents all that is intelligent, vigorous, courageous, and creative in man."[7] He is "a man who, starting with nothing but his wits and energy," becomes a beloved ruler.[8] That's why I believe that his actions up through the revelation of his true identity should be enough to establish him as one of the greatest heroes in all of literature. And so, for some scholars, not unreasonably, this quest for the truth is the most moving aspect of the play.[9] It certainly is one of the most moving aspects for me.

But then there's a second thing Oedipus does that sets him apart, something that exhibits enormous character and vaults him into his own heroic stratosphere.

THE MAN WHO MANNED UP

If Sophocles had ended the play right after the dramatic scene with the Theban shepherd in which the truth comes spilling out, it would still be one of the greatest works of literature of all time. And it would still contain all those moments and ideas that have thrilled me—everything that I've talked about thus far. But it does *not* end there. And though for a long time I paid little attention to what comes after the revelation, the older I got, the more important it became to me.

Over the course of the book, I've talked in general terms about the last third of the play, but to understand why it has come to mean so much to me, let's now look at exactly happens after the revelation.

When Oedipus staggers from the stage, he makes his way to Jocasta's room. The door is locked, and he bursts through it to find that she has hanged herself. Then Oedipus rips the golden brooches from her gown and plunges them into his eyes over and over, crying, "You, you'll see no more the pain I suffered, all the pain I caused! Too long you looked on the ones you never should have seen,, blind to the ones you longed to see, to know!" (lines 1405–09). None of this takes place on stage; it is described by a palace servant reporting to the chorus, telling them that "neither the waters of the Danube nor the Nile can wash this palace clean" (lines 1356–57).

Then Oedipus, his face and body covered with blood, reenters the stage, leaning on a boy for support. In dialogue with the chorus, he curses himself and his fate, bemoaning the fact that he was saved by the shepherd/servant who should have let him die, sparing him and the world the horror of what was to follow. Creon then enters. Oedipus acknowledges to Creon how wrong he has been and then begs Creon to drive him from the land, as the oracle advised. Creon says he would have done it already but thought it best to first consult the oracle again, to clarify his duty.

Oedipus asks to see his daughters, who are brought onto the stage by a nurse. After a tearful speech about their misery, he once again begs Creon to drive him into exile. Creon is noncommittal and orders Oedipus back into the palace. Guards remove his daughters from Oedipus and usher them into the palace, followed by Creon and Oedipus. And thus quietly ends one of the world's supreme masterworks.

Because the Sophocles version is so powerful and definitive, it's easy to fall into the trap of assuming that that's the way *Oedipus Rex* has to end. But the myth of Oedipus doesn't always end that way. In versions of the story dating from both before and after Sophocles, Oedipus continues to rule Thebes even after the revelation. That's how it is in Homer's brief account: "[H]e in growing pain ruled on in beloved Thebes—lording Cadmus' people—while she went down to Death."[10] Ending the play with Oedipus insisting on his own exile required a conscious decision on Sophocles's part, just as the use of the plague was a product of his artistic genius. The choice was not inevitable. But having made the choice, Sophocles created one of the most important and enduring symbols of human courage and integrity ever conceived.

I used to ignore this last third of the play. To me, the play's most important aspects were the Circular Detective story and the revelations, all of which happen by the end of the dialogue with the Theban shepherd. But measured by number of lines, a third of the play still remains after that dialogue. That's a lot of space for things to happen. And think about what *does* happens in that last third: Jocasta hangs herself, and Oedipus blinds himself. He comes out on stage and asks to be cast out of the city; Creon refuses. After some concluding thoughts by the chorus, the play ends.

So why did I downplay that last third? I think it's because for a long time, I was so intrigued by the idea that *Oedipus Rex* is a play about the unfolding of the past, an exploration of one's backstory, as I discussed in chapter 4. In fact, one commentator after another makes it sound as though that's *all* the play is about, from Schiller ("The *Oedipus* is, as it were, *only* a tragic analysis")[11] to Freud ("The action of the play consists in *nothing other than* the process of revealing")[12] and many modern commentators ("Inquiry and discovery . . . constitute *virtually the entire play*";[13] "*Nearly every crucial event in the action* has already happened";[14] "*Hardly anything happens*, beyond people arriving with news"[15]).

In time, though, I stopped fighting the last third. I realized it makes no sense to treat Jocasta's suicide and Oedipus's self-blinding as "hardly anything." For it's in the last third that we learn the most about Oedipus as a man and as a ruler, and about his true character. To ignore the last third, as I did for so long, is to cut out a portrait of unparalleled heroism—perhaps matched, but never exceeded—in Western literature.

How appropriate, then, that when the Czech novelist Milan Kundera was looking around for an example of this kind of greatness, he turned to Oedipus. In his novel *The Unbearable Lightness of Being*, set in 1960s communist Czechoslovakia, the protagonist, Tomas, a doctor, gets in trouble for writing a magazine piece contrasting the courage of Oedipus with the cowardice of his country's rulers. The latter blame their Soviet overlords for duping them into committing atrocities against their people: "We didn't know!

We were deceived! We were true believers [in communism]! Deep in our hearts we are innocent!" they cry. Oedipus, on the other hand, accepts full responsibility for his crimes despite his innocence. As Tomas writes:

> Oedipus did not know he was sleeping with his own mother, yet when he realized what had happened, he did not feel innocent. Unable to stand the sight of the misfortunes he had wrought by "not knowing," he put out his eyes and wandered blind away from Thebes.[16]

Oedipus could have argued that he was blameless. In fact, he does so in *Oedipus at Colonus*. But not in *Oedipus Rex*. As Dodds explains, "He accepts the responsibility for all his acts, including those which are objectively most horrible, though subjectively innocent."[17] Oedipus never asks, "Why me?" He accepts his fate without complaining.

Even while suffering the most horrible physical and mental pain imaginable, Oedipus continues to act as a responsible leader who puts the interests of others first. He has the presence of mind and moral sense to beg Creon to give Jocasta a proper burial (a foreshadowing of the other two Theban plays) and to take care of his young daughters. He shows, in other words, more character in a crisis and time of horror than any other literary figure I'm aware of.

I'm more moved by this extraordinary act of decency today than I was in the past. Again, this reflects changes in my own character. When I was younger, goodness struck me as kind of boring. Today, there's nothing I find more enthralling. That shift in my worldview is perfectly captured in a statement attributed to the great Jewish philosopher Abraham Joshua Heschel: "When I was young, I admired clever people. Now that I am old, I admire kind people."[18]

When scholars ask whether there's a moral lesson to be drawn from *Oedipus Rex*, they almost always focus on the negative lessons around hubris and anger and forgetting your place in the scheme of things—i.e., that you're not a god.[19] And, as I discussed, I myself have focused a lot at times on the moral lessons flowing from Oedipus's failure to accord a stranger the same consideration as a friend or relative. But over time, I've come to realize that the overriding moral lesson of the play is not negative but positive. It's about conduct not to avoid but to emulate—the conduct of Oedipus throughout the play, especially in the last third.

Some find *Oedipus Rex* depressing, a parable of the meaninglessness of life. I've never seen it that way. I've always found it inspiring. We all face setbacks; I certainly have had my share of failures. The real question is not whether you've had failures but how you deal with them. We always talk about building on success, but as Johnny Cash once put it, it's more important to build on failure. And for that life lesson, there is no greater role model than Oedipus the King—the man who, at the lowest possible point in his life, manned up.

There are two competing images of Oedipus in the public imagination: the bold and confident young man answering the Sphinx's riddle and the blind, helpless beggar dependent on his young daughter for everything. The cover of almost every book about Oedipus (including this one) features either one or the other. On one level, the contrast between these two iconic images couldn't be greater: strong vs. helpless. Yet on a deeper level, the difference melts away, for both are portraits of a man in the process of saving his city.

This is why I no longer ignore the last third of the play. The first two thirds offer one kind of heroism; the last third offers another, perhaps greater, kind. Together, they form a portrait of an incomparable hero.

"RIPENESS IS ALL"

Truth can be hard to grasp and understand even when it is handed to us on a silver platter, and this is perfectly demonstrated in *Oedipus Rex*. Earlier in the book, I noted in passing that in anger, Teiresias blurts out the entire truth about Oedipus's life:

> Listen to me closely: the man you've sought so long, proclaiming, cursing up and down, the murderer of Laius—he is here. A stranger, you may think, who lives among you, he soon will be revealed a native Theban but he will take no joy in the revelation. Blind who now has eyes, beggar who now is rich, he will grope his way toward a foreign soil, a stick tapping before him step by step. Revealed at last, brother and father both to the children he embraces, to his mother son and husband both—he sowed the loins his father sowed, he spilled his father's blood. (lines 510–23)

There it is—the whole truth in a nutshell. But it comes much too early for Oedipus to understand. He is given the answer he seeks, but he can't yet grasp it because sometimes it takes a while to see the truth of something. The same is true of two of the other great characters we discussed in chapter 1, in the context of the Circular Detective theme. In "The Great Stone Face," the main character, Ernest, takes a lifetime to realize that it is he who is the likeness of the Great Stone Face carved into the mountain. Similarly, Socrates was told by the oracle that he was the wisest man in Athens, but it took him many years to realize that he was, and why.

Robert M. Pirsig talks about this in *Zen and the Art of Motorcycle Maintenance*. "The truth knocks on the door and you say, 'Go away, I'm looking for the truth,' and so it goes away," he writes.[20] We have to be ready; or, as Shakespeare put it, "Ripeness is all."[21] This is why we sometimes miss the most obvious things. As my wife can attest, I have an inordinately thick skull; it sometimes takes me a long time to get things. That's true in general, but it has been especially true of my understanding of *Oedipus Rex*.

As a younger man, fixated on cleverness, I was most intrigued by the Circular Detective theme, which stretches from the oracle's prophecy to Oedipus's realization (during his dialogue with Jocasta) that he is almost certainly Laius's killer. I loved the surprise of always finding new examples of this theme in other works of literature and art, and I enjoyed pondering its philosophical implications.

But the Circular Detective story ends about a third of the way through the play, in the dialogue with Jocasta. My eventual realization of that very obvious fact led me to focus more on the play's middle third, including the two climactic dialogues with the Corinthian and the Theban. It's in this section of the play that Oedipus explores the deepest part of his backstory, his very origins.

Something terrible has been repressed, and Oedipus, using his renowned intellect, uncovers it. The repressed returns. This held a certain fascination for me at what was a particularly retrospective time in my life; few stories were as thrilling to me as that of a man searching for and discovering who he is. Over time, I teased apart the various implications of that discovery—that Oedipus committed incest and patricide, that the prophecies had been true all along, and that all this time, Oedipus has been home. I explored their broader philosophical meanings: the expanding circle of morality, the role of fate in our lives, the nature of the self-fulfilling prophecy, the tendency of truth to surface (or not), the all-along feeling, the circular arc of our lives, and the meaning of the tragic.

As I've argued, *Oedipus Rex* is the mother of all backstories, and I have long been caught in the gravitational pull of that backstory. But the play does more than bear us ceaselessly into the past. It faces forward as well, because it doesn't stop with the revelation of the truth; it also shows how people reckon with the past *and* try to forge a future, however bleak. Thus, at a certain point, my main attention shifted from Oedipus as an explorer of the past and a sufferer to Oedipus as a man of unparalleled character in the present. He went from being the Man Who Didn't Know He Was Home to the Man Who Manned Up.

This transformation wasn't as important to me when I was young. As the years went on, however, it became increasingly important. Only then was I ready to see *Oedipus Rex* in its fullness.

All of this is obvious to me now, but it took a long time to get there. I had to be ready to receive the message. Readiness arrived bit by bit, as my knowledge of and outlook on life evolved. That evolution brought a corresponding evolution in my view of the play.

In all of this, I was assisted by other stories—the movies and plays and novels I've discussed in this book. A great literary scholar named Northrop Frye (1912–1991) perfectly captured this process in his writings about the Bible and its impact on later literature: "[T]he more we study the literary developments of a myth the more we learn about the myth." He meant that you can learn a lot about the original myth (in that case, biblical stories) from later tellings of those myths. [22]

I think that observation applies to more than just stories that are express reinterpretations of a myth, like later versions of *Oedipus Rex* by Seneca or Voltaire, or something like *West Side Story*, which retells *Romeo and Juliet*. I think it also applies to stories that invoke the same themes as the original myth, such as *All My Sons* and any other narrative that is structured around the return of the repressed. I have learned just as much about the character of Oedipus the man from *All My Sons* and *Jean de Florette* and *The Sixth Sense* as I have from the Oedipus literature, and probably more. These stories helped me understand how and why *Oedipus Rex* struck various chords in me and, I think, in others as well. Obviously, I am not the only person to whom the play has meant so much.

One could liken the process to the peeling of an onion, in which one gradually gets closer and closer to the center. But that's not exactly it. I do think I've been zeroing in on the right answer, but onion peeling is the wrong metaphor. In thinking about the play over the years, I've been *adding* layers, not subtracting them. It's not that my earlier observations were false; they were simply earlier observations, and I now have a richer sense of the whole.

I'm sure there are some psychoanalysts out there who will tell you that all this is just a story I'm telling myself, that the real reason I'm fascinated by *Oedipus Rex* is the Oedipus complex, or some other Freudian or neo-Freudian or post-Freudian condition—perhaps unresolved father issues. Remember from chapter 3 that while Freud himself thought he had the answer, others came along and said that not only was he wrong in his interpretation but he had actually repressed the real reason for his own fascination with Oedipus (yes, father issues).

I don't think that's the case with me. I think I now understand pretty well why I'm so drawn to *Oedipus Rex*. But who knows? Self-analyses like the kind undertaken in this book, aren't always accurate. As *Oedipus Rex* itself teaches, we don't always know ourselves very well.

The title of this book is *Searching for Oedipus*. I thought about calling it *Finding Oedipus*, but on further reflection I decided that "searching" is the better word. Subjectively, I feel as though I've reached the final stage—that I've *found* him. But maybe I suffer from what has been called the "end of history illusion": the belief that one has settled on a final answer.

I've read *Oedipus Rex* countless times, but maybe next time I read it or see it performed, I'll see things in it I hadn't noticed before. Even as I was writing this book, I kept spotting new things, and I would realize that commentaries I had read years earlier that didn't make much of an impression on me back then suddenly seemed right on point. These days, I agree with the great American classicist Richmond Lattimore, who wrote, "We can read [*Oedipus Rex*] as many times as we like, and every time find new truths and throw away old falsehoods that once seemed to be true. *There is always a dimension that escapes*."[23]

It's more than possible that my views will continue to evolve and that dimensions of the play that loom large in my life now will fade into the background and vice versa, and this will affect how I see *Oedipus Rex*. Nothing ever really comes to a final rest. Zhou Enlai, the first premier of the People's Republic of China, was once asked what he thought of the French Revolution. His answer was "It's too early to tell."

The meaning of a person's life never stops changing, either. Sophocles was drawn to this idea, and he expressed it through the chorus in the final words of the play:

> People of Thebes, my countrymen, look on Oedipus.
> He solved the famous riddle with his brilliance,
> He rose to power, a man beyond all power.
> Who could behold his greatness without envy?
> Now what a black sea of terror has overwhelmed him.
> Now as we keep our watch and wait the final day,
> Count no man happy till he dies, free of pain at last. (lines 1678–84)

The same idea is reflected in the very first words of *The Women of Trachis* ("It was long ago that someone first said: You cannot know a man's life before the man has died, then only can you call it good or bad").[24] Before Sophocles, Aeschylus and Herodotus expressed the same exact sentiment.[25]

And that brings me to the final irony in *Oedipus Rex*: Even the chorus is wrong when it thinks it has seen the final state of Oedipus's life, for Oedipus, too, has another chapter. In his eighties, Sophocles wrote another masterpiece, *Oedipus at Colonus*, in which Oedipus is no longer a pollutant but a revered and holy figure. In the play, several cities, including Thebes, fight for the honor of being the site of Oedipus's grave. No one saw that coming back in the moment of his greatest agony.

But that's another story.

Conclusion

One Riddle, Many Answers

There's a character in *The Moonstone* (the detective novel discussed in chapter 1) named Gabriel Betteredge, the head butler of the manor where much of the novel takes place. He's a semicomical character with some interesting quirks, one of which is that he loves *Robinson Crusoe* so much that he thinks it contains the answers to all of life's questions and sees no need to read other books. Some people are that way about other books, especially religious texts like the Bible and the Koran.

Let me be clear: That is *not* how I feel about *Oedipus Rex*. It doesn't have all the answers. It deals with some of life's biggest issues, but not all of them. And I have certainly fallen in love with countless other writings, fictional and nonfictional, over the years, some of which I've discussed in this book.

Still, even after several decades of digesting an untold number of books and movies and plays, I have continued to be amazed by the sheer richness of *Oedipus Rex*. In the first place, there are few (or perhaps no) other works of literature upon which so many extraordinary claims can be made. And I'm not talking about subjective appraisals like D. H. Lawrence's assessment that it is "the finest drama of all times."[1] I'm talking about factual statements about its literary and cultural importance.

Start with the fact that it created the genre of detective fiction and bent it at the same time. Add to that the fact that it's the first true instance in literature of a person trying to discover who he is—the first existential search, if you will.[2] Then throw into the mix the fact that, from the era of Aristotle to the present, it has also been considered the paradigmatic tragedy.

Any one of these facts by itself would be enough to make *Oedipus Rex* a landmark in the history of literature. But that's just the beginning; the list goes on. It's *the* classic example of irony in literature—practically the textbook definition. Google "irony," and the myth of Oedipus is likely to be among the first examples to appear. The same is true for "tragedy of fate." Oedipus is the poster child for that concept, and it is one of the truly iconic images of suffering in Western culture. At the same time, the image of Oedipus solving the Sphinx's riddle is one of the preeminent depictions of riddle-solving and deep contemplation.

Further, the play is such a famous example of the self-fulfilling prophecy that Karl Popper coined the term "Oedipus effect" as a shorthand for that fascinating phenomenon. It's also the classic example of the slaying of an unrecognized kinsman and of the self-curse. And, as mentioned during the analysis of hero rankings in chapter 9, Oedipus is widely considered the paradigmatic mythological hero.

Then think about everything *else* Oedipus and his story have come to symbolize over the years: the state of blindness to reality, the swift fall of the mighty, the need to withhold judgment about a person's life until its end, the unpredictability of life, and a pivotal decision at a crossroad.[3] In fact, it could be reasonably argued that Oedipus is *the* leading literary symbol of all of these things.

Oedipus Rex has even been used as byword for the dangers of curiosity. Plutarch considered it a great symbol of how "the itch of curiosity is a sweetly bitter, uncontrollable thing."[4]

On top of all that, now consider the play's role in twentieth-century psychology, which of course began with Freud, who thought Oedipus offered a key to the unconscious and accorded him a central role in the study of the human mind. Is there another work of literature so intertwined with a major theory of human nature and behavior? Today, Oedipus's name is a shorthand for both an overly close relationship with one's mother *and* rebellion against one's father, or any authority figure for that matter. And it has been central to debates among anthropologists and others about the degree to which people differ from one culture to another. As I said earlier, I don't believe in the Oedipus complex, but there's no denying its cultural influence.

When you add all this up, you have an embarrassment of riches. So many roads lead to *Oedipus Rex*, which has worked its way into our cultural DNA as few other works of literature have. There's a joke about a person who reads *Hamlet* for the first time and says, "I don't see what the big deal is. It's just a bunch of famous quotations strung together." If you had never heard of *Oedipus Rex* but were otherwise culturally literate, and you read the play for the first time, you might have a similar reaction. You'd think it was just a bunch of famous episodes strung together that you hadn't realized were all originally from the same work.

But of course, *Oedipus Rex* is far more than the sum of these individual parts. It's a remarkable whole; each piece fits with every other. One episode flows into the next with a seamlessness bordering on perfection: The plague leads to the oracular response which leads to Oedipus's curse which leads to the interview with Teiresias which leads to the fight with Creon which leads to Jocasta's intervention, and on it goes, in one unbroken chain of events. Or, framing it in terms of the three-part structure I laid out in the last chapter: The Circular Detective story leads to the exploration of the past which leads to the three-part discovery which leads to Oedipus's self-blinding and acceptance of responsibility.

Nothing is extraneous; every element matters. There are no distractions or diversions, no subplots like those in some later versions (Voltaire, for example, gave Jocasta a lover). The play contains not a single unnecessary word, and the dialogues are models of economy and tension. If you want rapid-fire staccato, you will never find anything to exceed the climactic dialogue between Oedipus and the Theban—match, perhaps, but not exceed.

For these reasons, the sheer power of *Oedipus Rex* cannot be grasped without embracing the whole thing. Which is why the various theories I've discussed in this book—Freud's, Fromm's, Nietzsche's, Girard's, etc.—are interesting but don't help us understand the true power of the play. They call to mind the parable of the blind men and the elephant, each one touching a particular part but failing to grasp the whole.

Some commentators focus solely on the role of the gods, others solely on the role of fate. Freud's theory is about incest and patricide but nothing else; it doesn't even distinguish between the intentional and the unintentional. Fromm's is even narrower, focusing exclusively on patricide. Neither has anything to say, for example, about the Sphinx's role in the story, or the Circular Detective, or the exploration of Oedipus's childhood, or his self-blinding, and on and on.

My point is that *Oedipus Rex* is simply too rich to be captured by any narrowly focused theory. The anthropologist René Girard, as discussed in chapter 3, focuses solely on Oedipus's rivalry with Creon and Teiresias, others on the infanticide, and still others on Laius's crimes in the way-backstory. A few, like Thomas Cahill, author of the popular book *Sailing the Wine-Dark Sea*, focus on its political aspects. Cahill wrote, "Never in theatrical history has there been a more political play than [*Oedipus Rex*]," which strikes me as seeing too much politics in what is fundamentally a psychological story and a study in character.[5]

It's not that previous interpretations have nothing useful to say. I've gleaned many fascinating insights from the Oedipus literature. To offer just a handful of examples:

- Both Jocasta and the Sphinx—the two main females in Oedipus's life—commit suicide (Jocasta by hanging, the Sphinx by jumping off the cliff).[6]
- The Theban shepherd saved Oedipus as an infant and then was the one person who was spared at the crossroad by Oedipus. But in failing to kill the shepherd/servant at the crossroad, Oedipus preserved the life of the one person who was able to definitively identify him as the son of Laius and thereby bring him down.[7]
- Everything the Theban shepherd does in the story involves evasion: He evades the order to kill the infant Oedipus; he evades the killing at the crossroad by being the sole survivor; he evades detection by Oedipus by asking Jocasta permission to leave the city for the countryside; and he tries to evade Oedipus's questions.[8]
- Oedipus destroys the Sphinx when he solves her riddle about feet and destroys himself when he solves the riddle of his own feet—that is, why they have scars.[9]
- The name "Oedipus" is usually construed as a contraction of "swollen" and "foot." But because the "oed" part is similar to the Greek root for "to know," the name could also be construed as meaning "know foot," a clever play on words since, in addition to having a swollen foot, Oedipus, the solver of the Sphinx's riddle about feet, knows feet (including, by the end, the meaning of the scars on his).[10]
- The Sphinx is several animals in one, the creature of her riddle is several animals in one (or at least seems to be), and Oedipus turns out to be several creatures in one (husband/son, father/

> brother, etc.).[11] In fact, everyone in the play has a double role: Oedipus (husband/son), Jocasta (wife/mother), Creon (uncle/brother-in-law), Antigone (daughter/sister), the Corinthian (messenger/protector of the infant Oedipus), and the Theban shepherd (savior of the infant Oedipus/sole surviving witness to the crossroad incident). Even Teiresias has a dual nature (man/woman).

These are all neat observations. And the various close readings of the play, like that of Bernard Knox, have taught me much—for example, about the extraordinarily complex web of puns and the incomparable verbal ironies throughout the text. But as I've discussed throughout this book, my path to understanding *Oedipus Rex* did not run through the scholarly literature. It ran through life.

It's with good reason that we talk about the "Greek miracle." Even after millennia, Greek architecture of this period has never stopped being an inspiration. When we needed a good form of government at the birth of this country, we turned to the Greeks. When we wanted to organize an international sporting competition, we created something called "the Olympics" that features athletes throwing javelins and discuses and running a "marathon." When we need inspiring poetry and unparalleled tales of high adventure, we read Homer. When we want to know what a great history looks like, we pick up Herodotus or Thucydides. When we want to know how to debate an opponent, we read Plato's dialogues and learn about the "Socratic method." When we want a model of wisdom, we look to Socrates. When we want to learn how to think, we look to the system of logic developed by Aristotle.

And if we want a drama that will never fail to leave us breathless and spellbound, we return to *Oedipus Rex*, one of the milestones of that Greek miracle. It's a perfect work of art if ever there was one. Schiller was right when he said *Oedipus Rex* "is its own genus" to which there belongs "no second species."[12] That's why to me, Sophocles, too, like his best-known character, is a great hero.

Voltaire and others have complained that the play contains absurdities, like the fact that Oedipus never previously figured out he had killed Laius, or that he killed an older man and married an older woman right after being warned that he was destined to kill his father and marry his mother. It's easy to make fun of those aspects, as even its admirers have done. But in the first place, if one uses one's imagination, one can easily come up with good responses to these accusations.[13] And more importantly, so what if some things are implausible? While it's true that in some works of literature an absence of verisimilitude is a flaw that lessens their quality, in many other works it does not. Consider myth, or fantasy, or science fiction, or magical realism: In all of these, an absence of plausibility is often the point. An animal with the head of a woman and the body of a lion definitely lacks verisimilitude, but no one argues that the myth's power is undermined by the biological implausibility of the Sphinx. In real life, would the Trojans ever be so naïve as to wheel in a giant wooden horse left behind as a "gift" from the Greeks? Of course not. Does that lessen the greatness of the Trojan Horse as mythology?

People do strange, mystifying, inexplicable things all the time in great fiction. But once the play kicks into gear, the characters on the page or stage in front of us become real human beings whose pains and sorrows and fears and anxieties speak to us on a human level. At the end of the day, I feel about *Oedipus Rex* the way the late movie critic Roger Ebert felt about the noir classic *Laura*: "All of [the] absurdities and improbabilities somehow do not diminish the film's appeal. They may even add to it."[14]

People have been struggling for a long time to solve the Riddle of Oedipus. You see this struggle reflected in various ways—for example, the search for suitable analogies between the figure of Oedipus and other remarkable characters in fiction and history. In the titles of books and articles alone, Oedipus has been paired with Job,

Jonah, Akhenaten, Narcissus, Theseus, Jesus, Isaac, Joseph, Freud, and Hamlet.[15] People never tire of trying to get their arms around the Oedipus mystery. Another indicator of the story's timeless intrigue is the sheer number of different interpretations of Oedipus's interaction with the Sphinx. For Nietzsche, it was about stealing the secrets of the natural world. For others, it's about Oedipus's intellect. For still others, the encounter cements him as a dragon-slaying hero. For Jean-Joseph Goux, the Sphinx episode represents a "deviant initiation." For Carl Jung, the Sphinx is the Terrible Mother (whatever that is). The scholar John Irwin found deep numerological significance in the riddle.[16] André Gide had *his* Oedipus declare that he used the same answer for every riddle he encountered in his life. The Riddle of Oedipus, though, is the exact opposite: It is a single riddle with many answers.

Not that every answer is right. Some of them, in my view, are just plain wrong. For example, while I admire the creativity of Frederick Ahl's revisionist account (Oedipus was framed), it makes the play into something it's not. An Oedipus who didn't kill his father and marry his mother would not be Oedipus. He'd be some other character—Joseph falsely accused by Potiphar's wife, or one of those Alfred Hitchcock protagonists who have been wrongly accused, like Cary Grant's character, Roger Thornhill, in *North by Northwest.*[17] Similarly, I think the deconstructionist view—that there is no truth, even in the end—turns *Oedipus Rex* into a Kafka or Borges novel in which the protagonist is condemned to perpetually wander around in the dark, never learning anything (like those metaphysical detectives I mentioned in chapter 1). But the characters in the play don't act like characters in a postmodern novel; at no point does anyone question whether Oedipus committed the acts attributed to him. Jocasta doesn't hang herself because she decides that the world is radically ambiguous or because she is having trouble decoding the text of life. She hangs herself because she discovers an unbearable truth.

It's like the story of the rabbinical student who proposed an interpretation of a particular passage of the Torah that the rabbi rejected. The student protested, "But you said that for every passage in the Torah, there are sixty-three possible interpretations." The rabbi responded, "That's true, and yours isn't one of them."

That said, there are certainly plenty of legitimate responses to *Oedipus Rex*. As Harvard classicist Charles Segal put it, "If scholars differ about the meaning of the play, it is also because intelligent and sensitive men and women continue to differ over the meaning of life."[18] The fact that so many have debated its meaning for so long—and whether it even *has* any meaning—is testament to its richness and even adds to my fascination with it. Was Sophocles aware of all the meanings I've presented in this book? That's unlikely. But to limit myself to Sophocles's original purpose would make me guilty of the "intentional fallacy": the belief that in studying a work of art, the most important question is the author's intention. Nor should we limit ourselves to the historical analysis so brilliantly undertaken by scholars such as Segal and Knox. It's useful and interesting to know, for example, that Athens had just survived a terrible plague when *Oedipus Rex* was written. But that knowledge shouldn't blind us to Sophocles's genius in introducing the plague into the story.

Likewise, knowing what Athenians thought about the play may, as Knox argued, shed light on what we think about it today.[19] But such analysis can also be misleading and limiting. The classical scholar Alister Cameron put it well: "[While] it is important, and indeed necessary, to identify the play in its time and place . . . a work of art can be lost as well as found by [such] research and commentary."[20] For me, the most important thing about the play is the meaning we *here today* derive from it. We haven't just lived through a terrible plague, but I believe that the play is *more* powerful to us today than it was to its fifth-century audience, and how appropriate for a work of literature that so beautifully illustrates the fundamental truth that ripeness is all. The sixteenth-century French essayist Michel de Montaigne, another one of my intellectual heroes, wrote that "a competent reader can often find in another man's writings perfections other than those which the author knows that he put there, and endow them with richer senses and meanings."[21] I'm quite sure we'll continue to find richer senses and meanings in *Oedipus Rex*, just as I have kept doing so over the course of my life. Like other great works of art, it's a gift that never fails to give more. Oedipus rescued Thebes twice. It occurs to me that maybe, in a sense, he is able to rescue us, too. After all, we need his example of character more than ever.

After hearing Creon's report from the oracle, Oedipus says, "Then once more I must turn what is dark to light."[22] And so he did, at great personal cost. I suspect he is not done teaching us important things about life and about ourselves, and I think he continues to turn darkness to light.

Appendix

An Endless Controversy

It is hard to find a single issue about *Oedipus Rex* as to which there is scholarly consensus, or a single scholarly assertion that has gone uncontradicted. This table collects in one place a number of those disputes, using representative quotations to illustrate the opposing positions. The statements in italics are my summaries of the various positions.

Table 9.1. Appendix

Where does the Oedipus myth come from, and what inspired it?	
The Oedipus myth is based on history. • "[T]he legend of Oedipus grew from the real experiences of the Pharaoh Akhnaton and his family." (Velikovsky, 243) • Some scholars have "found in the myth the kernel of historical kings in Mycenaean Thebes." (Segal, 58)	***The myth is based on folktales, not history.*** • "I am persuaded that the origin of Oedipus is to be found not in history but in folk-tales." (Nilsson, 103)

The Oedipus story reflects widespread disgust with the practice of infanticide.

- "The emotional charge that Sophocles gives to the motif of exposing the infant suggests that he may be exploring the guilty feelings that parents would have over the practice." (Segal, 50)

The myth does not reflect disgust with infanticide, which was very common in the ancient world.

- "[Jocasta's] treatment of her newborn son would not revolt [ancient Athenians], for exposure of unwanted children was both frequent and legal in Athens." (Letters, 223)

The Sphinx episode was a late add-on to the myth.

- "The main purpose of this essay is to show that the Sphinx is a secondary element in the Oedipus legend, added at some point in the development of the legend to motivate the hero's marriage to his mother." (Edmunds, 147–48)

The Sphinx episode was long an integral part of the myth.

- "Both [Lowell Edmunds and Ulrich Hausmann] grappled with the question of the relation between the Sphinx and the larger Oedipus plot, that is, whether the riddle episode constituted an original part of the Oedipus story. . . . Both arrived at utterly divergent responses. . . . Hausmann concluded that the 'Sphinx-motif' was 'inseparably bound up with the Oedipus saga,' . . . and belonged 'since time immemorial at the apex of Oedipus' illustrious rise.'" (Renger, 24)

Oedipus is a great mythological hero—in fact, the archetypal hero.

- "He does not seem to have been regarded as a legislator; apart from that we may award him full marks [in the twenty-two point scale of mythological heroes]." (Somerset, 175)

The myth of Oedipus is a deviation and departure from the standard hero myth.

- "The difference between [standard hero myths like those of Jason and Perseus] and the Oedipus myth is striking. . . . [For example, the standard hero] has to fight, has to shed blood, in a struggle that mobilizes the energy of his entire being. He has to pierce with his sword or decapitate the horrible, dangerous, monstrous female . . . Oedipus's adventure lacks this lethal act. . . . [T]he Sphinx is not killed, but commits suicide. . . . In place of such noble deeds [as Jason's capture of the Golden Fleece] . . . Oedipus is condemned to a sordid and dishonoring combat in which he beats an old man to death with a stick." (Goux, 16, 23, 35)

Does the play have any broader meaning?

The play is highly symbolic and full of deep meaning.

- "Most critics who discuss this play assume that Sophocles put his whole soul and his deepest convictions into it, that he was trying to 'say something' and not merely trying to enthrall the audience." (O'Brien, 4)
- "The play is, above all other Greek tragedies we know anything about, a play of ideas." (Else, 105)
- "[The play is a] vehicle for the profoundest symbolism." (Whitman, 145)

The play has no meaning (not even that life is meaningless). We shouldn't try to extract any message from it.

- "[The argument that the play is about suffering] is just one more way of smuggling significance into the *Oedipus Tyrannus*; just one more expression of the feeling that this work, by hook or by crook, must be made to mean something. . . . There is no meaning in the *Oedipus Tyrannus*." (Waldock, 123, 128)
- "[T]he idea of the drama is the play itself, not something that can be extracted from it." (Owen, 36)

Oedipus is a symbol.

- "Oedipus is Everyman." (Whitman, 138)
- "[Sophocles's] Oedipus stands for human suffering." (Sheppard, 200)
- "Oedipus is a paradigm of all mankind." (Knox I, 196)
- "[W]e are moved because Oedipus represents man, and his tragedy [represents] the human condition. . . . Oedipus represents all of us." (Kaufmann, 108, 115)

Oedipus is not a symbol. He is just Oedipus.

- "Oedipus is not Everyman: he has been singled out by divinity for a unique fate." (Gould II, 158)
- "Attempts have been made to say that Oedipus 'stands for' something—ideal man, or all humanity, or the like . . . No one who knows the drama of the period will entertain such thoughts . . . Oedipus is not 'man,' but Oedipus." (Adams, 109)
- "Oedipus is a world-wonder in his suffering, in his peculiar destiny he is a freak. He is a man selected out of millions to undergo this staggering fate." (Waldock, 123)

The play is deeply philosophical.

- "Oedipus is the founder of philosophy:

***There is no "philosophy" in* Oedipus Rex.**

the prototypical philosopher." (Goux, 166)

- "I will now offer my own interpretation of *Oedipus Tyrannus* by calling attention to five central [philosophical] themes. . . . [For example] *Oedipus* is a play about *man's radical insecurity.*" (Kaufmann, 114–15)
- In the play, Sophocles steers away from "philosophical embroilment . . . [he] is so careful to allow nothing to divert him from the one thing with which he is concerned: that one thing being, of course, the writing of drama." (Waldock, 122)

What is the play about? What impact is it supposed to have on us?

It's a play about the meaninglessness of life, and therefore it should fill you with deep pessimism.

- "The only lesson to be drawn is one of *total pessimism*, and the only attitude encouraged is that of *uncomprehending resignation*." (Vellacott II, 208) (italics added)
- "How anyone . . . could view the end of the play as optimistic I cannot imagine." (Hester, 45)
- "The effect is to make the audience fear that perhaps the efforts of human beings to create lives for themselves may be devoid of human meaning." (Gould II, 2)
- "*Oedipus* touches another area of anxiety, existential rather than sexual or psychological: the fear of meaninglessness." (Segal, 14)

The play should you make you feel optimistic and hopeful because of the greatness of its hero.

- "[W]e go home from a performance of the *Oedipus* with a feeling of elevation." (Lesky, 132)
- "The end of *Oedipus* is . . . at once the most terrible and optimistic of Sophocles' plays." (Crossett, 141)
- "[Oedipus is] like a man who goes through hell but survives, and survives with the whole of himself—his courage, his passion, his goodness, and his anger—undiminished." (Cameron, 120)
- "The closing note of the tragedy is a renewed insistence on the heroic nature of Oedipus; the play ends as it began, with the greatness of the hero." (Knox I, 194)

The play is a cautionary tale about pride and overconfidence.

- "The *Tyrannus* . . . warns against overconfidence." (Letters, 229)

There is no message in* Oedipus Rex *about pride or overconfidence.

- "It seems unlikely that Sophocles intended to portray Oedipus as punished for wanton pride." (Bowra, 165)
- "Sophocles is certainly not suggesting that Oedipus' ruin is due to his pride." (Kaufmann, 66 n. 41)
- "Oedipus has no particular flaws." (Arrowsmith, 164)

There is an important moral to the play.

- "Oedipus accepts and preaches a further lesson. He knows he has become a signal example of the uncertainty of mortal welfare, and no less than the chorus will he draw the moral that Sophocles' characters so often do: the wisdom and happiness of the man, the danger of excess in mood, fortune and ambition." (Letters, 228)

The play has no moral.

- "There is no moral lesson here." (O'Brien, 15)
- We should reject "the unworthy attempts that have been made to turn this drama into one of sin and atonement and to reduce the unparalleled intensity of its tragic feeling to a mere story with a moral." (Lesky, 130)
- "I hope I have now disposed of the moralizing interpretation." (Dodds, 22)

The play teaches that our lives are ruled by fate. In other words, it's a "tragedy of fate"—in fact, the classic one.

- "[T]here is no doubt that the whole narrative of Oedipus has one main point: the fate was bestowed upon him at birth." (Megas, 141)
- The play stands for the theory that "even the most capable and best-intentioned of men might be marked by the gods for a grisly fate." (Gould II, 7)
- "He could no more have escaped the horror of his fate than he could have eluded birth." (Letters, 218)

Oedipus Rex *is not a "tragedy of fate." Oedipus is completely in charge of his fate, at least within the context of the play.*

- "*Oedipus*, as distinct from other Greek tragedies, is by no means a tragedy of human fate, for which it has so long served as a pattern . . . [I]n all its choruses, not a single one (as happens often enough elsewhere), sings about fate." (Reinhardt, 98)
- "The main events of the play are in fact not even part of the prophecy: Apollo predicted neither the discovery of the truth, the suicide of Jocasta, nor the self-blinding of Oedipus. In the actions of Oedipus in the play 'fate' plays no part at all." (Knox I, 6)
- "The central spring of the action of Sophocles' tragedy is not, as it well might have been, fate but rather Oedipus' imperious passion for the truth." (Kaufmann, 122)

To what extent, if any, was Sophocles influenced by events or circumstances in his life?

Sophocles obviously had the recent Athenian plague in mind while writing the play.

- "*Oedipus Tyrannus* is almost certainly a response to events of this period [such as the plague]." (Segal, 9)
- "The poet's Athenian audience could hardly have avoided thinking of the epidemic in the play in terms of the devastating plague of their own recent experience." (Ahl, 35)

Sophocles could not have had the recent Athenian plague in mind, because he wrote the play* before *the plague

- "Sophocles knew that an earlier playwright named Phrynicus was fined for depicting another real-life sad event (the sacking of Miletus, an Athenian colony, by Persia) and wouldn't have risked receiving a similar fine." (Hester, 60)
- "[T]he description of the plague that opens the play is often thought to have been influenced by the terrible plague that devastated Athens at the outset of the Peloponnesian War, in which Pericles died, along with a quarter of the Athenian population. But although this *may* be true, it is scarcely conclusive, especially since there is also a traditional of literary plague-descriptions going back to the opening of Homer's *Iliad*. Accordingly, some scholars have dated the play earlier than the beginning of the war." (Blondell I, 4)

Sophocles modeled Oedipus on his late friend Pericles, a great man who died from the plague of 429 BC.

- "Sophocles was a close friend of Pericles . . . Pericles' death from the plague may have inspired the theme of Oedipus's fall." (Segal, 10)

Oedipus represents all of Athens, not any particular figure.

- "[T]hese similarities [to Pericles] are only incidental details of a basic pattern which suggests a comparison of Oedipus not to any individual Athenian but to Athens itself." (Knox I, 64)

Sophocles was a very religious man and used the play to send a message about loosening religious standards in contemporary Athens.

- "[E]verything we know about Sophocles suggests that he was pious, even exceptionally so, and that he must have believed the gods' design to be somehow splendid and beneficial,

We don't know how religious Sophocles was—he might not have been very religious. And the play is* not *trying to send any religious message.

- "There is not one supernatural event in it, no gods . . . no monsters . . . nothing that is not, given the mythical situation, inexorably logical and however ruinous it was to the earthly life of this one excellent man." (Gould II, 8)

- The play "shows the power of the gods at every important turn in its development and leaves no doubt about the poet's theological intention. . . . [Oedipus's] failure is a lesson on the omnipotence of the gods and the insecurity of man." (Bowra, 175, 209)
- "Sophocles is supporting the traditional religion against contemporary attacks." (Webster, 102)

human. So far as the action is concerned, it is the most relentlessly secular of the Sophoclean tragedies." (Knox II, 134)

- "We know little of Sophocles' religion. When we sum up what we know of his beliefs we find them meagre in number and depressingly commonplace in quality. . . . There is religion in the *Oedipus Tyrannus* but it is not at all crucial in the drama." (Waldock, 127–28)
- "If Sophocles had wished to reawaken public religion, he could scarcely have chosen a worse way than by preaching the careless power of the gods and the nothingness of man—the very beliefs, in fact, which were themselves the concomitants of the Athenians' lawlessness and moral decay. . . . [T]here is no evidence for thinking that Sophocles differed greatly from the ingrained skepticism of his fellow Athenians." (Whitman, 134)

***Sophocles was trying to restore faith in oracles*.**

- The play demonstrates "that oracles always speak the truth—that nothing man can do will make them false. That . . . is the religious 'lesson' of the play." (Adams, 109)

***Sophocles wasn't trying to restore faith in oracles*.**

- "I would suggest that there is a simple reason for the frequency of oracles in his plays: they are excellent story material." (Waldock, 127)

How did Sophocles intend us to view Oedipus and Jocasta, in terms of their religiosity?

***Oedipus is disrespectful of the gods*.**

- Oedipus is "an autodidact, an atheist, and intellectual." (Goux, 19)

***Oedipus is not disrespectful of the gods*.**

- "[F]ar from being impious and sacrilegeous, he has twice shown his complete faith in the oracle." (Kitto, 226)

- "By no Athenian standards whatsoever are the king and queen godless or sinful in their religious attitude." (Whitman, 136)

***Jocasta is disrespectful of the gods*.**

- "[Jocasta] offends against religion. . . . The audience would expect her to be corrected, and before the scene is over she has been." (Bowra, 208)

***Jocasta is not disrespectful of the gods*.**

- "She is a pious woman." (Blondell II, 113)
- "Jocasta could hardly have avoided impiety more scrupulously." (Kitto, 225)

What's the relevance of mythical events outside of the play?

***The Laius backstory—i.e., the myth of Laius's abduction and rape of Chrysippus—sheds important light on what's really happening in* Oedipus Rex.**

- "The plot begins in infanticide. Parricide is a consequent. . . . Freud emphasizes parricide both in regard to the Oedipal urge and to the primal order, where sons kill the father. He says less about infanticide, about fathers killing their sons. This desire in the father to kill the child we ignore to our peril." (Hillman, 115)
- "The original fault in this story is therefore committed not by Oedipus . . . but by Laius. . . . A new inquiry into Sophocles' *Oedipus the King*, which has been analyzed so often, is indeed possible because we can now assert that the life of the son cannot be considered apart from the life of his father." (Balmary, 8, 13)

***Laius's mythical backstory crime is completely irrelevant to* Oedipus Rex.**

- Sophocles "is not occupied with the father and then the son and then his children. He is wholly occupied with Oedipus." (Cameron, 11)
- "[W]hereas Aeschylus' trilogy on the Oedipus theme . . . is organized around the motif of the inherited curse, it is precisely Sophocles' originality in *Oedipus the King* to have *suppressed* any such explanatory principle. All the material concerning the abduction of Chrysippus and Laius' 'hidden fault,' in other words, is drawn by Balmary from mythological handbooks and knowledge of other Greek sources, but *not* from Sophocles' tragedy." (Rudnytsky, 255)
- "In Sophocles' play there is none of this [focus on Laius's crimes], and Sophocles must have expected his audience to listen to what he was saying, and not to confuse themselves by trying to graft on, as they listened, recollections of perhaps half a dozen other Oedipus

plays that they might have heard." (Kitto, 203)

Sophocles intended us to look at* Oedipus Rex *as part of a greater whole with the other two Oedipus plays (*Antigone *and* Oedipus at Colonus*).

- "I wish to press the case for the unity of the Oedipus cycle." (Rudnytsky, 275)
- "While it is true that the trilogy was not written in this order . . . the three must nevertheless be interpreted as a whole. It makes little sense to assume that Sophocles described the fate of Oedipus and his children in three tragedies without having in mind an inner coherence of the whole." (Fromm, 202 n. 4)

Oedipus Rex *should be analyzed on a stand-alone basis; the other two Theban plays are essentially irrelevant*.

- "The *Oedipus Tyrannus*, single and self-complete, ignores everything but the immediate effect of the discovery on the calamitous hero himself." (Letters, 203)
- "[W]hatever our interpretation of the *Antigone*, there is no ground for drawing deductions from its supposed meaning to the meaning of the *Oedipus Tyrannus*." (Wheelwright, 256)
- In looking at *Oedipus Rex*, we should not "look ahead to a play not yet written," namely, *Oedipus at Colonus*. (Hester, 44)

***Sophocles did not intend us to ask questions about Oedipus's backstory life*.**

- "Such questions do not exist; they take us outside the frame of the picture." (Kitto, 202)
- "[W]hat is not mentioned in the play does not exist." (Dodds, 20)
- "In the *Oedipus Rex*, [Sophocles] passes over the question of whether or not Oedipus is morally guilty of parricide and incest and concentrates wholly on the extent of his knowledge." (Whitman, 124)

***Sophocles intended us to ask questions about Oedipus's backstory life*.**

- "Dodds is as unfair in trying to halt the questioning [of Oedipus's backstory] as he is in paraphrasing the question itself." (Ahl, 5)
- "Nor is it logical for the classicists to argue that a critic cannot bring a fictional character's previous life, conscious or unconscious, into a discussion of his present behavior." (Harshbarger, 10–11)

What should we think about Oedipus's backstory conduct?

It was absurd for Oedipus to allow the drunkard's words to set him on a course that eventually led to Delphi and the horrible prophecy.

- "A temperate man, with the Greek sense of fitness and decorum, would never have permitted the chance words of a man in his cups to send him to Delphi, in the first place." (Barstow, 159)

It made perfect sense for Oedipus to take seriously the drunkard at the banquet.

- "There was nothing extraordinary in his action [consulting his parents and the oracle] . . . [I]t was natural for him to be worried, natural for him to consult the oracle." (Waldock, 115)

It is absurd that Oedipus didn't ask the oracle a follow-up question about his parents.

- "He made the trek to Delphi to learn who his parents were and, upon hearing that he was destined to defile them, immediately abandoned the object of his journey., for the oracle manifestly did not resolve it. . . . Far from distracting him from his parents' identity as it did, the oracle's response made it imperative that he pursue just this quest. . . . The failure to consult the oracle further is an essential ingredient in his downfall and shifts the blame on to his own shoulders . . . Oedipus's ignorance results from his negligence." (Griffith, 52)
- "He assumes for no apparent reason that separation from [Polybus and Merope] must ensure avoidance of the predicted crimes. Yet doubt had sent Oedipus to Delphi in the first place, and that doubt had not been allayed. . . . There is no rational explanation for his assurance that separation from Polybus and Merope guarantees that he will [avoid the fate]." (Kaplan and Kloss, 108)

It's perfectly reasonable that Oedipus didn't ask the oracle a follow-up question about his origins.

- "The very ambiguity of the Delphic response can be construed as confirmation that Polybus and Merope are his real parents." (Crossett, 139)
- "The oracle would not answer his question directly, but *seemed* to warn him against the direst dangers at Corinth . . . [Oedipus's conclusion that the oracle meant that Polybus and Merope were his true parents] is assuredly as reasonable as another." (Waldock, 115)

After receiving the prophecy, it made sense for Oedipus to avoid Corinth.

- His decision to avoid Corinth is "logical and reasonably safe." (Waldock, 116)

It made no sense for Oedipus to avoid Corinth.

- "It might be argued that he cannot afford to return since that alone would be to risk the predicted crimes. But how can we understand that he now runs from Polybus and Merope *as though he had no doubt* of their being his true parents? He assumes for no apparent reason that separation from them must ensure avoidance of the predicted crimes." (Kaplan and Kloss, 208)

Oedipus was the aggressor at the crossroad.

- Oedipus "killed hot-headedly at the crossroads." (Grant, 198)
- "[M]en have suffered worse without recourse to killing." (Kaplan and Kloss, 109)
- "I myself have encountered many people at intersections without murdering any of them." (Griffith, 5)

Laius and his party were the aggressors at the crossroad.

- "Oedipus had not 'attacked' Laius, but merely struck back in self-defense." (Letters, 218)
- "Laius was the aggressor and got what he deserved." (Bowra, 164)
- "I would add from my own experience that it is very annoying and rather dangerous to meet someone who insists on having the road to himself, especially when you are driving a 'narrow' 'hidden' pass in the mountains in Europe." (Cameron, 148 n. 8)
- "The man I murdered: he'd have murdered me!" (Oedipus in *Oedipus at Colonus*, line 614)

Had he been charged with homicide against Laius, Oedipus would have been found innocent under Athenian law.

- "The act was wholly unpremeditated, prompted in equal shares by self-defense and righteous indignation." (Kaufmann, 130)
- "Legally Oedipus would be innocent of deliberate homicide, and by the law of Dracon would be acquitted." (Bowra, 165)
- "I am innocent! Pure in the eyes of the law." (Oedipus in *Oedipus at Colonus*, line 615)

Oedipus would have been found* guilty *under Athenian law.

- "[B]y murdering the belligerent stranger, his superior and elder, along with his retinue, including the sacred herald, while they were engaged upon official religious and state business, Oedipus violated the prerogatives of Zeus of Strangers, the respect due to superior and elders, and the principle of fitting retaliation; he is therefore guilty of murder." (Griffith, 5)

As to patricide (as opposed to ordinary homicide) and incest, Oedipus acted stupidly by killing a man older than himself and marrying an older woman right after receiving the oracle's prophecy.

- "The means to resist the prophecies are, after all, not difficult to achieve. He need only refrain from killing a man and marrying a woman, both a generation older than himself." (Kaplan and Kloss, 108)
- "In no circumstances should he have killed a man, or married a woman, twenty years or more older than himself." (Kitto, 227–28)
- After receiving the oracle, Oedipus should have adopted "a life of non-violence and celibacy rather than murdering the first people he met and marrying in the first city to which he came." (Griffith, 52)

Oedipus deserves no blame for killing his own father and marrying his own mother.

- "[W]hen anyone has had his head almost split open he can hardly be expected to weigh the possibilities of the assailant proving his unknown father . . . [A] man savagely struck on the head with a two-pronged goad is not for the moment required to act as a man of intellect." (Letters, 218)
- "He ought, we are told [by other scholars], to have been put upon his guard [by the oracle]. No jury, I venture to assert, and a fortiori no intelligent audience, would find him guilty on such grounds." (Sheppard, 194)

Oedipus bears the blame for the patricide and incest because he still had free will.

- "[T]he prediction does not exonerate Oedipus, for predestination does not, paradoxically, constitute a compulsion. Dodds know this. His own book *The Greeks and the Irrational* [said that a prediction leaves room for free will]. [H]e killed Laius by free choice, thereby abdicating any claim to essential moral innocence." (Griffith, 53)

Oedipus doesn't bear any blame for the patricide and incest, because those acts were preordained by the gods.

- "Sophocles has provided a conclusive answer to those who suggest that Oedipus could, and therefore should, have avoided his fate. The oracle was *unconditional* (line 790): it did not say 'If you do so-and-so you will kill your father'; it simply said 'You will kill your father, you will sleep with your mother.' And what an oracle predicts is bound to happen. Oedipus does what he can to evade his destiny. . . . But it is quite certain from the first that his best efforts will be unavailing." (Dodds, 21)

Oedipus was self-destructive, perhaps suicidal, in his early life.

- Oedipus exhibited at the crossroads and in the encounter with the Sphinx "a

Oedipus was never self-destructive or suicidal.

- "It was a mistake . . . to suggest (with some facile psychoanalysis) that suicidal despair." These were "the despairing act of a man who no longer cares to live [because of the horrible prophecy]." (Crossett, 136–39)

Oedipus somehow wished to destroy himself." (Vickers, 507)

Answering the Sphinx's riddle didn't require all that much intelligence.

- Oedipus wrongly thought "he had overcome the Sphinx sent by the mother-goddess merely because he had solved her childishly simple riddle." (Jung, 372)
- "His ability to decipher the riddle of the Sphinx has been much misinterpreted. Riddles are for children, particularly that one, and Oedipus's ability to solve it indicates no genius." (Cohen, 179)

Answering the Sphinx's riddle required great intelligence.

- "His decision to tackle the Sphinx . . . shows . . . extreme intelligence." (Crossett, 136)

It's absurd that Oedipus never inquired into the circumstances of his predecessor's death.

- "It is already contrary to the notion of verisimilitude that Oedipus, who has been king for such a long time, should not know how his predecessor died; but that he did not even know whether it was in the country or in town that this murder was committed, and that he should give neither the least reason nor the least excuse for his ignorance, I confess that I do not know any term to express such an absurdity." (Voltaire, 36)
- "There is no real way to explain this." (Waldock, 124)

There are perfectly plausible reasons why Oedipus never looked deeply into the matter.

- "Newly installed as king of a country being ravaged by a monster, involved with a new marriage and new duties, he would naturally have been far more concerned about the future than the past." (Segal, 79)
- "That he does not discover [the truth] earlier seems to me perfectly natural." (Crossett, 136)

What should we think about Oedipus's onstage conduct and character?

Oedipus is a great king who thinks of nothing but the good of his own city.

Oedipus is not nearly as great as his admirers claim.

- Oedipus is "extraordinarily good." (Adams, 110)
- Oedipus is "clearly a very great man." (Knox I, 50)
- "[Critics] have gone over the play with a microscope looking for moral faults and have duly found them—for neither here nor anywhere else did Sophocles portray that insipid and unlikely character, the man of perfect virtue. . . . The legitimate question is 'Did Sophocles intend us to think of Oedipus as a good man?' This *can* be answered . . . by looking at what the characters in the play say about him. And by that test the answer is 'Yes.'" (Dodds, 19)
- Oedipus is "a great man, a public benefactor, and a benevolent ruler." (Blondell II, 93)

- Oedipus's supposed civic-mindedness "should not be overstressed: which of us in his place would have let Thebes languish in the plague or have failed to pursue the hunt for the killer of Laius." (Gould I, 248)
- The picture of Oedipus as a selfless king who will do everything to rescue his city "founders on the simple fact that it never occurred to Sophocles to mention that the city in fact was delivered." (Kitto, 209)

Oedipus is a tyrant in the negative sense of that word.

- "[H]e acts like a tyrant." (Kitto, 221)
- "He is egocentric and paranoid: the very embodiment of Plato's tyrannical soul in so many ways." (Ahl, 262)

Oedipus is not a tyrant in the negative sense of that word.

- "King for some sixteen years, there is no suggestion that he had ever been anything but an admirable ruler, no hint that he had ever played the tyrant." (Letters, 223)

Oedipus represents all that is best and most civilized in Athenian society.

- Oedipus "embodies the ideal of the Sophistic enlightenment." (Ramfos, 5)
- "At every turn [the play] associates Oedipus with the scientific, questioning, and at the same time confident attitude of the fifth-century Greek, especially the Athenian, whose city was 'the council chamber of Greek wisdom.'" (Knox I, 16–20)

Oedipus is a throwback to a time much earlier than the enlightened fifth century BC of Sophocles.

- "He is stubborn, bullheaded, frequently stupid, often rude, and admittedly and unashamedly untutored; in short, a primitive, pre-Hellenic chieftain." (Cohen, 179)
- "He elevates his ignorance into his governing principle, acknowledging that he is 'the Know-Nothing Oedipus.'" (Griffith, 53)

Oedipus is full of arrogance and undue and excessive pride on stage—in short, hubris ("hybris" in Greek).

- Oedipus "shows fits of *hubris* in his over-confident, rash handling" of the situation. (Grant, 198)
- "What we may censure in him, if we choose to, is a kind of cocksureness. This it was that betrayed him into hybris." (Kitto, 225)
- "He has too much pride in his keen intelligence." (Winnington-Ingram, 203)

Oedipus doesn't exhibit excessive pride.

- "[T]here seems to be a tendency [among scholars] to seek in Oedipus some hybris to account for all that happens. It is not there." (Adams, 112)
- "Of course it is not true; Oedipus is not guilty of hubris." (Owen, 34)
- "A modern reader might be tempted to see [Oedipus's declarations of his own greatness] pronouncements as unattractively boastful. . . . But in the mouth of a Greek hero, they are simply statements of fact." (Blondell II, 97)

Oedipus is too masculine.

- Oedipus "[o]verestimat[ed] his intellect in a typically masculine way." (Jung, 373)
- Oedipus is "hypermasculine"—a man who "acts in such a way as to exaggerate 'masculine' traits as a defense against his knowledge that he is not a man." (Harshbarger, 51)

Oedipus is insufficiently masculine, having never achieved true manhood.

- "[T]he Oedipus myth is a myth of . . . avoided masculine initiation." (Goux, 3)
- "Cohabitation with Jocasta should thus be viewed primarily as a symbolically homosexual and only epiphenomenally as a heterosexual act, Oedipus' true love-hate object being the now feminized homosexual ogre Laius." (Devereux, 221)

Oedipus is a much better man than Creon.

- Oedipus is "far superior to the king Creon in character as well as in intellect." (Ehrenberg, 76)
- Creon is "essentially unheroic and scarcely admirable." (Blondell II, 112)
- "Creon is not a character who excites our sympathy." (Kirkwood, 131)

In the course of the play, Creon is the better man.

- "The modesty of Creon is a better example than the towering self-confidence of Oedipus." (Kitto, 242)

Oedipus is extremely intelligent.

- Oedipus is "exceptionally intelligent," "extraordinarily wise." (Kaufmann, 115, 121)
- "The swift action is firmly based on reflection, and that reflection is the working of a great intelligence." (Knox I, 18)
- Oedipus exhibits "extreme intelligence." (Crossett, 136)

Oedipus is not particularly intelligent.

- He is "not unusually bright." (Cohen, 179)
- "He does not possess, as far as we can make out, an intelligence of piercing quickness or very remarkable reach. . . . It seems difficult for him, when excited, to hold more than one thing before his gaze at a time, so that he rushes into actions that are absurdly ill-judged . . . [H]e lags noticeably in putting two and two together." (Waldock, 113, 124)
- Aside from the Sphinx episode, "there is nothing else in the legend that would characterize Oedipus as intelligent." (Edmunds, 160–61)

Oedipus is a great interrogator.

- "Anyone who has watched Oedipus ask one of his series of pointed and bulldog questions knows that he is shrewd and tenacious. He never wastes a question." (Crossett, 136)

Oedipus is not a particularly good interrogator.

- "True, Oedipus uses the vocabulary of such investigation, and he poses as a cross-examiner in the Socratic manner. But . . . he focuses so intently on one area of inquiry that he overlooks important details and ambiguities in other areas." (Ahl, 25)

Oedipus is unfair to Teiresias and Creon.

- Oedipus "is in fact unfair both to Tiresias and to Creon." (Gould II, 7)
- Oedipus's treatment of Teiresias and Creon is "grossly unfair" and "based on suspicions that are almost childish." (Ehrenberg, 76)
- "In his angry scenes with Teiresias and Creon he has lost some of our sympathy and revealed dangerous tendencies in his character." (Bowra, 185)

Oedipus is not unfair to Teiresias and Creon.

- "I would argue that his anger is excessive only because we know Creon and Teiresias are innocent." (Crossett, 144)
- "Why should he believe this preposterous statement about himself? Teiresias offered no proof for what he said, but based it simply upon his prophetic art, which is not sufficient in this case to convince even the naïve chorus. The suspicion which rises in Oedipus, though wrong, is in no sense unnatural." (Whitman, 130–31)

- "Oedipus can hardly be blamed for considering Creon guilty." (Kaufmann, 104)
- "[I]n his situation most of us would have done the same." (Kitto, 225)
- Consider also that "Oedipus has no monopoly on anger in the play." (Girard, 69)

Oedipus is a great hero of the truth.

- Oedipus "goes boldly to meet it and grapples it with a burning passion for the truth and a readiness to suffer that makes him one of the greatest figures of the tragic stage." (Lesky, 131)
- Oedipus has a "passion for truth." (Crossett, 140)
- "Characteristic of his intelligence is his insistence on complete knowledge and clarity. . . . [H]e admits no mysteries, no half-truths, no half-measures. He will never rest content with less than the full truth . . . [H]e will accept nothing incomplete, nothing untested, only the full truth." (Knox I, 18, 30)

In hunting down the truth, Oedipus didn't do anything all that special.

- "[I]s Oedipus' persistence really a feat that none of us would be capable of? . . . And who wouldn't keep searching for the identity of his parents in response to Tiresias' absurd-sounding accusations or Jocasta's sudden, inexplicable plea?" (Gould I, 247)
- "It should be clear from this [this discussion] that Oedipus cannot always be described as a man who must have 'complete knowledge and clarity,' or as one whose 'intelligence will accept nothing incomplete, nothing untested, only the full truth.'" (Harshbarger, 9, quoting Knox)

The truth surfaced only because of Oedipus's efforts.

- "I cannot understand Sir Maurice Bowra's idea that the gods *force* on Oedipus the knowledge of what he has done. They do nothing of the kind; on the contrary, what fascinates us is the spectacle of a man freely choosing, from the highest motives, a series of actions which lead to his own ruin. . . . The immediate cause of Oedipus' ruin is not 'Fate' or 'the gods'—no oracle said that he must discover the truth—and still less does it lie in his own weakness; what causes his ruin is his own strength and courage, his loyalty to Thebes, and his loyalty to the truth." (Dodds, 23)

The truth would have surfaced whatever Oedipus did or didn't do.

- "[S]o many signs point to Oedipus's state as incestuous parricide that in the random workings of the world [not much needed to happen] for the Truth to be revealed." (Griffith, 63)
- "It is often presented as self-evident, indeed blazingly clear, that Sophocles chose to dramatize Oedipus' discovery of his old crimes, not the actual commission of those crimes, because the former are self-willed, whereas the latter were not. Only in this way, it is asserted, could he play down the traditional role of fate in the legend and make of it a

- "The catastrophe of Oedipus is that he discovers his own identity; and for this discovery he is first and last responsible. . . . The autonomy of his actions is emphasized by the series of attempts made by others to stop the investigation. He is four times advised to drop the matter and be content with ignorance . . . He rejects the advice every time." (Knox I, 6, 12)

moving play, one about a free agent acting on his own. But . . . the self-revelation was not really self-caused. The gods sent the plague, then directed Oedipus to find the killer of Laius; and perhaps the god sent the messenger from Corinth as well." (Gould I, 249)

What did Oedipus know and when did he know it?

Sophocles intended us to believe that by the time of his marriage to Jocasta, and certainly long before the play begins, Oedipus must have known that he was guilty of patricide and incest.

- "The thesis which I hope to establish by a detailed examination of the whole play is that Sophocles intended the *careful reader* (and perhaps some unusually acute spectators) to see Oedipus as having been aware of his true relationship to Laius and Jocasta ever since the time of his marriage." (Vellacott I, 104)

Sophocles never intended us to think that Oedipus remained married to Jocasta for all those years knowing she was his mother.

- "Vellacott's thesis is unconvincing, and has deservedly met with general condemnation." (Rudnytsky, 269)
- "[Sophocles's treatment of the story] not only makes it impossible for Oedipus to infer correctly who he is, and why, but also guarantees his innocence. Failure to observe this crucial point has led recently to a remarkable misinterpretation of the play by Philip Vellacott." (Vickers, 547 n. 9)

Did Oedipus even commit the "oedipal" acts?

There's no solid evidence that Oedipus committed patricide or incest; we believe that he did because we know the myth, not because of anything in the play itself.

- "The charges against Oedipus are

Oedipus did of course commit the acts for which his name is a byword—patricide and incest.

- "This chapter critiques the argument of [Frederick] Ahl . . . and advocates the traditional idea that Oedipus did in based entirely on his own testimony against himself and unsupported hearsay." (Ahl, 21)

fact do what he convicts himself of." (Griffith, 29)

- "The longer one ponders [the thesis that Oedipus was framed] the more far-fetched [it] seem[s]." (Rudnytsky, 354)

Oedipus was a scapegoat.

- "Oedipus is responsible for the ills that have befallen his people. He has become a prime example of the human scapegoat. . . . The entire investigation is a feverish hunt for a scapegoat, which finally turns against the very man who first loosed the hounds." (Girard, 77–78)

Oedipus was not a scapegoat.

- René Girard's scapegoat theory "differs from Sophocles' [play] on four major points," involves "double" and "incompatible" reasoning, and is just generally "odd." (Griffith, 32–34)
- "Girard's argument breaks down in several crucial respects. . . . Beginning in plausibility, Girard by imperceptible steps arrives at absurdity." (Rudnytsky, 346)

What about the Oedipus complex?

The Oedipus complex accounts for the power of the play.

- "His destiny moves us only because it might have been ours—because the oracle laid the same curse upon us before our birth as upon him. It is the fate of all of us, perhaps, to direct our first sexual impulse toward our mother and our first hatred and our first murderous wish against our father." (Freud, 296)

The Oedipus complex does not account for the power of the play.

- "[T]here is an immediate, obvious difficulty with the Freudian hypothesis as applied to this play, that if its appeal lies in the 'peculiar material,' then there is no explanation of why Voltaire's *Oedipe*, for example, is not as effective as Sophocles.'" (Cameron, ix)
- "It can still be argued that the Oedipus myth is evocative of universal human psycho-sexual experience; however, the common denominator of this experience is incest aversion, not incestuous desire." (Sugiyama, 311–12)

Oedipus himself has an Oedipus complex. In other words, Oedipus is not just a convenient symbol of the Oedipus complex but a living, breathing case of it.

- "By setting out to seek his fortune (and giving himself over to free associations) Oedipus is going to fulfill his destiny (that is to say his fantasy). . . . One thing is certain, that Oedipus finds happiness in his mother's bed. In repossessing his mother he rediscovers that first happiness that he lost when he was so early separated from her and exposed on Cithaeron." (Vernant, 103–108, quoting Didier Anzieu)
- "The man Oedipus, as we have him in this play, is as much possessed of oedipal wishes as any character we can find in fiction. . . . The oedipally driven neurotic who weds a much older woman, or who rages unjustifiably against authority figures, relates to such people for their resemblance to his own parents. . . . And so we have further reason to believe he murders the one, and weds the other, in part because they are parental figures to him." (Kaplan and Kloss, 7, 109)

It makes no sense to claim that Oedipus himself has an Oedipus complex.

- "His marriage to Jocasta was a matter of civic duty. . . . There is no indication in Sophocles' play or in any of the surviving records of the ancient myth that Oedipus and Jocasta were drawn to each other erotically." (Wheelwright, 252)
- "If Sophocles had wanted to, he could easily have suggested it [an oedipal feeling toward Jocasta]. But instead he wiped out everything in the personal relations between the husband and wife that, before the final revelation, might hint at the links between a son and a mother." (Vernant, 108–109)

The play is deeply sexual, at least symbolically.

- Oedipus "describes the place where Laius was killed in terms that anatomically are highly suggestive of the outer female genitalia." (Harshbarger, 33)
- The triumph over the Sphinx "had something to do with sexual knowledge" because solving the riddle "enabled Oedipus to come into his kingdom by marrying his own mother." (Bettelheim, 128)

The play is not about sex in any way and is not the least bit erotic.

- "[I]t seems difficult to avoid the conclusion that the play itself is not very much concerned with sexual desire as such, or with deep-hidden sexual urges toward one's parent, combined with aggressive wishes toward one's parental rival. . . . So far as the intentional content of his desire is concerned, Jocasta is simply a well-placed eligible stranger." (Nussbaum, 43)
- "Lust and the Complex, then, have nothing to do with this play but are intruders from our own age, and like other intruders do nothing but cause confusion." (Kitto, 23)

Creon has an incestuous relationship with his sister Jocasta.

- "[There is an] incestuous attachment between Creon and Jocasta." (Vernant, 109, quoting Didier Anzieu)

There is no incestuous relationship between Creon and Jocasta.

- "There is not a scrap of evidence for an incestuous attachment between the brother and sister." (Vernant, 109)

The play is fundamentally about hostility to, and rebellion against, the father.

- "If we interpret *King Oedipus* in light of the whole trilogy, the assumption seems plausible that the real issue . . . is the conflict between father and son and not the problem of incest." (Fromm, 204)

In the course of the play, Oedipus shows nothing but love for his father, whether Laius or Polybus.

- "[A]lthough Oedipus does commit the two crimes for which his name is a byword, in the course of the play he actually shows his love for his father [Laius] and tries to kill his mother." (Rudnytsky, 258)
- "Fromm distorts the evidence by speaking repeatedly of the three Theban plays as a 'trilogy.'" (Wheelwright, 256)

Two strange debates: What was the width of the road? And did Oedipus walk with a limp?

The road was narrow.

- "[Karl] Abraham points out that Oedipus' encounter with Laius is said to take place at . . . a 'narrow pass.'" (Rudnytsky, 261)

The road was wide.

- The road is wide enough that "giving way would not be difficult." (Cuddihy, 56, quoting Freud's letter to Karl Abraham in response to the latter's assertion that the road is narrow)

Oedipus walks with a limp.

- Oedipus is "majestic, but for his tell-tale limp" and "lame" (Fergusson, 31, 43)

Oedipus does not walk with a limp.

- "Francis Fergusson's assumption that Sophocles' Oedipus has a 'tell-tale limp' is surely false." (Kaufmann, 113)
- "[T]here is no reason to think that Oedipus is portrayed with a limp." (Griffith, 32)

What is the name of the play?	
• Many scholars call it *Oedipus Rex* or *King Oedipus* or *Oedipus the King* (e.g., C. M. Bowra, Ruby Blondell, Alister Cameron, Thomas Gould, Albert Cook, Michael O'Brien). Evidently, they believe the play should be so called because Oedipus is the hereditary king of Thebes.	• Many scholars call it *Oedipus Tyrannus* (e.g., Charles Segal, Bernard Knox, A. J. A. Waldock, Luci Berkowitz and Theodore F. Brunner, E.T. Owens, J.T. Sheppard). Evidently, they believe it should be so called because Oedipus obtained power through his own deeds.

SOURCES CITED IN TABLE

The information in the table above is derived from the following sources, generally referred to in parentheses by the last name of the author. Reference names for those sources identified other than by the author's last name are given in parentheses following the bibliographical information about the source.

Adams, S. M. *Sophocles the Playwright*. Toronto: University of Toronto Press, 1957. Excerpt reprinted as "Oedipus Tyrannus" in *Oedipus Tyrannus*, edited by Luci Berkowitz and Theodore Brunner, 108–12. New York: W. W. Norton & Co., 1970.

Ahl, Frederick. *Sophocles' Oedipus: Evidence and Self-Conviction*. Ithaca, NY: Cornell University Press, 1991.

Arrowsmith, William. "The Criticism of Greek Tragedy." *Tulane Drama Review* 3, no. 3 (1959). Reprinted in *Oedipus Rex: A Mirror for Greek Drama*, edited by Albert Cook, 155–69. Belmont, CA: Wadsworth Publishing, 1963.

Balmary, Marie. *Psychoanalyzing Psychoanalysis: Freud and the Hidden Fault of the Father*. Translated by Ned Lukacher. Baltimore: Johns Hopkins University Press, 1982.

Barstow, Marjorie L. "Oedipus Rex: A Typical Greek Tragedy." In *The Greek Genius and Its Influence*, edited by Lane Cooper, 156–62. Ithaca, NY: Cornell University Press, 1972.

Bettelheim, Bruno. *The Uses of Enchantment: The Meaning and Importance of Fairy Tales*. New York: Vintage Books, 2010.

Blondell, Ruby. "Introduction." In Sophocles. *King Oidipous*. Translated by Ruby Blondell. Newburyport, MA: Focus Publishing, 2003. ("Blondell I")

_____. "Essay." In Sophocles. *King Oidipous*. Translated by Ruby Blondell. Newburyport, MA: Focus Publishing, 2003. ("Blondell II")

Bowra, C. M. *Sophoclean Tragedy*. London: Oxford University Press, 1964.

Cameron, Alister. *The Identity of Oedipus the King*. New York: New York University Press, 1968.

Cohen, Robert. "Oedipus and the Absurd Life." In *Oedipus Tyrannus*, edited by Luci Berkowitz and Theodore Brunner, 178–82. New York: W. W. Norton & Co., 1970.

Crossett, John. "The *Oedipus Rex*." In *Oedipus Rex: A Mirror for Greek Drama*, edited by Albert Cook, 134–55. Belmont, CA: Wadsworth Publishing, 1963.

Cuddihy, John Murray. *The Ordeal of Civility: Freud, Marx, Lévi-Strauss, and the Jewish Struggle with Modernity*. Boston: Beacon Press, 1987.

Devereux, George. "Why Oedipus Killed Laius: A Note on the Complementary Oedipus Complex in Greek Tragedy." In *Oedipus: A Folklore Casebook*, edited by Lowell Edmunds and Alan Dundes, 215–33. Madison: University of Wisconsin Press, 1995.

Dodds, E. R. "On Misunderstanding the *Oedipus Rex*." *Greece & Rome* 13, no. 1 (1966). Reprinted in *Twentieth Century Interpretations of Oedipus Rex*, edited by Michael J. O'Brien, 17–29. Englewood Cliffs, NJ: Prentice-Hall Inc., 1968.

Edmunds, Lowell. "The Sphinx in the Oedipus Legend." In *Oedipus: A Folklore Casebook*, edited by Lowell Edmunds and Alan Dundes, 147–73. Madison: University of Wisconsin Press, 1995.

Ehrenberg, Victor. *Sophocles and Pericles*. Oxford: Basil Blackwell & Mott Ltd., 1954. Excerpt reprinted in *Twentieth Century Interpretations of Oedipus Rex*, edited by Michael J. O'Brien, 74–80. Englewood Cliffs, NJ: Prentice-Hall Inc., 1968.

Else, Gerald F. *Aristotle's Poetics: The Argument.* Cambridge, MA: Harvard University Press, 1957. Excerpt reprinted in *Oedipus Rex: A Mirror for Greek Drama*, edited by Albert Cook, 104–106. Belmont, CA: Wadsworth Publishing, 1963.

Fergusson, Francis. *The Idea of a Theater: A Study of Ten Plays; The Art of Drama in Changing Perspective*. Garden City, NY: Doubleday Anchor Books, 1955.

Freud, Sigmund. *The Interpretation of Dreams*. Translated by James Strachey. New York: Avon Books, 1965.

Fromm, Erich. *The Forgotten Language: An Introduction to the Understanding of Dreams, Fairy Tales, and Myths*. New York: Random House, 1956.

Girard, René. *Violence and the Sacred*. Translated by Patrick Gregory. Baltimore: Johns Hopkins University Press, 1979.

Gould, Thomas. "The Innocence of Oedipus: The Philosophers on Oedipus the King." Pt. 3, *Arion* 5, no. 4 (1966). Excerpt reprinted in *Oedipus Tyrannus*, edited by Luci Berkowitz and Theodore Brunner, 246–49. New York: W. W. Norton & Co., 1970. ("Gould I")

———. "Introduction." In Sophocles, *Oedipus the King*. Translated by Thomas Gould, 1–12. Englewood Cliffs, NJ: Prentice-Hall, 1970. ("Gould II")

Goux, Jean-Joseph. *Oedipus, Philosopher*. Translated by Catherine Porter. Stanford, CA: Stanford University Press, 1993.

Grant, Michael. *Myths of the Greeks and Romans*. New York: New American Library, 1962.

Griffith, R. Drew. *The Theatre of Apollo: Divine Justice and Sophocles'* Oedipus the King. Montreal: McGill-Queen's University Press, 1996.

Harshbarger, Karl. *Sophocles' Oedipus*. Washington, DC: University Press of America, 1979.

Hester, D. A. "Oedipus and Jonah." *Proceedings of the Cambridge Philological Society* 23 (1977): 32–60.

Hillman, James. "Oedipus Revisited." In *Oedipus Variations: Studies in Literature and Psychoanalysis*. Woodstock, CT: Spring Publications, 1995.

Jung, Karl. "Symbols of Transformation." In *Oedipus: Myth and Drama*, edited by Martin Kallich, Andrew MacLeish, and Gertrude Schoenbohm, 368–73. Indianapolis: The Odyssey Press, 1968.

Kaplan, Morton, and Robert Kloss. *The Unspoken Motive: A Guide to Psychoanalytic Literary Criticism*. New York: The Free Press, 1973.

Kaufmann, Walter. *Tragedy and Philosophy*. Princeton, NJ: Princeton University Press, 1992.

Kirkwood, G. M. *A Study of Sophoclean Drama*. Ithaca, NY: Cornell University Press, 1994.

Kitto, H. D. F. *Poiesis: Structure and Thought*. Berkeley: University of California Press, 1965.

Knox, Bernard. *Oedipus at Thebes: Sophocles' Tragic Hero and His Time*. New Haven, CT: Yale University Press, 1998. ("Knox 1998")

———. "Introduction." In *Sophocles: Three Theban Tragedies*. Translated by Robert Fagles, 131–53. New York: Penguin Books, 1984. ("Knox 1984")

Lesky, Albin. *A History of Greek Literature*. Translated by James Willis and Cornelis de Heer. New York: Thomas Y. Crowell Co., 1966. Excerpt reprinted in *Oedipus Tyrannus*, edited by Luci Berkowitz and Theodore Brunner, 128–32. New York: W. W. Norton & Co., 1970.

Letters, F. J. H. *The Life and Work of Sophocles*. London: Sheed and Ward, 1953.

Megas, Giorgio A. "On the Oedipus Myth." In *Oedipus: A Folklore Casebook*, edited by Lowell Edmunds and Alan Dundes, 133–46. Madison: University of Wisconsin Press, 1995.

Nilsson, Martin. *The Mycenaean Origin of Greek Mythology*. Berkeley: University of California Press, 1972.

Nussbaum, Martha C. "The Oedipus Rex and the Ancient Unconscious." In *Freud and Forbidden Knowledge*, edited by Peter L. Rudnytsky and Ellen Handler Spitz, 42–71. New York: New York University Press, 1994.

O'Brien, Michael. "Introduction." In *Twentieth Century Interpretations of Oedipus Rex*, edited by Michael J. O'Brien, 1–16. Englewood Cliffs, NJ: Prentice-Hall Inc., 1968.

Owen, E. T. "Drama in Sophocles' *Oedipus Tyrannus*." Reprinted in *Twentieth Century Interpretations of Oedipus Rex*, edited by Michael J. O'Brien, 30–40. Englewood Cliffs, NJ: Prentice-Hall Inc., 1968.

Plutarch. *On Curiosity*. Translated by Michael J. O'Brien. Reprinted in *Twentieth Century Interpretations of Oedipus Rex*, edited by Michael J. O'Brien, 99. Englewood Cliffs, NJ: Prentice-Hall Inc., 1968.

Ramfos, Stelio. *Fate and Ambiguity in* Oedipus the King. Translated by Norman Russell. Boston: Somerset Hall Press, 2006.

Reinhardt, Karl. *Sophokles*. Translated by Carol R. Cook and Albert Cook. Excerpt reprinted in *Oedipus Rex: A Mirror for Greek Drama*, edited by Albert Cook, 97–99. Belmont, CA: Wadsworth Publishing, 1963.

Renger, Almut-Barbara. *Oedipus and the Sphinx: The Threshold Myth from Sophocles through Freud to Cocteau*. Translated by Duncan Smart and David Rice with John Hamilton. Chicago: University of Chicago Press, 2013.

Rose, H. J. *Modern Methods in Classical Mythology*. St. Andrews: W. C. Henderson & Son, 1930.

Rudnytsky, Peter L. *Freud and Oedipus*. New York: Columbia University Press, 1987.

Segal, Charles. *Oedipus Tyrannus: Tragic Heroism and the Limits of Knowledge*. New York: Twayne Publishers, 1993.

Sheppard, J. T. *The Oedipus Tyrannus of Sophocles*. Cambridge: Cambridge University Press, 1920. Excerpt reprinted as "The Innocence of Oedipus" in *Oedipus Tyrannus*, edited by Luci Berkowitz and Theodore Brunner, 191–204. New York: W. W. Norton & Co., 1970.

Somerset, FitzRoy Richard (Lord Raglan). *The Hero: A Study in Tradition, Myth and Drama*. Mineola, NY: Dover Publications Inc., 2003.

Sophocles. *Oedipus at Colonus*. Translated by Robert Fagles. New York: Penguin Books, 1984. ("Oedipus in *Oedipus at Colonus*")

Sugiyama, Michelle Scalise. "New Science, Old Myth: An Evolutionary Critique of the Oedipal Paradigm." In *Evolution, Literature, and Film: A Reader*, edited by Brian Boyd, Joseph Carroll, and Jonathan Gotschall, 306–15. New York: Columbia University Press, 2010.

Van Nortwick, Thomas. *Oedipus: The Meaning of a Masculine Life*. Norman: University of Oklahoma Press, 1998.

Velikovsky, Immanuel. *Oedipus and Akhnaton: Myth and History*. New York: Pocket Books, 1960.

Vellacott, Phillip. *Sophocles and Oedipus: A Study of Oedipus Tyrannus*. London: Macmillan Press, 1971. ("Vellacott 1971")

———. "The Guilt of Oedipus." In *Oedipus Tyrannus*, edited by Luci Berkowitz and Theodore Brunner, 207–18. New York: W. W. Norton & Co., 1970. ("Vellacott 1970")

Vernant, Jean-Pierre. "Oedipus without the Complex." In *Myth and Tragedy in Ancient Greece*. Translated by Janet Lloyd. New York: Zone Books, 1990.

Vickers, Brian. *Towards Greek Tragedy*. London: Longman, 1973.

Voltaire, F. M. A. "Letters on Oedipus, Letter III: Containing the Critique of the *Oedipus* of Sophocles." Reprinted in *Sophocles: The Classical Heritage*, edited by R. D. Dawe, 35–44. New York: Garland Publishing, Inc., 1996.

Waldock, A. J. A. *Sophocles the Dramatist*. Cambridge: Cambridge University Press, 1951. Excerpt reprinted in *Oedipus Tyrannus*, edited by Luci Berkowitz and Theodore Brunner, 113–28. New York: W. W. Norton & Co., 1970

Webster, T. L. *An Introduction to Sophocles*. Oxford: The Clarendon Press, 1936. Excerpt reprinted in *Twentieth Century Interpretations of Oedipus Rex*, edited by Michael J. O'Brien, 102. Englewood Cliffs, NJ: Prentice-Hall Inc., 1968.

Wheelwright, Philip. *The Burning Fountain: A Study in the Language of Symbolism*. Bloomington: Indiana University Press, 1954. Excerpt reprinted in *Oedipus Tyrannus*, edited by Luci Berkowitz and Theodore Brunner, 250–59. New York: W. W. Norton & Co., 1970.

Whitman, Cedric. *Sophocles: A Study of Heroic Humanism*. Cambridge, MA: Harvard University Press, 1951.

Winnington-Ingram, R. P. *Sophocles: An Interpretation*. Cambridge: Cambridge University Press, 1990.

Acknowledgments

I want to thank the following people:

My editor, Adam Rosen, for helping me get it ready for prime time and for often figuring out before I did what I was trying to say; my copy editor, Molly Pisani, for improving it in ways that went way beyond catching typos and conforming the text and notes to the style manual, and for teaching me much useful information about the rules of writing (including the fact that there should be commas around her name just now!); and Alex Tritell, for invaluable research assistance and, in the last couple of months before completion, excellent company.

For many helpful suggestions and unbounded encouragement over the years: Ronald Collins; Dr. Sinan Duzyurek; Gabrielle Glaser; Dorothy Hearst; Edward Hearst; Professor Marti Hearst of the University of California, Berkeley; Professor Patrick Hogan of the University of Connecticut; Professor Douglas Keesey of Cal Poly, San Luis Obispo; Father Ronald Murphy of Georgetown University; Dr. Kenneth X. Robbins; and John Schneider. I'm particularly grateful to Ronald Collins and John Schneider for the amount of time they spent speaking with me about the concept of the Circular Detective.

My mother, my brother, and my late father, for love and support over many years, with advance apologies to my mother for any grief she might be given about her son's obsession with Oedipus!

My wonderful children, Adam and Sophia, for all those times when I was busy pondering and researching *Oedipus Rex* when I could have been doing something with them (although I'm sure that as they got older they minded less and less).

Sophocles, for writing a masterpiece the meaning of which we will be pondering and debating until the heat death of the universe.

Above all others, my beloved wife, Elisa. Without her love, support, and faith, this book would not exist. In every possible sense, it's as much her book as it is mine. She suffered through it for more years than anyone should have to suffer through *anything*. But she did a lot more than suffer. She supported me, every step of the way, and made countless invaluable suggestions. As is the case with most husbands and wives, she's a lot smarter than I am and saw long before I did the form this book should take. It took me ridiculously long to figure out she was right (once again, ripeness is all). After many years, it finally entered my inordinately thick skull, and it is due to her that the book not only exists but is in the form in which you see it. For all that, and for more things than could ever be listed, I dedicate this book to her.

COPYRIGHT PERMISSIONS

Publishing Group, a division of Penguin Random House LLC.

Excerpts from *All My Sons* by Arthur Miller, copyright © 1947, renewed 1975 by Arthur Miller. Used by permission of Penguin Books, an imprint of Penguin Publishing Group, a division of Penguin Random House LLC, and by permission of the Wylie Agency LCC for UK and Commonwealth (excluding Canada).

Excerpt from "Oedipus Rex" by Tom Lehrer, copyright by Tom Lehrer. Reprinted by permission of Tom Lehrer.

Notes

INTRODUCTION

1. This description of ancient Greek theater and the Dionysian festival is drawn from several sources, including F. J. H. Letters, *The Life and Work of Sophocles* (London: Sheed & Ward, 1953), 16–21; Albert Cook, "The Greek Theater," in *Oedipus Rex: A Mirror for Greek Drama*, ed. Albert Cook (Belmont, CA: Wadsworth Publishing, 1963), 1–3; Ruby Blondell, "Introduction," in Sophocles, *King Oidipous*, trans. Ruby Blondell (Newburyport, MA: Focus Publishing, 2003), 7–15.

2. Charles Segal, *Oedipus Tyrannus: Tragic Heroism and the Limits of Knowledge* (New York: Twayne Publishers, 1993), 42.

3. Apollodorus, *The Library of Greek Mythology*, trans. Robin Hard (Oxford: Oxford University Press, 2008), 100–107; Timothy Gantz, "Thebes," in *Early Greek Myth: A Guide to Literary and Artistic Sources*, vol. 2 (Baltimore: Johns Hopkins University Press, 1993); Robert Graves, *The Greek Myths* (New York: Penguin Books, 1992), chapters 50, 105, 106. For a useful summary of the overall Theban saga focused on intergenerational violence, see Kenneth X. Robbins, "Oedipus: Uncovering Intergenerational Cycles of Violence," in *Rediscovering Childhood Trauma*, ed. Jean M. Goodwin (Washington, DC: American Psychiatric Press, 1993).

4. See, e.g., Cook, "The Greek Theater," in *Oedipus Rex: A Mirror*, ed. Cook; Bernard Knox, *The Heroic Temper: Studies in Sophoclean Tragedy* (Berkeley: University of California Press, 1983), 166.

5. Lowell Edmunds, *Oedipus* (New York: Routledge, 2006), 32–33; Segal, *Oedipus Tyrannus*, 44–46.

6. H. D. F. Kitto, *Poiesis: Structure and Thought* (Berkeley: University of California Press, 1966), 203; Lowell Edmunds, *Oedipus: The Ancient Legend and Its Later Analogues* (Baltimore: Johns Hopkins University Press, 1996), 8–9.

7. Compare Letters, *The Life and Work of Sophocles*, 205 (the Hera versus Semele theory) with Graves, *The Greek Myths*, 372 (sent by Hera to punish Laius for a crime I'll mention later in this book).

8. Segal, *Oedipus Tyrannus*, 55; Ruby Blondell, "Introduction," in Sophocles, *King Oidipous*, trans. Blondell, 18. For the origins and variations of the Sphinx legend, see Gantz, *Early Greek Myth*, 2: 494–98.

9. Michael Grant, *Myths of the Greeks and Romans* (New York: New American Library, 1962), 195. For a different interpretation of the pinning of the feet, see Letters, *The Life and Work of Sophocles*, 204 ("in order that even if a stranger found the child alive, its probably permanent incapacity might deter him from rearing it"). See also Blondell, "Essay," in Sophocles, *King Oidipous*, trans. Blondell, 105 n. 1.

10. Robin Hard, explanatory notes to Apollodorus, *Library*, 225 n. 105; R. Drew Griffith, *The Theatre of Apollo: Divine Justice and Sophocles'* Oedipus the King (Montreal: McGill-Queen's University Press, 1996), 72–75.

11. Homer, *Odyssey*, trans. Robert Fagles (New York: Penguin Books, 1996), XI.307–11.

12. For a discussion of the many different versions of the Oedipus story told in antiquity, see Gantz, *Early Greek Myth*, 2: 492–502; R. C. Jebb, "Introduction," *Oedipus Tyrannus*, trans. R. C. Jebb (Cambridge: Cambridge University Press, 1883), excerpt reprinted in *Oedipus Rex: A Mirror*, ed. Cook , 88–92.

13. Walter Kaufmann, *Tragedy and Philosophy* (Princeton, NJ: Princeton University Press, 1992), 112; Alister Cameron, *The Identity of Oedipus the King* (New York: New York University Press, 1968), 13–14; Richmond Lattimore, "Sophocles: *Oedipus Tyrannus*," in *Oedipus: Myth and Dramatic Form*, ed. James Sanderson and Everett Zimmerman (Boston: Houghton Mifflin, 1968), 286; Gantz, *Early Greek Myth*, 2: 499–500; *Oedipus Tyrannus*, trans. R. C. Jebb, 91–92 (the process of discovery in the lost Aeschylus version was "not comparable" to that in the Sophoclean version).

14. Blondell, "Essay," in Sophocles, *King Oidipous*, trans. Blondell, 107 n. 2.

15. Preface to John Dryden and Nathaniel Lee, *Oedipus: A Tragedy* (London: printed for R. Bentley and M. Magnes, 1679), reprinted in *Oedipus: Myth and Drama*, ed. Martin Kallich, Andrew MacLeish, and Gertrude Schoenbohm (Indianapolis: The Odyssey Press, 1977), 48.

16. Schiller to Johann Wolfgang von Goethe, October 2, 1797, in *The Correspondence between Schiller and Goethe*, vol. 1, trans. L. Dora Schmitz (London: George Bell, 1877), reprinted in *Oedipus Rex: A Mirror for Greek Drama*, ed. Albert Cook (Belmont, CA: Wadsworth Publishing, 1963), 86.

17. *The Letters of D.H. Lawrence*, vol. 1 (1901–13), ed. James T. Boulton (Cambridge: Cambridge University Press, 2002), 261 (letter 257, April 26, 1911).

18. S. M. Adams, *Sophocles the Playwright* (Toronto: University of Toronto Press, 1957), excerpt reprinted as "Oedipus Tyrannus," in *Oedipus Tyrannus*, ed. Luci Berkowitz and Theodore Brunner (New York: W. W. Norton & Co., 1968), 112.

19. Stelios Ramfos, *Fate and Ambiguity in* Oedipus the King (Boston: Somerset Hall Press, 2006), 20.

20. Philip Vellacott, *Sophocles and Oedipus: A Study of* Oedipus Tyrannus (London: Macmillan Press, 1971), 121 (quoting H. D. F. Kitto).

21. Segal, *Oedipus Tyrannus*, 12.

22. Suetonius, *The Twelve Caesars*, trans. Robert Graves and Michael Grant (New York: Penguin Books, 1980), 39.

23. Jean-Pierre Vernant and Pierre Vidal-Naquet, *Myth and Tragedy in Ancient Greece*, trans. Janet Lloyd (New York: Zone Books, 1990), 372 (referencing a dissertation by Christian Biet).

24. Ibid., 375.

25. Segal, *Oedipus Tyrannus*, 32.

26. Edmunds, *Oedipus*, 116 (quoting Gide).

27. Cameron, *The Identity of Oedipus the King*, vii, xiii.

28. Bernard Knox, "Introduction," in Sophocles, *The Three Theban Plays*, trans. Robert Fagles (New York: Penguin Books, 1984), 131; Martin Kallich, Andrew MacLeish, and Gertrude Schoenbohm, "Preface," in *Oedipus: Myth and Drama*, ed. Martin Kallich, Andrew MacLeish, and Gertrude Schoenbohm (Indianapolis: The Odyssey Press, 1977).

29. Kaufmann, *Tragedy and Philosophy*, chapter 4.

30. Michael J. O'Brien, "Introduction," in *Twentieth Century Interpretations of Oedipus Rex*, ed. Michael J. O'Brien (Englewood Cliffs, NJ: Prentice-Hall Inc., 1968), 2.

31. Jean-Joseph Goux, *Oedipus, Philosopher*, trans. Catherine Porter (Stanford, CA: Stanford University Press, 1993), 3.

32. For a discussion of some twentieth-century literature using various pieces—or "mythemes"—of *Oedipus Rex* and how they reflect back upon it, see Debra A. Moddelmog, *Readers and Mythic Signs: The Oedipus Myth in Twentieth-Century Fiction* (Carbondale and Edwardsville: Southern Illinois University Press, 1993).

1. THE CIRCULAR DETECTIVE

1. Nathaniel Hawthorne, "The Great Stone Face," in *The Complete Short Stories of Nathaniel Hawthorne* (Garden City, NY: Hanover House, 1959), 473.

2. Ray Bradbury, *The Martian Chronicles* (New York: Simon & Schuster, 2001), 241.

3. Sigmund Freud, "The 'Uncanny,'" *Imago*, Bd. V., 1919, trans. Alix Strachey, reprinted in Sigmund Freud, *On Creativity and the Unconscious: The Psychology of Art, Literature, Love, and Religion*, ed. Benjamin Nelson (New York: Harper & Row Publishers, 1986).

4. Rudyard Kipling, "That Day," in *The Seven Seas* (London: Methuen, 1905), 179.

5. John Scaggs, *Crime Fiction: The New Critical Idiom* (New York: Routledge, 2005), 9–11.

6. Sophocles, *Three Theban Plays*, trans. Robert Fagles (New York: Penguin Books, 1984), lines 108–11. Unless otherwise cited, the quotations from *Oedipus Rex* in this book are from this translation by Robert Fagles and will be referenced parenthetically in the text by the line number or numbers in this edition.

7. Robert Graves, *The Greek Myths* (New York: Penguin Books, 1992), 372–73.

8. *Detecting Texts: The Metaphysical Detective Story from Poe to Postmodernism*, ed. Patricia Merivale and Susan Elizabeth Sweeney (Philadelphia: University of Pennsylvania Press, 1999). See also Stefano Tani, *The Doomed Detective: The Contribution of the Detective Novel to Postmodern American and Italian Fiction* (Carbondale and Edwardsville: Southern Illinois University Press, 1984), which uses the term "anti-detective fiction" to describe essentially the same thing. I am grateful to Douglas Keesey for making me aware of the term and the genre.

9. Debra A. Moddelmog, *Readers and Mythic Signs: The Oedipus Myth in Twentieth-Century Fiction* (Carbondale and Edwardsville: Southern Illinois University Press, 1993), 63.

10. Gen. 22:6–8 (King James Version).

11. Plato, *The Apology*, trans. Benjamin Jowett, in *The Apology, Phaedo, and Crito of Plato*, vol. 2 (New York: P. F. Collier & Son, 1909), 7.

12. Ibid., 8.

13. Sophocles, *The Oedipus Cycle*, trans. Dudley Fitts and Robert Fitzgerald (New York: Harcourt Brace Jovanovich, 1977), 9.

14. Thomas De Quincey, "The Theban Sphinx," in *Collected Writings*, vol. 6, ed. T. K. Masson (London: A & C Black, 1897), excerpted in *Oedipus Rex: A Mirror for Greek Drama*, ed. Albert Cook (Belmont, CA: Wadsworth Publishing Co., 1963), 87. See also R. Drew Griffith, *The Theatre of Apollo: Divine Justice and Sophocles'* Oedipus the King (Montreal: McGill-Queen's University Press, 1996), 79; Charles Segal, *Oedipus Tyrannus: Tragic Heroism and the Limits of Knowledge* (New York: Twayne Publishers, 1993), 56–57; Sophocles, *King Oidipous*, trans. Ruby Blondell (Newburyport, MA: Focus Publishing, 2003), 104–105.

15. See, e.g., Alister Cameron, *The Identity of Oedipus the King* (New York: New York University Press, 1968), 22; Peter L. Rudnytsky, *Freud and Oedipus* (New York: Columbia University Press, 1987), 265; Segal, *Oedipus Tyrannus*, 57; Sophocles, *King Oidipous*, trans. Blondell, 93; and R. P. Winnington-Ingram, *Sophocles: An Interpretation* (Cambridge: Cambridge University Press, 1990), 203.

16. August Wilhelm Schlegel, "Lecture VII," in *Lectures on Dramatic Art and Literature*, trans. John Black (London: George Bell & Sons, 1889), 101. Available at http://www.gutenberg.org/cache/epub/7148/pg7148-images.html.

2. KNOW THYSELF

1. For an overview of the Delphic oracle, see William J. Broad, *The Oracle: Ancient Delphi and the Science Behind Its Lost Secrets* (New York: The Penguin Press, 2006).

2. Michael J. O'Brien, "Introduction," in *Twentieth Century Interpretations of Oedipus Rex*, ed. Michael J. O'Brien (Englewood Cliffs, NJ: Prentice-Hall Inc., 1968), 11; Charles Segal, *Oedipus Tyrannus: Tragic Heroism and the Limits of Knowledge* (New York: Twayne Publishers, 1993), 137–38. See also R. Drew Griffith, *The Theatre of Apollo: Divine Justice and Sophocles'* Oedipus the King (Montreal: McGill-Queen's University Press, 1996), 78; Ruby Blondell, "Essay," in Sophocles, *King Oidipous*, trans. Blondell (Newburyport, MA: Focus Publishing, 2003), 94.

3. Justin Kruger and David Dunning, "Unskilled and Unaware of It: How Difficulties in Recognizing One's Own Incompetence Lead to Inflated Self-Assessments," *Journal of Personality and Social Psychology* 77, no. 6 (1999): 1122.

4. Ambrose Bierce, *The Unabridged Devil's Dictionary*, ed. David E. Schultz and S. T. Joshi (Athens: University of Georgia Press, 2001), 164.

5. Daniel Gilbert, *Stumbling on Happiness* (New York: Doubleday Publishing Group, 2006), 230.

6. Steven Pinker, *The Stuff of Thought: Language as a Window into Human Nature* (New York: Viking, 2007), 131.

7. Jonathan Haidt, *The Happiness Hypothesis: Finding Modern Truth in Ancient Wisdom* (New York: Basic Books, 2006), 1.

8. Adam Alter, *Drunk Tank Pink: And Other Unexpected Forces That Shape How We Think, Feel, and Behave* (New York: Penguin Books, 2013).

9. Timothy Wilson, *Strangers to Ourselves: Discovering the Adaptive Unconcious* (Cambridge, MA: Harvard University Press, 2002), 165.

10. See, e.g., Henri F. Ellenberg, *The Discovery of the Unconscious: The History and Evolution of Dynamic Pyschiatry* (New York: Basic Books, 1981); Peter Gay, *Freud: A Life for Our Time* (New York: Anchor Books, 1989), 127–29.

11. Stanislas Dehaene, *Consciousness and the Brain: Deciphering How the Brain Codes Our Thoughts* (New York: Penguin, 2014), 52. But see Gay, *Freud*, 128 ("His particular contribution was to take a shadowy, as it were poetic, notion, lend it precision, and make it into the foundation of a psychology by specifying the origins and contents of the unconscious and its imperious ways of pressing toward expression"); Peter L. Rudnytsky, *Freud and Oedipus* (New York: Columbia University Press, 1987), 93–94 (criticizing those who fail to give Freud sufficient credit for the distinctiveness of his contribution).

12. William Makepeace Thackeray, *The History of Pendennis: His Fortunes and Misfortunes, His Friends and His Greatest Enemy*, quoted in Peter Gay, *The*

Naked Heart, vol. 4 of *The Bourgeois Experience: Victoria to Freud* (New York: W. W. Norton, 1995), 5.

13. Quoted in Wilson, *Strangers to Ourselves*, 168.

14. Daniel Wegner, *The Illusion of Conscious Will* (Cambridge, MA: Massachusetts Institute of Technology, 2002), 54 (describing Benjamin Libet's experiments); Dehaene, *Consciousness and the Brain*, 47–88.

15. Ambrose Bierce, *The Devil's Dictionary*, quoted in Wegner, *The Illusion of Conscious Will*, iii.

16. Paul Bloom, *Against Empathy: The Case for Rational Compassion* (New York: HarperCollins Publishers, 2016), chapter 6.

17. Steven Pinker, *How the Mind Works* (New York: W.W. Norton and Co., 1997), 424. See also Haidt, *The Happiness Hypothesis*, 77.

18. Pinker, *How the Mind Works*, 305.

19. Haidt, *The Happiness Hypothesis*, 40.

20. Robert Wright, *The Moral Animal: Why We Are the Way We Are: The New Science of Evolutionary Psychology* (New York: Vintage Books, 1994), 269.

21. Benedict Carey, "Stumbling Blocks on the Path to Righteousness," *New York Times*, May 5, 2009.

22. Steven Pinker, *The Better Angels of Our Nature: Why Violence Has Declined* (New York: Penguin Books, 2011).

23. Quoted in Wright, *The Moral Animal*, 371.

24. Mark Twain, *Pudd'nhead Wilson* (New York: Signet, 1964), 113.

25. Wilson, *Strangers to Ourselves*, 38.

26. Ibid., 38.

27. August Wilhelm Schlegel, "Lecture VII," in *Lectures on Dramatic Art and Literature*, trans. John Black (London: George Bell & Sons, 1889), 101. Available at http://www.gutenberg.org/cache/epub/7148/pg7148-images.html.

28. 2 Sam. 12:5–7 (KJV).

29. *Hamlet* (New York: The Modern Library, 1994), 2.2.596.

30. Herodotus, *The Histories*, trans. Aubrey de Sélincourt (New York: Penguin Books, 2003), 41.

31. André Gide, *Two Legends: Oedipus and Theseus*, trans. John Russell (New York: Vintage Books, 1958), 28.

32. For a good discussion of this historical shift, see Yuval Noah Harari, *Homo Deus: A Brief History of Tomorrow* (New York, Random House, 2016), 222.

3. FROM ARISTOTLE TO FREUD AND BEYOND

1. Aristotle, *Poetics*, trans. Malcolm Heath (New York: Penguin Books, 1996), 18.

2. Ibid., 18–19.

3. Ibid., 19 (italics added).
4. Ibid., 22 (italics added).
5. Bernard Knox, *Oedipus at Thebes: Sophocles' Tragic Hero and His Time* (New Haven, CT: Yale University Press, 1998), 31.
6. Frederick Ahl, *Sophocles' Oedipus: Evidence and Self-Conviction* (Ithaca, NY: Cornell University Press), 16.
7. Charles Segal, *Oedipus Tyrannus: Tragic Heroism and the Limits of Knowledge* (New York: Twayne Publishers, 1993), 76; E. R. Dodds, "On Misunderstanding the *Oedipus Rex*," *Greece & Rome* 13, no. 1 (1966), reprinted in *Twentieth Century Interpretations of Oedipus Rex*, ed. Michael J. O'Brien (Englewood Cliffs, NJ: Prentice-Hall Inc., 1968), 20. For a useful discussion of what Aristotle meant by "hamartia," see Walter Kaufmann, *Tragedy and Philosophy* (Princeton, NJ: Princeton University Press, 1992), 61–69.
8. Clarence W. Mendell, *Our Seneca* (New Haven, CT: Yale University Press, 1941), reprinted in *Oedipus: Myth and Dramatic Form*, ed. James Sanderson and Everett Zimmerman (Boston: Houghton Mifflin, 1968), 309.
9. Lowell Edmunds, *Oedipus* (New York: Routledge, 2006), 64.
10. Martin Mueller, *Children of Oedipus and Other Essays on the Imitation of Greek Tragedy 1550–1800* (Toronto: University of Toronto Press, 1980), 105.
11. F. M. A. de Voltaire, "Letters on Oedipus, Letter III: Containing the Critique of the *Oedipus* of Sophocles," in *Sophocles: The Classical Heritage*, ed. R. D. Dawe (New York: Garland Publishing, Inc., 1996).
12. Ibid., 37.
13. Ibid., 36.
14. Henry C. Lancaster, "Enter Voltaire," in *Oedipus*, eds. Sanderson and Zimmerman, 319–20.
15. Bernard Knox, "Introduction," in Sophocles, *Three Theban Plays*, trans. Robert Fagles (New York: Penguin Books, 1984), 132.
16. Voltaire, "Letters on Oedipus, Letter III," in *Sophocles*, ed. R. D. Dawe, 41.
17. Quoted in Peter L. Rudnytsky, *Freud and Oedipus* (New York: Columbia University Press, 1987), 105.
18. Rudnytsky, *Freud and Oedipus*, 96.
19. Ibid., chapter 6.
20. Friedrich Nietzsche, *The Birth of Tragedy*, trans. Walter Kaufmann (New York: Vintage Books, 1967), 68.
21. Ibid., 69.
22. Martin Heidegger, *An Introduction to Metaphysics*, trans. Ralph Manheim (New Haven, CT: Yale University Press, 1959), quoted in Rudnytsky, *Freud and Oedipus*, 231.
23. James Hillman, "Oedipus Revisited," in *Oedipus Variations: Studies in Literature and Psychoanalysis* (Woodstock, CT: Spring Publications, 1987), 102; Erich Fromm, *The Forgotten Language: An Introduction to the Understanding of Dreams, Fairy Tales, and Myths* (New York: Random House, 1956), 200.

24. Hillman, "Oedipus Revisited," 102.

25. "Oedipus, n." OED Online. January 2018. Oxford University Press. http://www.oed.com/view/Entry/130510?redirectedFrom=oedipus+complex (accessed January 25, 2018).

26. "Tom Lehrer—Oedipus Rex," YouTube video, 3:43, from the album *An Evening Wasted with Tom Lehrer*, posted by "Freddie21," January 27, 2008, https://www.youtube.com/watch?v=mScdJURKGWM.

27. Discussed in Rudnytsky, *Freud and Oedipus*, 103.

28. Martha Nussbaum, "The *Oedipus Rex* and the Ancient Unconscious," in *Freud and Forbidden Knowledge*, ed. Peter L. Rudnytsky and Ellen Handler Spitz (New York: New York University Press, 1994), 53; Ahl, *Sophocles' Oedipus*, 168.

29. Sigmund Freud, "A Special Type of Choice of Object Made by Men (Contributions to the Psychology of Love, I) (1910)," in *The Standard Edition of the Complete Psychological Works of Sigmund Freud*, trans. and ed. James Strachey, vol. 11 (London: Hogarth, 1957), 163–75. Cited in Debra A. Moddelmog, *Readers and Mythic Signs: The Oedipus Myth in Twentieth-Century Fiction* (Carbondale and Edwardsville: Southern Illinois University Press, 1993), 30.

30. Sigmund Freud, *The Interpretation of Dreams*, trans. James Strachey (New York: Avon Books, 1965), 294.

31. Ibid., italics added.

32. Ibid., 296.

33. Freud, *The Interpretation of Dreams*, 297.

34. Ibid.

35. Ibid.

36. Ibid., 298–300.

37. Otto Rank, *The Incest Theme in Literature and Legend*, trans. Gregory C. Richter (Baltimore: Johns Hopkins University Press, 1992).

38. Erich Wellisch, *Isaac and Oedipus: A Study in Biblical Psychology of the Sacrifice of Isaac* (London: Routledge and Kegan Paul, 1954).

39. Jean-Pierre Vernant and Pierre Vidal-Naquet, *Myth and Tragedy in Ancient Greece*, trans. Janet Lloyd (New York: Zone Books, 1990), 94 (discussing French psychoanalyst Didier Anzieu).

40. Clare Garner, "Psychiatrist Puts Jesus on the Couch," *Independent* (UK), August 22, 1998, http://www.independent.co.uk/news/psychiatrist-puts-jesus-on-the-couch-1173548.html.

41. Michelle Scalise Sugiyama, "New Science, Old Myth: An Evolutionary Critique of the Oedipal Paradigm," in *Evolution, Literature, and Film: A Reader*, ed. Brian Boyd, Joseph Carroll, and Jonathan Gotschall (New York: Columbia University Press, 2010), 5.

42. Allen W. Johnson and Douglass Price-Williams, *Oedipus Ubiquitous: The Family Complex in World Folk Literature* (Stanford, CA: Stanford University Press, 1996), 13.

43. Rudnytsky, *Freud and Oedipus*, 4.

44. Morton Kaplan and Robert Kloss, *The Unspoken Motive: A Guide to Psychoanalytic Literary Criticism* (New York: Free Press, 1973), 109; Vernant and Vidal-Naquet, *Myth and Tragedy in Ancient Greece*, trans. Lloyd, 103–108 (quoting Didier Anzieu, without citation).

45. Rudnytsky, *Freud and Oedipus*, 271.

46. Vernant and Vidal-Naquet, *Myth and Tragedy in Ancient Greece*, trans. Lloyd, 103–108.

47. Sándor Ferenczi, "The Symbolic Representation of the Pleasure and Reality Principles in the Oedipus Myth," reprinted in *Sex in Psycho-Analysis: Contributions to Psycho-Analysis*, trans. Ernest Jones (Boston: The Gorham Press, 1916), 263–64.

48. Karl Abraham, "'The Trifurcation of the Road' in the Oedipus Myth," part 2 of "Two Contributions to the Study of Symbols," in *Clinical Papers and Essays on Psychoanalysis*, trans. Hilda Abraham and D. R. Ellison (New York: Basic Books, 1922), 83–85. Cited in Rudnytsky, *Freud and Oedipus*, 261. See also Karl Harshbarger, *Sophocles' Oedipus* (Washington, DC: University Press of America, 1979), 33 (Oedipus "describes the place where Laius was killed in terms that anatomically are highly suggestive of the outer female genitalia").

49. Harshbarger, *Sophocles' Oedipus*, 26–27.

50. Géza Róheim, *The Riddle of The Sphinx*, trans. R. Money-Kyrle (New York: Harper Torchbooks, 1974), 8.

51. Vernant and Vidal-Naquet, *Myth and Tragedy in Ancient Greece*, trans. Lloyd, 109.

52. Carl Jung, "Symbols of Transformation," in *Oedipus: Myth and Drama*, ed. Martin Kallich, Andrew MacLeish, and Gertrude Schoenbohm (Indianapolis: The Odyssey Press, 1968), 372.

53. On the application of Freud's concept of "condensation" to *Oedipus Rex*, see Geoffrey H. Hartman, "The Voice of the Shuttle: Language from the Point of View of Literature," in *Beyond Formalism: Literary Essays 1958–1970* (New Haven, CT: Yale University Press, 1970), 347–48. Hartman's work is discussed in Rudnytsky, *Freud and Oedipus*, 379 n. 52.

54. Harshbarger, *Sophocles' Oedipus*.

55. John Crossett, *The Oedipus Rex* (1962), reprinted in *Oedipus Rex: A Mirror for Greek Drama*, ed. Albert Cook (Belmont, CA: Wadsworth Publishing Co., 1963), 134–35.

56. Translation of C. M. Bowra in Bowra, *Sophoclean Tragedy* (London: Oxford University Press, 1965), 162.

57. Kaplan and Kloss, *The Unspoken Motive*, 112 and 115. See also, e.g., Harshbarger, *Sophocles' Oedipus*, 9 ("In this study I will argue that Oedipus is driven by powerful unconscious needs which push him in directions he cannot admit to himself and which he must hide from others").

58. Patrick Lee Miller, "Oedipus Rex Revisited," *Modern Psychoanalysis* 31, no. 2 (July 2006): 234.

59. Philip Vellacott, *Sophocles and Oedipus: A Study of Oedipus Tyrannus* (Bristol, UK: Macmillan Press, 1971).

60. Ibid.,132.
61. Ibid., 213.
62. Hillman, "Oedipus Revisited," 115.
63. Kenneth X. Robbins, "Oedipus: Uncovering Intergenerational Cycles of Violence," in *Rediscovering Childhood Trauma*, ed. Jean M. Goodwin (Washington, DC: American Psychiatric Press, 1993), 17–18.
64. Apollodorus, *The Library of Greek Mythology*, trans. Robin Hard (Oxford: Oxford University Press, 2008), 104; Timothy Gantz, *Early Greek Myth: A Guide to Literary and Artistic Sources*, vol. 2 (Baltimore: Johns Hopkins University Press, 1993), 489–91.
65. Robin Hard, explanatory note to Apollodorus, *The Library of Greek Mythology*, 225 n. 106.
66. George Devereux, "Why Oedipus Killed Laius: A Note on the Complementary Oedipus Complex in Greek Drama," in *Oedipus: A Folklore Casebook*, ed. Lowell Edmunds and Alan Dundes (Madison: University of Wisconsin Press, 1995).
67. Devereux, "Why Oedipus Killed Laius," 220–21.
68. Marie Balmary, *Psychoanalyzing Psychoanalysis: Freud and the Hidden Fault of the Father*, trans. Ned Lukacher (Baltimore: Johns Hopkins University Press, 1982), 8–9.
69. Ibid., 20.
70. Irvin Yalom, *Existential Psychotherapy* (Basic Books, 1980), 70.
71. Balmary, *Psychoanalyzing Psychoanalysis*, 27.
72. John Murray Cuddihy, *The Ordeal of Civility: Freud, Marx, Lévi-Strauss, and the Jewish Struggle with Modernity* (Boston: Beacon Press, 1987), chapter 4.
73. Ibid., 54.
74. Ibid., 55–56.
75. Michel Bréal, *Mélanges de mythologie et de linguistique* (Paris: Hachette, 1877), 184, cited by William A. Lessa, "Oedipus-Type Tales in Oceania," in *Oedipus*, ed. Edmunds and Dundes, 69.
76. See Segal, *Oedipus Tyrannus*, 58 (discussing theory of H. J. Rose).
77. Robert Graves, *The Greek Myths* (New York: Penguin Books, 1992), 375.
78. Immanuel Velikovsky, *Oedipus and Akhnaton: Myth and History* (New York: Pocket Books, 1960).
79. See Lowell Edmunds, "The Sphinx in the Oedipus Legend," in *Oedipus: A Folklore Casebook*, ed. Lowell Edmunds and Alan Dundes (arguing for the Sphinx episode as a late add-on) and Almut-Barbara Renger, *Oedipus and the Sphinx: The Threshold Myth from Sophocles through Freud to Cocteau*, trans. Duncan Smart and David Rice with John Hamilton (Chicago: University of Chicago Press, 2013), 24 (discussing the conclusion of Ulrich Hausmann that the Sphinx motif was inseparably bound up with the Oedipus saga).
80. Segal, *Oedipus Tyrannus*, 52 (citing Hesiod's *Theogony*, 326–32).
81. Otto Rank, *The Myth of the Birth of the Hero: A Psychological Interpretation of Mythology* (Redditch, UK: Read Books Ltd., 2013), 106–107.

82. Lord Raglan, *The Hero: A Study in Tradition, Myth and Drama* (Mineola, NY: Dover Publications Inc., 2003).

83. Ibid., 175.

84. Jean-Joseph Goux, *Oedipus, Philosopher*, trans. Catherine Porter (Stanford, CA: Stanford University Press, 1993).

85. Ibid., 35.

86. Ibid., 79.

87. Sir James George Frazer, *The Golden Bough*, excerpted in *Oedipus: Myth and Drama*, ed. Kallich, MacLeish, and Schoenbohm, 354.

88. Mark R. Anspach, "Introduction," in René Girard, *Oedipus Unbound: Selected Writings on Rivalry and Desire* (Stanford, CA: Stanford University Press, 2004), xxxi.

89. René Girard, *Violence and the Sacred*, trans. Patrick Gregory (Baltimore: The John Hopkins University Press, 1979), 78. For a good takedown of Girard, see R. Drew Griffith, *The Theatre of Apollo: Divine Justice and Sophocles' Oedipus the King* (McGill-Queen's University Press, 1996), 29–44; Rudnytsky, *Freud and Oedipus*, 344–50.

90. Girard, *Violence and the Sacred*, 84.

91. Vernant and Vidal-Naquet, *Myth and Tragedy in Ancient Greece*, trans. Lloyd, 128–29.

92. Rudnytsky, *Freud and Oedipus*, 236–50; Michael P. Carroll, "Lévi-Strauss on the Oedipus Myth: A Reconsideration," *American Anthropologist* 80 (1978): 805–14.

93. Claude Lévi-Strauss, *Structural Anthropology*, trans. Claire Jacobson and Brooke Grundfest Schoepf (New York: Basic Books, 1963), chapter 11.

94. Ibid., 213.

95. Claude Lévi-Strauss, *The Jealous Potter*, trans. Bénédicte Chorier (Chicago: University of Chicago Press, 1985), 198–206.

96. D. A. Hester, "Oedipus and Jonah," *Proceedings of the Cambridge Philological Society* 123 (1977): 32–60.

97. Dodds, "On Misunderstanding the *Oedipus Rex*," 26–27.

98. Bowra, *Sophoclean Tragedy*, 175.

99. T. B. L. Webster, *An Introduction to Sophocles* (Oxford: The Clarendon Press, 1936), 23, excerpted in *Twentieth Century Interpretations of Oedipus Rex*, ed. O'Brien, 103.

100. Cedric H. Whitman, *Sophocles: A Study of Heroic Humanism* (Cambridge, MA: Harvard University Press, 1951), 136. See also F. J. H. Letters, *The Life and Work of Sophocles* (London: Sheed & Ward, 1953), 225.

101. Dodds, "On Misunderstanding the *Oedipus Rex*," 26.

102. As quoted in Letters, *The Life and Work of Sophocles*, 221.

103. See, e.g., Segal, *Oedipus Tyrannus*, 9.

104. Ibid., but see citations in the appendix.

105. Ibid., 10.

106. Knox, "Introduction," in Sophocles, *Three Theban Plays*, trans. Fagles, 134.

107. Bernard Knox, *Oedipus at Thebes: Sophocles' Tragic Hero and His Time* (New Haven, CT: Yale University Press, 1998), 67.
108. Ibid., 63.
109. Ibid., 64.
110. Karl Harshbarger, "Who Killed Laius?" *Tulane Drama Review* 9, no. 4 (Summer 1965): 120–31.
111. Ahl, *Sophocles' Oedipus*.
112. Ibid., 21.
113. Ibid., x.
114. Ibid., 264.
115. Ibid.
116. "Jacques Derrida 'Dies,'" *The Onion*, October 20–26, 2004.
117. See Simon Goldhill, *Reading Greek Tragedy* (Cambridge: Cambridge University Press, 1986), 221.
118. Patricia Merivale, "Gumshoe Gothics: 'The Man of the Crowd' and His Followers," in *Detecting Texts: The Metaphysical Detective Story from Poe to Postmodernism*, ed. Patricia Merivale and Susan Elizabeth Sweeney (Philadelphia: University of Pennsylvania Press, 1999), 103.
119. John T. Irwin, *The Mystery to a Solution: Poe, Borges, and the Analytic Detective Story* (Baltimore: Johns Hopkins University Press, 1994). See also Moddelmog, *Readers and Mythic Signs*, chapter 6 (arguing that we're drawn to the Oedipus myth because it reflects the modern, Kuhnian, relativistic recognition of the limits of knowledge).
120. Ann Scales, "Introduction," in J. C. Smith and Carla J. Ferstman, *The Castration of Oedipus: Feminism, Psychoanalysis, and the Will to Power* (New York: New York University Press, 1996), 8.

4. BORNE BACK CEASELESSLY

1. As quoted in T. J. Stiles, "The Ghost That Haunts Grant's Memoirs," *New York Times*, October 13, 2017, https://www.nytimes.com/2017/10/13/books/review/john-marszalek-personal-memoirs-of-ulysses-s-grant.html.
2. Arthur Miller, *Timebends: A Life* (London: Methuen Publishing, 1999), 134.
3. Arthur Miller, *All My Sons* (New York: Penguin Books, 1975), 65.
4. Philip Vellacott, *Sophocles and Oedipus: A Study of* Oedipus Tyrannus (Bristol, UK: Macmillan Press, 1971), 107: "There is no other extant Greek tragedy which contains a comparable proportion of lines devoted to circumstantial narrative of past events."
5. Sophocles, *The Oedipus Cycle*, trans. Dudley Fitts and Robert Fitzgerald (New York: Harcourt Brace Jovanovich, 1977), 9.
6. Sigmund Freud, *The Interpretation of Dreams*, trans. James Strachey (New York: Avon Books, 1965), 295.

7. Jonathan Engel, *American Therapy* (New York: Gotham Books, 2008), 90 (discussing Ellis).

8. James Baldwin, *Notes of a Native Son* (Boston: Beacon Press, 1955), 20, as quoted in Isabel Wilkerson, *The Warmth of Other Suns: The Epic Story of America's Great Migration* (New York: Random House, 2010), 302.

9. F. Scott Fitzgerald, *The Great Gatsby* (New York: Charles Scribner's Sons, 1953), 73.

10. Ibid., 121.

5. "THE LIVES I CUT DOWN WITH THESE HANDS"

1. Paul Bloom, *Against Empathy: The Case for Rational Compassion* (New York: HarperCollins Publishers, 2016), 94.

2. Peter Singer, *The Expanding Circle: Ethics, Evolution, and Moral Progress* (Princeton, NJ: Princeton University Press, 2011).

3. Steven Pinker, "The Moral Instinct," *New York Times Magazine*, January 13, 2008, http://www.nytimes.com/2008/01/13/magazine/13Psychology-t.html.

4. Exod. 22:21 (KJV).

5. Lev. 19:34 (KJV) ("But the stranger that dwelleth with you shall be unto you as one born among you, and you shalt love him as thyself; for ye were strangers in the land of Egypt: I am the Lord your God"); Deut. 10:19 (KJV) ("Love ye therefore the stranger: for ye were strangers in the land of Egypt").

6. See also George Polti, *The Thirty-Six Dramatic Situations*, trans. Lucille Ray (Boston: The Writer Inc., 1995), 63–66.

7. Arthur Miller, *All My Sons* (New York: Penguin Books, 1975), 83.

8. Ibid., italics added.

9. Ibid., 77.

10. Ibid., 84.

11. Tenzin Gyatso, the Fourteenth Dalai Lama, "Compassion and the Individual," https://www.dalailama.com/messages/compassion-and-human-values/compassion, accessed January 25, 2018.

12. Bloom, *Against Empathy*, 94–95 (italics added).

13. Sigmund Freud, *The Interpretation of Dreams*, trans. James Strachey (New York: Avon Books, 1965), 296.

14. Daniel Goleman, "As a Therapist, Freud Fell Short, Scholars Find," *New York Times*, March 6, 1990, http://www.nytimes.com/1990/03/06/science/as-a-therapist-freud-fell-short-scholars-find.html?pagewanted=1.

15. See, e.g., Martin Daly and Margo Wilson, *Homicide* (New York: Aldine de Gruyter, 1988), 107; Jonathan Engel, *American Therapy* (New York: Gotham Books, 2008), 257–58; Bloom, *Against Empathy*, 216.

16. Walter Kaufmann, *Tragedy and Philosophy* (Princeton, NJ: Princeton University Press, 1992), 108; Alister Cameron, *The Identity of Oedipus the King* (New York: New York University Press, 1968), ix.

17. Michelle Scalise Sugiyama, "New Science, Old Myth: An Evolutionary Critique of the Oedipal Paradigm," in *Evolution, Literature, and Film: A Reader*, ed. Brian Boyd, Joseph Carroll, and Jonathan Gottschall (New York: Columbia University Press, 2010), 311–12; Engel, *American Therapy*, 221 (citing M. L. Gross, *The Psychological Society* [1978]).

18. Sugiyama, "New Science, Old Myth," 315.

19. Ibid.

20. Lowell Edmunds and Alan Dundes, "Introduction," in *Oedipus: A Folklore Casebook*, ed. Lowell Edmunds and Alan Dundes (Madison: University of Wisconsin Press, 1995).

21. Allen W. Johnson and Douglass Price-Williams, *Oedipus Ubiquitous: The Family Complex in World Folk Literature* (Stanford, CA: Stanford University Press, 1996).

22. Ibid., 123.

23. Melford Spiro, "The Oedipus Complex in Burma," in *Oedipus: A Folklore Casebook*, ed. Edmunds and Dundes, 212.

24. See, e.g., Daly and Wilson, *Homicide*, 107–21.

25. Mark R. Anspach, "Introduction," in René Girard, *Oedipus Unbound: Selected Writings on Rivalry and Desire* (Stanford, CA: Stanford University Press, 2004), xliii.

26. To get a feel for the excitement felt by Freudians in those early, heady days, see Ernest Jones, *Hamlet and Oedipus* (New York: W. W. Norton & Co., 1976), 14–15.

27. Frederick Ahl, *Sophocles' Oedipus: Evidence and Self-Conviction* (Ithaca, NY: Cornell University Press), 28.

28. Thomas Gould, "The Innocence of Oedipus: The Philosophers on *Oedipus the King*, pt. 3," *Arion* 5, no. 4 (1966): 502.

29. Erich Fromm, *The Forgotten Language: An Introduction to the Understanding of Dreams, Fairy Tales, and Myths* (New York: Random House, 1956), 201.

30. Ibid., 204.

31. See, e.g., Peter L. Rudnytsky, *Freud and Oedipus* (New York: Columbia University Press, 1987), 258.

32. See Ruby Blondell, "Introduction," in Sophocles, *King Oidipous*, trans. Ruby Blondell (Newburyport, MA: Focus Publishing, 2003), 5–6 (noting that the story was probably apocryphal).

33. Timothy Gantz, *Early Greek Myth: A Guide to Literary and Artistic Sources*, vol. 1 (Baltimore: Johns Hopkins University Press, 1993), 44 (castration of Cronus by Zeus); Robert Graves, *The Greek Myths* (New York: Penguin Books, 1992), 37 (castration of Uranus by Cronus); Apollodorus, *The Library of Greek Mythology*, trans. Robin Hard (Oxford: Oxford University Press, 2008), 27.

34. Rudnytsky, *Freud and Oedipus*, 200.

35. James Schroeter, "The Four Fathers: Symbolism in *Oedipus Rex*," *Criticism* 3, no. 3 (1961), 185–200, reprinted in *Oedipus Rex*, ed. Cook, 121–33.

36. Ibid., 124.
37. Ibid., 130–31.
38. Ibid., 131.
39. Rudnytsky, *Freud and Oedipus*, 21 (quoting Freud's *Studies on Hysteria* [1895]).
40. Ibid., 271.
41. Charles Segal, *Oedipus Tyrannus: Tragic Heroism and the Limits of Knowledge* (New York: Twayne Publishers, 1993), 62.
42. See Karl Harshbarger, *Sophocles' Oedipus* (Washington, DC: University Press of America, 1979), 13.

6. "CURSED IN MY BIRTH"

1. Bernard Knox, "Introduction," in Sophocles, *Three Theban Plays*, trans. Robert Fagles (New York: Penguin Books, 1984), 131 (noting that it is "almost universally regarded as the classic example of the 'tragedy of fate,'" though disagreeing with the idea); Michael Grant, *Myths of the Greeks and Romans* (New York: New American Library, 1962), 200–201 ("*Oedipus* has been used more than any other play to support the view that Greek tragedy deals with puppets in the grip of destiny").
2. Georgios A. Megas, "On the Oedipus Myth," in *Oedipus: A Folklore Casebook*, ed. Lowell Edmunds and Alan Dundes (Madison: University of Wisconsin Press, 1995), 141.
3. Martha Nussbaum, "The *Oedipus Rex* and the Ancient Unconscious," in *Freud and Forbidden Knowledge*, ed. Peter L. Rudnytsky and Ellen Handler Spitz (New York: New York University Press, 1994), 64.
4. Ibid.
5. Jean Cocteau, *The Infernal Machine and Other Plays*, trans. Albert Bermel (New York: New Directions Publishing, 1963), 6.
6. Homer, *Iliad*, trans. Robert Fagles (New York: Viking, 1990), 6.582–84.
7. Lucius Annaeus Seneca, *Oedipus*, trans. F. J. Miller (lines 1204–08), in *Oedipus: Myth and Dramatic Form*, ed. James Sanderson and Everett Zimmerman (Boston: Houghton Mifflin, 1968).
8. See, e.g., H. D. F. Kitto, *Poiesis: Structure and Thought* (Berkeley: University of California Press, 1966), 210–11; E. R. Dodds, "On Misunderstanding the *Oedipus Rex*," *Greece & Rome* 13, no. 1 (1966), reprinted in *Twentieth Century Interpretations of Oedipus Rex*, ed. Michael J. O'Brien (Englewood Cliffs, NJ: Prentice-Hall Inc., 1968), 19; Kaufmann, *Tragedy and Philosophy*, 104.
9. See, e.g., Peter L. Rudnytsky, *Freud and Oedipus* (New York: Columbia University Press, 1987), chapter 10; Brian Vickers, *Towards Greek Tragedy* (London: Longman Group Ltd., 1979), 497–99, 546 n. 2 (citing others making

same point); Kitto, *Poiesis*, 203; Bowra, *Sophoclean Tragedy* (London: Oxford University Press, 1965), 163–64.

10. Herodotus, *The Histories*, trans. Aubrey de Selincourt (New York: Penguin Books, 2003), 23.

11. Yuval Noah Harari, *Homo Deus: A Brief History of Tomorrow* (New York: Random House, 2016), 56.

12. Karl Popper, *The Poverty of Historicism* (London: Routledge Classics, 2002), 11.

13. Dodds, "On Misunderstanding the *Oedipus Rex*," 22–23 ("[N]o oracle said that he must discover the truth"); Bernard Knox, *Oedipus at Thebes: Sophocles' Tragic Hero and His Time* (New Haven, CT: Yale University Press, 1998), 6.

14. *Hamlet* (New York: The Modern Library, 1994), 1.2.256–57.

15. Knox, *Oedipus at Thebes*, 10.

16. Dodds, "On Misunderstanding the *Oedipus Rex*," 23; Knox, *Oedipus at Thebes*, chapter 1.

17. Thomas Gould, "The Innocence of Oedipus: The Philosophers on *Oedipus the King*, pt. 3," *Arion* 5, no. 4 (1966), excerpted in *Oedipus Tyrannus*, ed. Luci Berkowitz and Theodore Brunner (New York: W. W. Norton & Co., 1968), 248.

18. R. Drew Griffith, *The Theatre of Apollo: Divine Justice and Sophocles'* Oedipus the King (Montreal: McGill-Queen's University Press, 1996), 60–61.

19. Charles Segal, *Oedipus Tyrannus: Tragic Heroism and the Limits of Knowledge* (New York: Twayne Publishers, 1993), 47; Kitto, *Poiesis*, 208–09. See also Griffith, *The Theatre of Apollo*, 39–40 (arguing that Sophocles introduced the plague because of his interest in medicine).

7. THE MAN WHO DIDN'T KNOW HE WAS HOME

1. See, e.g., Bernard Knox, *Oedipus at Thebes: Sophocles' Tragic Hero and His Time* (New Haven, CT: Yale University Press, 1998), 54; Thomas Van Nortwick, *Oedipus: The Meaning of a Masculine Life* (Norman: University of Oklahoma Press, 1998), 23; Blondell, "Essay," Sophocles, *King Oidipous*, trans. Ruby Blondell (Newburyport, MA: Focus Publishing, 2003), 107; C. M. Bowra, *King Oedipus* (London: Oxford University Press, 1964), 186; Philip Wheelwright, *The Burning Fountain: A Study in the Language of Symbolism* (Bloomington: Indiana University Press, 1954), excerpted in *Oedipus Tyrannus*, ed. Luci Berkowitz and Theodore Brunner (New York: W. W. Norton & Co., 1968), 257.

2. Knox, *Oedipus at Thebes*, 57.

3. Eccles. 1:7 (KJV).

4. Ibid., 1:5.

5. Job 1:21 (KJV).

6. Gen. 3:19 (KJV).

7. For a book-length exploration of our love of and fascination with circles from a design standpoint, see Manuel Lima, *The Book of Circles: Visualizing Spheres of Knowledge* (Princeton, NJ: Princeton Architectural Press, 2017). See also Mary Douglas, *Thinking in Circles: An Essay on Ring Composition* (New Haven, CT: Yale University Press, 2007) (discussing ring composition in literature, in which the ending of a tale often joins up with the beginning).

8. "Planet of the Apes (5/5) Movie CLIP—Statue of Liberty (1968) HD," YouTube video, 2:42, posted by "Movieclips," August 17, 2015, https://www.youtube.com/watch?v=mDLS12_a-fk.

9. R. Drew Griffith, *The Theatre of Apollo: Divine Justice and Sophocles'* Oedipus the King (Montreal: McGill-Queen's University Press, 1996), 79.

10. See, e.g., Nigel Wilson, *Encyclopedia of Ancient Greece* (New York: Routledge, 2013), 127; David L. Braddock and Susan L. Parish, "An Institutional History of Disability," in *Handbook of Disability Studies*, ed. Gary L. Albrecht, Katherine D. Seelman, and Michael Bury (Thousand Oaks, CA: Sage Publications, 2001), 15. See also F. J. H. Letters, *The Life and Work of Sophocles* (London: Sheed and Ward, 1953), 223 ("[Jocasta's] treatment of her newborn son would not revolt the audience, for exposure of unwanted children was both frequent and legal in Athens").

11. Charles Segal, *Oedipus Tyrannus: Tragic Heroism and the Limits of Knowledge* (New York: Twayne Publishers, 1993), 131.

8. "IS THERE A MAN MORE AGONIZED?"

1. Walter Kaufmann, *Tragedy and Philosophy* (Princeton, NJ: Princeton University Press, 1968/1992), 310.

2. Adrian Poole, *Tragedy: A Very Short Introduction* (Oxford: Oxford University Press, 2005), 5.

3. Aristotle, *Poetics*, trans. Malcolm Heath (New York: Penguin Books, 1996), 10 (italics added).

4. But see Gerald Else, *Aristotle's Poetics: The Argument* (London: Oxford University Press, 1957) (arguing that it's not about the audience).

5. Kaufmann, *Tragedy and Philosophy*, 43–49.

6. F. J. H. Letters, *Sophocles* (London: Sheed & Ward, 1953), 97.

7. One scholar defines tragedy as a "story with an unhappy ending that is memorably and upliftingly moving rather than simply sad." Terry Eagleton, *Sweet Violence: The Idea of the Tragic* (Malden, MA: Blackwell Publishing, 2003), 2–3, citing Paul M. Allen, *Alan Ayckbourn: Grinning at the Edge* (London: Bloomsbury, 2001), 224.

8. Eagleton, *Sweet Violence*, 4 (quoting Samuel Johnson).

9. Ibid., 3.

10. Ibid., citing Leo Aylen, *Greek Tragedy and the Modern World* (London: Methuen, 1964).

11. Jennifer Wallace, *The Cambridge Introduction to Tragedy* (Cambridge: Cambridge University Press, 2007), 117.

12. Eagleton, *Sweet Violence*, 15 (discussing the views of A. C. Bradley, C. S. Lewis, and Ulrich Simon).

13. Arthur Miller, "Tragedy and the Common Man," *New York Times*, February 27, 1949, http://www.nytimes.com/books/00/11/12/specials/miller-common.html?mcubz=0.

14. A. J. A. Waldock, *Sophocles the Dramatist* (Cambridge: Cambridge University Press, 1951), excerpted in *Oedipus Tyrannus*, ed. Luci Berkowitz and Theodore Brunner (New York: W. W. Norton & Co., 1968), 113.

15. Alister Cameron, *The Identity of Oedipus the King* (New York: New York University Press, 1968), xiv.

16. Charles Segal, *Oedipus Tyrannus: Tragic Heroism and the Limits of Knowledge* (New York: Twayne Publishers, 1993), 14.

17. Philip Vellacott, "The Guilt of Oedipus," in *Oedipus Tyrannus*, ed. Berkowitz and Brunner, 208 (citation added).

18. For one recent discussion of the difference between the modern world view of chaos and the older view based on a cosmic plan, see Yuval Noah Harari, *Homo Deus: A Brief History of Tomorrow* (New York: Random House, 2016), 200.

19. Thomas Cahill, *Sailing the Wine-Dark Sea: Why the Greeks Matter* (New York: Anchor Books, 2004), 128.

20. Jonathan Haidt, *The Happiness Hypothesis: Finding Modern Truth in Ancient Wisdom* (New York: Basic Books, 2006), 47–48.

21. Segal, *Oedipus Tyrannus*, 12.

22. Werner Jaeger, *Paideia: The Ideals of Greek Literature*, trans. Gilbert Highet (Oxford: Basil Blackwell & Mott Ltd., 1954), 284, excerpted in *Twentieth Century Interpretations of Oedipus Rex*, ed. Michael J. O'Brien (Englewood Cliffs, NJ: Prentice-Hall Inc., 1968), 103.

23. Wendy Doniger, *Splitting the Difference: Gender and Myth in Ancient Greece and India* (Chicago: University of Chicago Press, 1999), 181; Eric Wellisch, *Isaac and Oedipus: A Study in Biblical Psychology of the Sacrifice of Isaac,* The Akedah (London: Routledge & Kegan Paul, 1954), 38.

24. Thomas Gould, "Notes," in Sophocles, *Oedipus the King*, trans. Gould (Englewood Cliffs, NJ: Prentice-Hall, 1970), 158.

25. Victor Ehrenberg, *Sophocles and Pericles* (Oxford: Basil Blackwell & Mott Ltd., 1954), 66–73. Reprinted as "Sophoclean Rulers: Oedipus" in *Twentieth Century Interpretations of Oedipus Rex*, ed. O'Brien, 77.

26. Gilbert Murray, *The Literature of Ancient Greece* (Chicago: University of Chicago Press, 1956), excerpted in *Oedipus: Myth and Drama*, ed. Martin Kallich, Andrew MacLeish, and Gertrude Schoenbohm (Indianapolis: The Odyssey Press, 1968), 279.

27. Kitto, *Poiesis*, 217–18.

9. THE MEANING OF HEROISM

1. Robert Cohen, "Oedipus and the Absurd Life," in *Oedipus Tyrannus*, ed. Luci Berkowitz and Theodore Brunner (New York: W. W. Norton & Co., 1968), 179.

2. Bernard Knox, *Oedipus at Thebes: Sophocles' Tragic Hero and His Time* (New Haven, CT: Yale University Press, 1998), 25.

3. Dodds, "On Misunderstanding the *Oedipus Rex*," *Greece & Rome* 13, no. 1 (1966), reprinted in *Twentieth Century Interpretations of Oedipus Rex*, ed. Michael J. O'Brien (Englewood Cliffs, NJ: Prentice-Hall Inc., 1968), 19.

4. Ibid., 28.

5. Knox, *Oedipus at Thebes*, 18–19.

6. Charles Segal, *Oedipus Tyrannus: Tragic Heroism and the Limits of Knowledge* (New York: Twayne Publishers, 1993), 26 (quoting Schopenhauer).

7. Knox, *Oedipus at Thebes*, 50.

8. Ibid.

9. Alister Cameron, *The Identity of Oedipus the King* (New York: New York University Press, 1968), xx.

10. Homer, *Odyssey*, trans. Robert Fagles (New York: Viking, 1996), 11.312–14; see also *Iliad*, trans. Robert Fagles (New York: Viking, 1990), 23.756–58.

11. Friedrich von Schiller to Johann Wolfgang von Goethe, October 2, 1797, in *The Correspondence between Schiller and Goethe*, vol. 1, trans. L. Dora Schmitz (London: George Bell, 1877), reprinted in *Oedipus Rex: A Mirror for Greek Drama*, ed. Albert Cook (Belmont, CA: Wadsworth Publishing, 1963), 86 (italics added).

12. Sigmund Freud, *The Interpretation of Dreams*, trans. James Strachey (New York: Avon Books, 1965), 295 (italics added).

13. Michael J. O'Brien, "Introduction" in *Twentieth Century Interpretations of Oedipus Rex*, ed. O'Brien (Englewood Cliffs, NJ: Prentice-Hall Inc., 1968), 7–8 (italics added).

14. Segal, *Oedipus Tyrannus*, 83–84 (italics added).

15. A. J. A. Waldock, *Sophocles the Dramatist* (Cambridge: Cambridge University Press, 1951), excerpted in *Oedipus Tyrannus*, ed. Berkowitz and Brunner, 128 (italics added).

16. Milan Kundera, *The Unbearable Lightness of Being*, trans. Michael Henry Heim (New York: Harper & Row, 1984), 177.

17. Dodds, "On Misunderstanding the *Oedipus Rex*," 28.

18. Harold Kushner, *When All You've Ever Wanted Isn't Enough: The Search for a Life That Matters* (New York: Fireside, 2002), 58.

19. See, e.g., Michael O'Brien, "Introduction," in *Twentieth Century Interpretations of Oedipus Rex*, ed. O'Brien, 13–14 (discussing J. T. Sheppard).

20. Robert M. Pirsig, *Zen and the Art of Motorcycle Maintenance: An Inquiry into Values* (New York: Bantam Books, 1982), 5.

21. *King Lear* (New York: The Modern Library, 1994), 5.2.10.
22. See also Debra A. Moddelmog, *Readers and Mythic Signs: The Oedipus Myth in Twentieth-Century Fiction* (Carbondale and Edwardsville: Southern Illinois University Press, 1993), 41 ("Our interpretation of the fictional renderings of a mytheme [a piece of *Oedipus Rex*] are as likely to inform our later meetings with that same mytheme as are our readings of critical exegesis").
23. Richmond Lattimore, "The Poetry of Greek Tragedy," reprinted as "The Chorus in the *Tyrannus*" in *Oedipus Tyrannus*, ed. Berkowitz and Brunner, 177 (italics added).
24. Sophocles, *The Women of Trachis*, trans. Michael Jameson (Chicago: University of Chicago Press, 1969), 1–3.
25. Herodotus, *The Histories*, trans. Aubrey de Sélincourt (New York: Penguin Books, 2003), 15–16; Aeschylus, *Agamemnon*, trans. Philip Vellacott (New York: Penguin Books, 1980), 74 (lines 926–27).

CONCLUSION

1. *The Letters of D. H. Lawrence*, vol. 1 (1901–13), ed. James T. Boulton (Cambridge: Cambridge University Press, 2002), 261 (letter 257, April 26, 1911).
2. Alister Cameron, *The Identity of Oedipus the King* (New York: New York University Press, 1968), 50.
3. H. D. F. Kitto, *Poiesis: Structure and Thought* (Berkeley: University of California Press, 1966), chapter 4 (on the unpredictability of life); John Crossett, "The *Oedipus Rex*," in *Oedipus Rex: A Mirror for Greek Drama*, ed. Albert Cook (Belmont, CA: Wadsworth Publishing, 1963), 137 (on a pivotal decision at a crossroad).
4. Quotation from Plutarch's *On Curiosity*, translated by Michael J. O'Brien, reprinted in *Twentieth Century Interpretations of Oedipus Rex*, ed. O'Brien (Englewood Cliffs, NJ: Prentice-Hall Inc., 1968), 99.
5. Thomas Cahill, *Sailing the Wine-Dark Sea: Why the Greeks Matter* (New York: Anchor Books, 2004), 124.
6. Peter L. Rudnytsky, *Freud and Oedipus* (New York: Columbia University Press, 1987), 259.
7. Crossett, "The *Oedipus Rex*," in *Oedipus Rex*, ed. Cook, 138.
8. Charles Segal, *Oedipus Tyrannus: Tragic Heroism and the Limits of Knowledge* (New York: Twayne Publishers, 1993), 94.
9. Frederick Ahl, *Sophocles' Oedipus: Evidence and Self-Conviction* (Ithaca, NY: Cornell University Press), 28.
10. Bernard Knox, *Oedipus at Thebes: Sophocles' Tragic Hero and His Time* (New Haven, CT: Yale University Press, 1998), 182–83; Blondell, "Essay," in Sophocles, *King Oidipous*, trans. Ruby Blondell (Newburyport, MA: Focus Publishing, 2003), 98.

11. Blondell, "Introduction," in *King Oidipous*, trans. Blondell, 18.

12. Friedrich von Schiller to Johann Wolfgang von Goethe, October 2, 1797, in *The Correspondence between Schiller and Goethe*, vol. 1, trans. L. Dora Schmitz (London: George Bell, 1877), reprinted in *Oedipus Rex: A Mirror for Greek Drama*, ed. Albert Cook (Belmont, CA: Wadsworth Publishing, 1963), 86.

13. For some responses to some of the play's supposed flaws, see Segal, *Oedipus Tyrannus*, 78–79; Crossett, "The *Oedipus Rex*," in *Oedipus Rex*, ed. Cook, 134–55; Walter Kaufmann, *Tragedy and Philosophy* (Princeton, NJ: Princeton University Press, 1992), 129; Sophocles, *King Oidipous*, trans. Blondell, 114.

14. Roger Ebert, review of *Laura*, 20th Century Fox, RogerEbert.com, January 20, 2002, https://www.rogerebert.com/reviews/great-movie-laura-1944.

15. Eric Wellisch, *Isaac and Oedipus: A Study in Biblical Psychology of the Sacrifice of Isaac*, The Akedah (London: Routledge & Kegan Paul, 1954); D. A. Hester, "Oedipus and Jonah," *Proceedings of the Cambridge Philological Society* 23 (1977): 32–60; Meyer Fortes, *Oedipus and Job in West African Religion* (New York: Cambridge University Press, 1959); Peter L. Rudnytsky, *Freud and Oedipus* (New York: Columbia University Press, 1987); Immanuel Velikovsky, *Oedipus and Akhnaton: Myth and History* (New York: Pocket Books, 1960); Victoria Hamilton, *Narcissus and Oedipus: The Children of Psychoanalysis* (London: Routledge & Kegan Paul, 1982); John T. Irwin, "Oedipus and Theseus," in Irwin, *The Mystery to a Solution: Poe, Borges, and the Analytic Detective Story* (Baltimore: Johns Hopkins University Press, 1994); Ernest Jones, *Hamlet and Oedipus* (New York: W. W. Norton & Co., 1976); Gerhard Vinnai, *Jesus und Ödipus* (Frankfurt: Fischer Taschenbuch Verlag GmbH, 1999); René Girard, "The Myth of Oedipus, the Truth of Joseph," in *Oedipus Unbound: Selected Writings on Rivalry and Desire* (Stanford, CA: Stanford University Press, 2004), 107–13.

16. Irwin, *The Mystery to a Solution*, 224.

17. For a detailed refutation of Ahl's thesis, see R. Drew Griffith, *The Theatre of Apollo: Divine Justice and Sophocles' Oedipus the King* (Montreal: McGill-Queen's University Press, 1996), 29–44. See also Rudnytsky, *Freud and Oedipus*, 350–57 (refuting Sandor Goodhart's similar thesis).

18. Segal, *Oedipus Tyrannus*, 35.

19. Knox, *Oedipus at Thebes*, 1–2.

20. Cameron, *The Identity of Oedipus the King*, xii.

21. Michel de Montaigne, *The Complete Essays*, trans. M. A. Screech (New York: Penguin Books, 1991), 144.

22. Sophocles, *The Oedipus Cycle*, trans. Dudley Fitts and Robert Fitzgerald (New York: Harcourt Brace Jovanovich, 1977), 9.

Index

A

B

C

D

E

F

G

H

I

J

K

L

M

T

U

V

W

Y

About the Author

Kenneth Glazer practiced law for many years after graduating from the University of California, Berkeley, where he studied history and philosophy, and Stanford University Law School. He and his wife live in Bethesda, Maryland and have two grown children. He has a perfectly normal relationship with his mother.